Islam, Arabs, and the Intelligent World of the Jinn

Contemporary Issues in the Middle East

Islam, Arabs, and the Intelligent World of the Jinn

Amira El-Zein

Syracuse University Press

∞ The paper used in this publication meets the minimum requirements of American National Standard for Information Sciences—Permanence of Paper for Printed Library Materials, ANSI Z39.48–1992.

For a listing of books published and distributed by Syracuse University Press, visit our Web site at SyracuseUniversityPress.syr.edu

ISBN-13: 978-0-8156-3200-9

Library of Congress Cataloging-in-Publication Data

El-Zein, Amira.

  Islam, Arabs, and the intelligent world of the jinn / Amira El-Zein.

    p. cm. — (Contemporary issues in the Middle East)

  Includes bibliographical references and index.

  ISBN 978-0-8156-3200-9 (cloth : alk. paper)

  1. Jinn.   2. Demonology, Islamic   I. Title.

  BP166.89.E49 2009

  297.2'17—dc22

                                        2009026745

TO MUNIR,

husband and dearest friend

AMIRA EL-ZEIN is a scholar, poet, and translator. She was the director of the Arabic Program at Tufts University from 2002 to 2008. She holds an M.A. in French Literature from Lebanese University, an M.A. in Arabic and Islamic studies from La Sorbonne Nouvelle University, Paris, and a Ph.D. in Arabic language and literature from Georgetown University. She is currently a visiting associate professor at Georgetown University in Doha, Qatar. The range of her scholarly interest in comparative literature, medieval and modern Arabic thought, Islamic studies, and comparative folklore has resulted in numerous and multilingual lectures, articles, and book and encyclopedia chapters, in addition to editions of her own poetry and translations of other poets. Her latest book of poetry, *The Jinn and Other Poems,* is published by Arrowsmith.

Contents

Introduction

He created the jinn from a fusion of fire
So which of your Lord's blessings do you both deny?
—QUR'AN 55:15

$\mathcal{T}$his book is long overdue. After years of painstaking investigation, this thorough work is based on an extensive and intricate research in Arabic and several European languages. I have attempted to present an all-embracing examination of the jinn's concept in classical Islam including most types of supposed interactions of the jinn with humans, angels, and animals.

I was often confronted with, on one hand, Western sources simply dismissing the whole concept of the jinn as superstitions, primitivism, animism, and the like; and on the other hand, contemporary Arab and Muslim sources, which, in general, expand on the predecessors' work, but rarely innovate.[1] I would read thousands of pages to finally fall upon some original ideas on the topic. Western scholars in general concentrate on the political and social manifestations of Islam, totally neglecting this concept, while Arab and Muslim contemporary scholars find it enough to reiterate what the Qur'an and prophetic tradition Hadith mention, or try to apply a Western methodology that would lead them to maintain that these "spiritual beings" simply pertain to the domain of fantasy.

This book deals with the concept of the jinn in classical Islam only, corresponding to Islam's golden age, which witnessed an extraordinary flourishing of intellectual and spiritual debates. No other era has known such a thriving of the mind, the heart, and the spirit. It is during this time theologians, Sufis, Qur'an commentators, poets, literary critics, historians, and geographers mused and deliberated on the concept of the jinn among other things.

But why write a book on the jinn? People in the West currently are more interested to learn about jihad, the veil, the status of women in Islam, and the various fundamentalist movements. For them Islam is solely all of the above. They assume the jinn is a topic better left to Disney and popular culture, or at best to anthropologists. Broadly speaking, many would argue this subject matter is very marginal, and would not add anything to the understanding of a religion such as Islam, while others assert its significance, but acknowledge at the same time it is a particularly thorny topic to address. For how would one classify the jinn mentioned in the Qur'an? Are they psychic powers? Are they spiritual powers? Are they the product of the imagination? Do they really exist? And if so, how to prove their existence to the skeptics, how to be in contact with them, and how to describe them?

For all of the above reasons, scholars on both sides prefer not to embark on this venture. It was clear there was an urgent need for a serious academic work that goes beyond the Western bias, the Arab/Muslim redundancy, and the folkloric simplification of the jinn in Disney, while attempting as much as possible to describe the phenomenon *from within* the culture.

I argue, on the contrary, examining such a concept is essential to understanding Islam inasmuch as it is a concept at the heart of the religion. It is, first, an important constituent of the hierarchical view of the world Islam espouses because jinn are thought to be "intermediary" or "imaginal" beings, above our terrestrial realm but below the celestial realm, as shall be seen in the first chapter. In other terms, one has to deeply grasp the concept of the jinn to understand Islamic cosmology.

Second, although belief in the jinn is not one of the five pillars of Islam, one can't be Muslim if he/she doesn't have faith in their existence because they are mentioned in the Qur'an and the prophetic tradition. Indeed, the Qur'anic message itself is addressed to both humans and jinn, considered the only two intelligent species on Earth. The prophetic tradition mentions them in several instances. Therefore, exploring the concept of the jinn in classical Islam would shed light on the complexity of a religion that has long been overshadowed in the West and misinterpreted. It would unravel the originality of a religious system that systematically takes into consideration the impact of the intermediary realm on humans.

Third, although there exists a prolific literature on angels in Islam, there is still very little serious academic work devoted solely to the investigation of the jinn's concept in Islam. Analyzing angels is always easier and thought to be more rewarding in the sense that these spiritual entities are good, beautiful, universal, and eternally obedient to God. There is no paradox, no contradiction in their nature. Simply put, these "divine messengers" and beings of light are bringers of peace and quietude. Intermediary beings such as the jinn, on the other hand, are more complex, multifarious, intricate, and hesitant between obscurity and glow. They are go-between beings. Like humans, they could at anytime shift toward goodness or toward evil.

Finally, the West persists in interpreting Islam as a rigorous monotheism that leaves no room for imagination and creativity. My research shows this is a sweeping prejudice because Islam, on the contrary, developed an ingenious and sophisticated concept of the imagination and the imaginal. It also contends the originality of Islam lies precisely in being a monotheism that highlights the existence of intelligent spiritual entities without necessarily demonizing them. As a matter of fact, jinn in Islam are not demons opposed to angels. They are a third category of beings different from both angels and demons. Moreover, the analysis of these diverse spiritual beings will reveal to us the belief in them never deterred Muslims from the worship of God's oneness. Generally speaking, it is difficult for westerners to understand how one can be monotheist and still believe in spiritual beings such as the jinn. Some westerners summarize this issue as follows: either you are polytheist and you believe in spirits, or you are monotheist and you believe only in God, angels, and the devil. That is why in the eyes of some orientalists such as Samuel Zwemer (d. 1952) all religions other than Judaism and Christianity are dismissed as "animist," including Islam.[2]

THE UNIVERSAL BELIEF IN SPIRITUAL ENTITIES

Since time immemorial, humans have maintained across traditions that the invisible realm occupies in the universe a much larger part than the manifest or visible domain. Belief in spiritual entities is universal. Humans seem to have at all times thought there is more than what meets the eye. No civilization known to anthropology, regardless of its cultural patterns or historical development, is without a corpus of narratives that tell of the human belief and interaction with spiritual entities. Humans have attempted to tune in to them, knowing spirits actually operate in the same real world in which they live, accepting as true the existence of a world of powers beyond, or alongside, the visibly perceived world of everyday life.

It is to this plethora of the invisible world that William James, American philosopher and psychologist (d. 1910), characterized the life of religion in the broadest and most general terms possible: "One might say that it consists of the belief that there is an unseen order, and that our supreme good lies in harmoniously adjusting ourselves thereto."[3] Further, James added this all-encompassing remark: "The whole universe of concrete objects, as we know them, swims in a wider and higher universe of abstract ideas, that lend it its significance."[4]

Humans have constantly maintained that different spirits inhabit different elements. Thus, it is claimed gnomes, elves, and brownies prefer to dwell in the element earth, while salamanders and jinn inhabit the element fire. As for the element air, it is alleged it contains the sylphs and the jinn as well. And, finally, the element of water holds all kinds of undines, such as mermaids, nymphs, and naiads.

What follows is not a comprehensive survey of all the traditions believing in the spirits' existence. That is not the purpose of this book. Besides highlighting that most traditions incorporate belief in spiritual entities and the intermediary realm in their dogmas, the purpose is to emphasize the specificity of the Islamic spiritual tradition when compared to the other traditions.

Native Americans are among the nations who are the most tuned to the world of spirits. For them, all creatures have a self, and interact somehow with humans. One of their most persistent beliefs is the soul as a cosmic breath that endows everything with its energy. A Hopi Indian of high cult rank once pointed out, "The universe is endowed with the same breath; rocks, trees, grass, earth, all animals, and men."[5]

For Native Americans, all beings are interconnected and interdependent. Within this spiritual perspective, one owes respect to all forms of life; one needs to be in constant dialogue with them as well as with all kinds of spirits, that of the wind, the earth, the animals, and act in harmony and cooperation with them. This belief, however, in all kinds of spirits has never put off Native Americans from the belief in one God, contrary to what some Western interpretations have claimed. Indeed, Native Americans call him the Great Spirit and are aware of his manifestations in nature around them. "Things are not mysterious themselves, but manifestations of mysteries, and the Great Spirit, or the Great Mystery, synthesizes them in its transcendent unity."[6]

In accordance with the Japanese Shinto religion, it is claimed that a huge number of spirits dwell everywhere in nature. "Central to these experiences is the concept—and felt presence—of *kami:* the 'spirits' that invest every tree, rock, flower, mountain, river, and other natural objects."[7] Spirits are believed to be of two kinds: one gentle, *nigi-mi-tama,* and the other violent, *ara-mi-tama.* "Nine out of ten Japanese claim some affiliation with Shinto, but in the West the religion remains the least studied of the major Asian spiritual traditions."[8]

In general, the Shinto religion emphasizes the bond that ties humans to nature and stresses the sacred character of the latter. Finally, the Shinto revolves around the notion of *ki,* which is thought to be a force that dwells within the individual as well as in nature.

Broadly speaking, Buddhism describes two kinds of spirits—good and evil. Good spirits are those that work to protect the people and the Buddha's teachings, while evil spirits are malevolent and try to harm people and the Buddha's teachings. The latter are often referred to as "demons." In addition to these spirits, Boddhisatvas are considered souls who could have passed to Nirvana, but out of compassion for other humans, they remain in the world to help them.

In Mahayana Buddhism, the dominant form of religion in Tibet, China, Korea, Japan, and Vietnam, the presence of spiritual entities in everyday life remains strong. Most village monks offer to help their followers with a wide range of specific intercessions such as reciting sutras thought to impart protection from evil. The most significant words of these sutras are printed on the fans monks hold.

In Theravada Buddhism, which is mostly spread in Thailand, Laos, Nepal, and some parts of Sri Lanka, people believe they are surrounded by spirits called *Phi* who exist almost everywhere—in trees, hills, water, animals, the earth, and so on. Some are evil, others favorable to humans.

In Indian religion, there is an abundance of spirits of all kinds, such as demons, ogres, evil spirits called *Rakshas* or *Asuras,* goblins, and the like.[9] The *Gandharvas* are spirits of the air, mountains, and forests. Some of these spirits are called *Yaksas.* They bear a resemblance to fairies and are friendly to humans, especially men. In the epic story of the *Mahabharata,* they often enter into contact with humans, either to help them or punish them when they go beyond the bounds of their natural realms. Kubera, their king, is the guardian of treasures and precious gems. He and his people watch diligently over their domain for fear of any human transgression.[10]

In Irish and Celtic folklore, Fairies are thought of as spiritual entities concerned with human affairs, and that long to interfere in their lives. They were not thought to live in a separate realm, but rather close to humans and intermingling with them. They are like humans, male and female, and have their own families.[11]

Ancient Egypt was one of the richest civilizations of the Near East, if not the richest with regard to the concept of spirits. Ancient Egyptian religion had a host of all kinds of evil spirits the Egyptians searched to placate, but it also had many spiritual powers within the human, among them the *ka* or life force, which is a double of the person, a kind of guide that accompanies the human, similar to what Socrates says of his own *daimon*. There is also the *ba* or vital energy that subsists after death. Neither ka nor ba were visible during life or after death. Egyptians used to represent "the ka as a human with a pair of upraised arms on his head, while the ba was a human headed bird that could move freely in and out of the tomb."[12]

Spiritual power in Ancient Egypt seems to be within the human, but it could also materialize and go out of him, in the physical world, similar to the jinn perceived as spirits, powers, or energies within us and outside of us as well, as shall be seen in this book.

In the mythologies of Assyria, Sumer, and Babylonia, spirits existed everywhere. They were structured in armies and hierarchies; each spirit had a particular responsibility. Some were good while others were bad. It is not simple to clearly distinguish the function assigned to each spirit, nor is here the place to mention the numerous spirits existing in these mythologies. What is of interest is the distinction in this mythology of two kinds of *genii*, like the Muslim jinn. There were the good genii called *Shedu* or *Lamasu* and the bad genii called *Utuku*.

In Greek mythology and religion, the term *daemon* was ubiquitous, referring to supernatural agents or intelligences, lower in rank than a god and holding a middle place between gods and humans, such as the *Corybantes, Curetes, Dactyls, Satyrs,* and *Sileni.* Spirits of forests, rivers, mountains, and cities presided over public and family life, and were also referred to as daemons that could be either good or evil. Even good ones were believed to be capable of evil acts if angered by humans.

Ancient Greeks considered daimons as guardian spirits of a sort, giving headship and protection to the ones they watched over, while bad daimons led people astray. In Greek philosophy, Socrates (470–399) means specifically by daimon a companion to the human. In his *Apology,* he speaks of his daimon: "My familiar prophetic voice of the spirit in all times past has always come to me frequently, opposing me even in every small thing, if I was about to do something not right."[13] Socrates often referred to the fact that each person has his/her own guide that is his or her own daimon. As for Plato (d. 347 BCE), "The intermediary world must have been of the utmost significance. It is the idea or view of the daemonic as an 'intermediate' realm between the human level and the divine, a realm that because of its intermediate position unites the cosmos to itself."[14]

In ancient Rome, the term genii means a group of spirits in the classical Roman and Etruscan mythologies. Genii were considered guardian spirits of the individual beings and of some nature phenomena. There is, for example, a genius for crops, trees, water, and mountains as well as for each kind of animal and for each human male to whom it was assigned at birth. Interesting enough, women had a different kind of guardian spirit called *Juno*. It should be mentioned here that in pre-Islam and in Islam as well, *jinni* is a masculine spiritual entity that has its feminine counterpart called *jinniyah*.

In Persian mythology, there existed two classes of spiritual entities: the *Daevas* who were demons and fighters against the supreme god, Ahura Mazda, while the *Peris* were good spirits, some say fallen angels who guided the soul to the world of the deceased. *Peris* were similar to fairies in Irish and Celtic mythologies and to jinn as well, and, like them, could be either compassionate or malign toward humans.

In the Arab Muslim tradition, as shall be seen in the following chapters, the jinn are not the souls of the dead, kind of ghosts roaming the earth; they are not forces of evil battling forces of good. Jinn are intelligent and subtle beings. Their free will initiates their activities, so each jinni is responsible before God for his or her own deed.

Muslims recognize the intervention of the jinn in their lives, and acknowledge these spirits are not indifferent to humans and that they have a desire to influence their destinies. The Qur'an refers to these relations between jinn and humans, and specifically to the fact some humans have sought the help of the jinn. In Qur'an 6:128–130, the close proximity of the communities of jinn and humans is mentioned:

> On the day when He shall muster them all together;
> "Company of jinn, you have made much of mankind."

Then their friends among mankind will say, "Our Lord,
we have profited each of the other, and we
have reached the term determined by Thee for us"

Like the traditions depicted above, Islam stresses that the invisible realm with its beings is vaster than the manifest realm. One saying of the Prophet mentions that "God divided the jinn and the humans into ten parts. One part makes up the human race, and the other nine parts is made up of the jinn."[15]

The Arabic language itself bears witness to how the invisible realm invades major aspects of life. In Arabic, each time the two letters *jim* and *nun* occur together, like in jinn, they convey the meaning of invisible, unseen, or hidden. Thus, paradise is *jannah* because it is hidden from the human sight. *Janin* is the fetus in the womb because we do not see it. The expression *ajannahu al-layl* means the night covered him or hid him, etc.

SPIRITUAL ENTITIES AND THE WEST

Broadly speaking, almost all traditions seem to have believed, and still believe one way or another, in the existence of an invisible realm that constantly interacts with our own physical or manifest domain. However, a majority of westerners reject today these beliefs, and qualify them as "animistic." As Patrick Harpur, contemporary writer on the history of imagination in the West, eloquently comments, "The very people who have emptied Nature of soul and reduced it to dead matter obeying mechanical laws, pejoratively call the traditional world view animism—a term which effectively writes off what it claims to describe. To 'animistic' cultures there is no such thing as animism. There is only Nature presenting itself in all its immediacy as daimon-ridden."[16] Western Judeo-Christianity in general is thought to have introduced a vision of the world where "Man is against God, Nature is against God, and Man and Nature are against each other. God's own likeness (Man), God's own creation (Nature) and God himself,—all three are at war."[17]

This perception of the world was initiated in Europe with Descartes, surnamed the father of modern philosophy, (d. 1650). Descartes divided the world into religious and material.[18] Since that time, Westerners in general have the tendency to see things through opposite pairs: logos versus mythos, sensation versus intellect, metaphorical versus literal, inner versus outer, object versus subject, spiritual versus supernatural, nature versus culture, and humans versus the Divine. Nothing seems to mediate between these pairs. Newton (d. 1727) later depicted the material universe as a mechanism that functions under the laws of nature. He viewed the world through the eyes of "casual determinism," which stipulates any movement can be calculated exactly given the laws of motion. Classical physics asserted that consciousness is separated from nature and psyche from physics. Locke (d. 1704), the philosopher of the Newtonian system, pictured humans as passive in front of a robotic nature that should be manipulated as dead matter rather than being respected as alive, sacred, and conscious.

Subsequently, French sociologist Auguste Comte (d. 1857) maintained European science alone was behind the intellectual evolution of humanity. Comte described this progress as being from mythology to metaphysics and finally to science. Comte and his contemporaries considered myth as substantiation of a prelogical mentality, and as representative of the childhood of humanity. They argued non-European civilizations lived and continue to live in a world of fantasy while European society alone became enlightened through reason and science.

This "scientific" perception of the world was in total opposition to religion, which was consigned to the inner sphere, while science evolved in the rational and manifest realm. Irrevocably separated from each other, they remained on good terms as long as they didn't intervene in each other's affairs. In contrast to this dualistic view of the world, science and religion in the Muslim classical world worked hand in hand. Most of the scientists at that point in time were themselves great Sufis. Suffice it to mention here that physician Avicenna (d. 1037) made important discoveries in medicine, and wrote beautiful mystical treatises as well.

One would think today's relations between science and religion would be changed after the revolutionary discoveries in quantum physics, which reinterpreted the relations of man to matter. Unfortunately, this isn't the case. "After the bombing of Hiroshima and Nagasaki, Karl Barth, Europe's most famous Protestant theologian, was asked to speak with physicians concerning the moral implications of atomic weapons. He refused, as did all of his students. When asked why, Barth said that scientists had one world, he had another, and they had no common ground to speak about. He believed it was a logical impossibility that they, the scientists, could have anything to say about the morality or the immorality of the bomb, even though they had built this device."[19]

Despite this general Western doubt about the existence of an unseen world, one should acknowledge there were in the past several exceptions to the rule; in particular the Romantic Movement, which genuinely opened up to the invisible realm. Poets like William Blake (d. 1827), John Keats (d. 1821), Samuel Coleridge (d. 1834), and later W. B. Yeats (d. 1919) have described their wanderings beyond the seen physical world. They maintained they were able to access it through the power of imagination, which they cherished and almost venerated.

Hermetic philosophers and alchemists like Paracelsus (d. 1541), Giordano Bruno (d. 1600), Sir Francis Bacon (d. 1626), and the Count of St. Germain (d. 1784) underscored the unity between microcosm and macrocosm, and highlighted in their writings the power of the invisible world over human lives.

CHAPTER STRUCTURE

Chapter 1 sets the theoretical grounding for the whole concept of the jinn as intermediary beings, constantly moving from the visible domain to the invisible, and vice-versa. One can say, without exaggeration, that the whole of Islam is based upon these two facets of visible and invisible: *'alam al-ghayb wa al-shahadah.*

Moreover, the concept of the jinn is tightly linked to the notion of the intermediary realm or *imaginal.* There is no understanding of this concept without first unraveling the seminal role of imagination and the imaginal world in classical Islamic thought.

The next chapter analyzes the ways classical Islam establishes correspondences between jinn and humans in the major aspects of life, and then turns to the analysis of human superiority over jinn.

This is followed by the theme of jinn preceding humans on Earth and the elaborate relationships between the two spiritual entities: jinn and angels. Chapter 3 makes obvious how Islam expounds always on the angels' superiority.

In chapter 4, a quick survey of divination in the ancient Near East precedes the narration of the encounters of the Prophet of Islam with the jinn, as found in Islamic sources. The very important issue that was raised in medieval times—did the Prophet Muhammad see the jinn or only hear them?—is also raised.

Chapter 5 discusses the correlations between magic, medicine, and faith from the perspective of traditional Islam. It delves into the different means invented to ward off evil jinn, such as the recitation or the writing of specific Qur'anic verses, the use of the Most Beautiful Names of God (*asma' allah al-husna*) and the Arabic letters. It also addresses the phenomenon of possession and madness, as well as their remedies.

The next chapter elaborates on the nature of jinn as tricksters and especially stresses the jinn's embodiment of animal forms and their many maneuvers when luring humans. This is followed by chapter 7 revealing how the jinn take the shapes of humans when they fall in love with a man or a woman from the human world and analyzing the love stories found in the original sources.

Chapter 8 treats the intriguing question of poetical inspiration and its relation and difference from revelation. It analyzes the Qur'an's attitude toward poets and includes the many stories told about poets' encounters with their inspirers, the jinn. As in the preceding chapters, it attempts to answer the question: Are the jinn physical entities, or rather imaginal beings coming from within the self?

Finally, an appendix presents the many kinds of the jinn. In the realm of imaginable beings, variety remains of essence.

METHODOLOGY

There are five aspects to my methodology for this book.

The first aspect examines the concept of the jinn in classical Islam from within a combination of the three major layers of Islam: orthodox or official Islam, folk or popular Islam, and Sufism.

(a) Official or orthodox Islam is essentially based on the Qur'an and the *Hadith* (the prophetic tradition), considered the backbone of its teachings. From them the *shari'ah,* or Islamic Law, is derived. Official Islam tends to be literalist, and generally doesn't encourage interpretations of the Qur'an, which often puts it in contradiction with the two other layers, popular or folk Islam and Sufism. With regard to the Qur'an, I have essentially adopted the translation of Arthur John Arberry (d. 1969). However, as a native speaker of Arabic, and as a scholar of Islam and Arabic, I have made modifications each time I felt Arberry's translation did not mirror the Arabic meaning and indicated it with an asterisk.

As for the Hadith, I have used different sources (refer to Arabic bibliography). Because the purpose of this research is to interpret the jinn's phenomenon as it manifested itself at that point in time, I have used these pertinent sources as they appeared and widely spread among Muslims, generation after generation. These sources are a phenomenon in itself. Their data are of sensible intuition. That is, they very likely involve *mental projections.* A historical and theological critique of this wide variety of sources would need a volume of its own. Moreover, it would gravely disrupt the reader's focus on the main topic. In brief, I generally relied on the two most well-known works of Hadith, namely *Sahih Muslim* and *Sahih Bukhari.* Occasionally, I turned to the Hadith compiled by Muhammad ibn Yazid ibn Majah (d. 887) entitled *Sunan ibn Majah.* I also used the collection of forty Hadiths by one of the most notable compilers, Muhyiddin abu Zakariyya Yahya ibn Sharaf al-Nawawi (d. 1277).

(b) The second layer of Islam is popular or folk Islam. I define it as the corpus dealing with legends, myths, popular stories, and heroic tales. I especially worked, however, with the text of *The Arabian Nights* that contains an impressive number of stories on the jinn. I have adopted the translation of Husain Haddawy in its two volumes (see bibliography). However, because Haddawy limits himself to earlier manuscripts of *The Nights,* and leaves out a number of stories, I have also used Richard Burton's translation, which is more complete. Unfortunately, the English is somehow Victorian and archaic. In this same category, I have also used the popular tale entitled "Sirat Sayf bin Zi Yazan" translated by Lena Jayyusi. (see bibliography).

(c) Regarding the third layer, or Sufism, I define it as mystical Islam. It is a path toward purification and attaining unity with the Divine. Sufism uses a highly symbolical language that sometimes puts it in conflict with official Islam.

I have incorporated several Sufi texts from different periods to present the reader with a great variety of texts. For example, I have used the work of Nur al-din 'Abd al-Rahman Jami (d. 1492), and 'Abdul Qader al-Gilani (d. 1166.) However, I have especially focused on the work of Andalusian Sufi, Muhyi-al-din ibn 'Arabi (d. 1240), and some figures belonging to his school of thought. This is because his work, more than any other Sufi's work, deals extensively with the topic of the jinn. He remains the most original writer on this issue. His treatment of this complex topic is unequaled.

It should be mentioned these three layers of Islam are far from being entrenched categories. They sometimes flow in each other. For example, in which layer of Islam should one place the Qur'an's commentaries, *tafasir*? One finds literalist Qur'an commentaries as well as Sufi ones. Henceforth, the tafasir do not really belong to orthodox Islam only; it would also be wrong to put them under Sufism. In fact, I have used both kinds of tafasir to offer an all-inclusive view on the concept of the jinn. In the Sufi tradition, I have referred to *Tafsir al-safi* of al-Fayd al-Kashani (d. 1680), *Tafsir al-hasan al-basri* (b. 642), *Tafsir al-qur'an al-karim* by ibn 'Arabi (d. 1240), and the tafsir entitled *Lata'if al-isharat* by the Sufi Abd al-Kabir al-Qushairi (d. 1074).

Regarding the Orthodox tafasirs, I have essentially used the Qur'anic commentaries written by Isma'il ibn Kathir (d. 1373); ibn Qayyim al-Jawziyyah, renowned scholar of Islamic tradition (d. 1350); Fakhr al-din al-Razi (d. 1209), *al-Tafsir al-kabir li al-qur'an,* called also *Mafatih al-ghayb;* Abdullah ibn 'Umar al-Baydawi (d. 1286), *Anwar al-tanzil wa asrar al-ta'wil;* and Muhammad ibn Jarir al-Tabari (d. 923), *Tafsir al-qur'an.*

Another example of the overlap of these three layers is found in the works of medieval Muslim historians and geographers I have used amply in this book. I have looked at them as texts that are halfway between official Islam and folk Islam. Many Muslim historians were well grounded in the Qur'an and the Hadith. In fact, some historians were Qur'an commentators, like historian Isma'il ibn Kathir who composed his own commentary of the Qur'an. He also wrote his own version of the "Stories of the Prophets," a corpus closer to folk Islam than it is to official Islam. As for classical Muslim geographers, they were very much tuned to the eerie world of marvels to the point they were considered the principal inventors of this literary genre. Their depictions of jinn in far away countries are filled with intriguing details. They are constantly looking for the uncanny and all that lies beyond the conventional. In this sense, their work could be looked upon as closer to folk Islam than to orthodox Islam.

In simultaneously analyzing these three layers of Islam, my intent is: (a) to demonstrate that, despite the differences existing between the three major layers, the Islamic belief in the jinn is always represented as embedded in the Qur'an and the prophetic tradition; and (b) to illustrate the jinn's concept in the three layers is depicted sometimes as an external energy, and sometimes as an internal energy within the self.

I believe it is almost impossible to comprehend the phenomenon of the jinn in classical Islam without concomitantly taking into consideration these three layers. Otherwise, it would be difficult to obtain a more complete picture regarding the jinn. I maintain part of the incomprehension characterizing the field of

Islamic studies is the stress on one side of Islam, especially the dogmatic, legal, literal, and official at the expense of the two others, which, obviously, distorts Islam, and presents it as an abrasive monotheism.

The second aspect is thematic. In addition to the works mentioned above, each chapter has its own additional references because each chapter deals with a specific theme or aspect of the jinn. For example, chapter 6 deals with the trickster aspect of jinn and their frequent manifestation in animal forms; and therefore, works consulted and cited in this chapter refer essentially to this luring aspect of the jinn.

The third aspect of my approach is a close reading of the original texts. Throughout this book I have opted to give the original sources the chance to speak, to show their uniqueness, and open up to their readers. I argue that to figure out the complexity and subtleness of the jinn's concept, it is imperative to carefully listen to the original texts and to meditate while reading them. I am an advocate of intimate attentiveness to the original texts, which eventually allow concealed meanings to surface, and masked connotations to appear in the daylight. I consider that close reading is a journey one undertakes from the visible, manifest, and literal reading of the texts to their hidden and invisible message.

The fourth aspect espouses a decoding of the symbols contained in the original texts. This is a continuation and a culmination of the close reading technique mentioned above, which takes it up to a higher level. I contend that behind everything and every word hides a symbol, especially in the domain of religion.

The fifth aspect of my approach relates universal patterns to particular ones. I have endeavored to seek the universal across traditions while stressing at the same time the specificity and originality of Islam. This is why I have examined the beliefs of the major traditions pertaining to each chapter's theme. In fact, this book contains a large amount of narratives related to spiritual entities from all over the world. In this sense, it is truly encyclopedic; all through this research, I have intentionally chosen to enrich the study with an abundance of stories, gathered from multilingual sources and tens of thousands of pages to create a rare *Golden Bough* of the jinn.

My analysis is certainly more phenomenological than historical. I have decided to look at the concept of the jinn with an open mind and with empathy, letting the sources unfold their meanings.

This book contains many stories and anecdotes translated for the first time from Arabic into English.

Finally, I believe the dramatic growth of Islamic and Arab studies in the West in general, and in the United States in particular, necessitates new approaches to the study of Islam. I hope to have presented a rather unorthodox topic in a unique manner.

Islam, Arabs, and the Intelligent World of the Jinn

I
The Poetics of the Invisible

Muslim Imagination and the Jinn

> Imagination is like the image that a human sees in the mirror.
> —IBN 'ARABI (d. 1240)

*A*s spiritual entities, the jinn are considered dual dimensional, with the ability to live and operate in both manifest and invisible domains. The traffic between them is the focus of discussion in Islam, because believing in *al-ghayb,* the unseen and the unknown, is central and fundamental in Islamic faith. God himself is referred to in the Qur'an as the Outward and the Inward.[1] This means God unveils himself through infinite external manifestations and veils himself in absolute secrecy in his Oneness. "From that unitary point of view, the Principle of the Source is seen as not the Inward but also the Outward, not only the One but also the essential reality of the many which is but the reflections of the One."[2]

THE NOTION OF MULTIPLE WORLDS IN ISLAM

It is difficult to grasp this constant and complex interchange between the manifest and the invisible without unraveling from the outset the concept of multiple worlds that is at the heart of the Muslim vision of existence. It profoundly implies there is always more than meets the eye.

Muslims begin their prayers each time with the *fatiha* (the opening chapter of the Qur'an), which begins with these words: "Praise belongs to God, the Lord of the worlds," *rabb al-'alamin.*[3] Muslims repeat the expression *rabb al-'alamin* (the Lord of the worlds) in the *fatiha* several times during their prayers, which deeply ensconces the idea of numerous realms in their hearts and minds. Despite the preeminence of our Earth because the human is God's vice-regent on it,[4] Islam

1

emphasizes the existence of yet other domains in general, and of other earths in particular.[5] It is this belief in the infinite possibilities of other dimensions that triggered the great development of sciences during medieval times. Nothing in the new religion hinders the exploration of these worlds mentioned in the Holy Book. Muslims believe God created many worlds and subjected them to humans and jinn to explore them, benefit from them, and come to a deeper discernment of the Divine and a genuine glorification of his wonders.[6]

Muslim compilers speak of not one earth but of seven earths as being one on top of the other, exactly like the seven heavens. The analogy between seven earths and seven heavens is worthy of note inasmuch as the number seven is considered "the number of the universe, the macrocosm."[7] It is also "the first number which contains both the spiritual and temporal"[8] and that joins heaven and Earth. However, in Arabic the term "seven" could also be used emphatically to refer to more than seven, to numerous things or beings.[9] In the context of earths and heavens, it could therefore allude to a great number of earths and heavens, and not just to seven.

Although details on the seven earths are so scarce in the Qur'an that it mentions it only once,[10] the prophetic tradition provides additional details. The imam Muhammad al-Bukhari (b. 810), author of one of the most authentic collections of prophetic traditions, states

> The Prophet asked once his Companions, "Do you know what is below the earth?" We replied, "God and his Prophet know better." He said, "There is an earth. Do you know what is underneath it?" We replied, "God and his Prophet know better." He said, "Another earth. Do you know what distance separates both of them?" We replied, "God and his Prophet know better." He said, "Seven hundred years apart," and he continued so forth until he counted seven earths. Then he said, "By God, if any of you go downwards, he will reach the seventh earth." Then he recited from the Qur'an: "He is the First and the Last and the Outward and the Inward, and He has knowledge of everything."[11]

The Prophet not only asserts the existence of multiple earths, but he also underscores the need to respect and nurture our Earth because it is alive, sacred, and ranked above other earths: "He who takes anything from the earth that doesn't belong to him or that is not his right will be thrown on the Day of Judgment downwards to the seventh earth."[12]

Muslim theosophists depicted the marvels of these earths, claiming, "Between each earth and the next there is a distance similar to that between each heaven and the next. On each earth, there are beings created by the Almighty."[13] Each earth is more picturesque than the other. One of them, for example, is totally white, embodying transcendence and purity, a gem among the other earths: "God has a white Earth where the sun's rotation is of 30 days, so that the days there are thirty times longer than the day on our Earth. This white Earth is filled with people who don't know that God's orders are being disobeyed and they don't know either that God created Adam and the devil, Iblis."[14]

Another earth is stupendous. It is called "the earth which was created from what remained of the clay of Adam" as ibn 'Arabi (d. 1240) illustrates: "This Earth was created from 'a remainder that was the equivalent of sesame seed.'"[15] Then he adds, "A multitude of things exist there which are rationally impossible, that is, a multitude of things about which reason has established decisive proof that they are incompatible with real being. And yet! All these things do indeed exist in that Earth."[16]

Therefore, from a remainder the equivalent of a sesame seed, God created this marvelous Earth. From the extremely small came the infinitely vast, because this remarkable Earth is itself an illustration of the multiple worlds. "In the whole of all the universes that make up that Earth, God has especially created one universe in our image (a universe corresponding to each one of us)."[17]

Interestingly enough, this Earth contains in its vastness many universes instead of they containing it! One of these universes hosts beings similar to those living in our own Earth. If we visit them, we will encounter our own homologues. However, not everything is truly identical to our Earth because beings there are eternal and in our Earth, every living creature is subject to eventual decay. That is why this white earth "does not allow access to any of our physical bodies made of perishable human clay; its nature is such that it allows access only to bodies of the same quality as that of its own universe or the world of Spirits."[18] It is possible for the spiritually gifted to visit it in spirit, as did ibn 'Arabi whose depiction surpasses the most stunning stories in Western science fiction, except for ibn 'Arabi it is not fantasy. It really exists because it pertains to the imaginal realm, which is, for him, as real as our own physical world, albeit in a different manner, as shall be seen. Everything found on that earth, absolutely everything, "is alive and speaks, has a life analogous to that of every living being endowed with thought and speech."[19] Ibn 'Arabi uncovers that the visitor could speak with these beings if he wishes despite the fact they "speak different languages, but this Earth has the gift, peculiar to it, of conferring on whomsoever enters the ability to understand all the tongues that are spoken there."[20]

Everything on this astounding earth moves with an extraordinary speed, faster than the twinkling of the eye. Moreover, time there is different from ours: "The times of that Earth are qualitatively of different kinds. Every event, every person, has his own time there."[21] More astonishing, "Light which reigns there is not that of the physical sun but nevertheless night and day alternate, just as with us. However, the darkness of the nights in this place is never a veil; it never prevents an object from being seen."[22] The ocean there is similar to ours, but instead of water, it has earth. However, it has the same appearance and behaves like our oceans.

In all the earths described above with their numerous universes, our laws of physics seem to be shattered and replaced by different laws particular to the imaginal realm.[23]

Medieval texts speak in general of an infinite number of beings of all kinds. "On each of these levels, species exist analogous to those in our world, but they are infinite. Some are peopled by Angels and the human Elect. Others are peopled by Angels and genii, others by demons."[24]

Within the perspective of multiple realms, Islam expands on the notion of God's permanent creation of universes in which different beings are brought into existence. "He creates what you know not" (Qur'an 8:16*). Through an unremitting process of creating and destroying, God discloses himself differently each time. The creation is thus renewed at each instant. The Qur'an mentions that "Each day He is upon some task" (Qur'an 55:29). Every moment witnesses the unfolding of a novel universe. In fact, "the universe experiences rebirth eternally, so the final world never ends."[25] Persian poet and Sufi, Nur al-din 'Abd al-Rahman Jami (b. 1414), who was one of the commentators of the work of ibn 'Arabi and a follower of his school of thought, praised God's continuous Creation of worlds in his verse: At every moment brings a world to naught/And fashions such another in its place.[26]

Ibn 'Arabi in turn commented on the endless creation of the universes, "As there is no end to the Ipseity of God or to His qualifications, consequently the Universes have no end or number, because the Universes are the places of manifestation for the Names and Qualities. As that which manifests is endless, so the places of manifestation must be endless."[27]

Islam is far from being the only religion that stipulates the never-ending creation and destruction of universes. Hinduism, like Islam, emphasizes in its philosophy of Vedanta the idea of multiple worlds constantly being born, then annihilated. This goes on forever, cycle after cycle. The many universes abide by the same rhythm, creation and dissolution. "Beyond the farthest vision, crowding outer space, the universes come and go, an innumerable host. Like delicate boats they float on the fathomless, pure waters that form the body of Vishnu."[28] These universes could be pictured as existing in a state of manifestation, then in an invisible state; expanding outwardly, then withdrawing inwardly.

Buddhism adopts the Hindu vision of multiple universes appearing and disappearing in the flux of cyclic time. Buddhism, however, conceives them as corresponding to different mental states, and compares cyclic time to a wheel of twelve spokes. In ancient Greek philosophy, the notion of multiple worlds was also prevalent. Democritus (b. about 460 BCE) held the view "there are infinite worlds both like and unlike this world of ours. For the atoms being infinite in number, as was already proved, are borne on far out into space."[29] And Greek Anaximander (b. 610 BCE) "proposed a model of the cosmos cycling over time, with the old universe destroyed and a new universe produced at the end of each cycle and the start of the next."[30]

THE IMAGINAL AND THE IMAGINATION

To distinctly understand the jinn in the Islamic imagination, we should first explore what is commonly called "the hierarchical view of the cosmos," to which Islamic imagination strongly adheres, as well as the imagination of all traditional societies. This perspective is seminal inasmuch as it unveils to us that visible matter alone does not define the cosmos.

The term hierarchy here has no pejorative meaning. If we go back to its etymology, we will find it does not necessarily entail an authoritarian and oppressive structured world where the patriarchal god is ruling over his creatures inasmuch as it indicates everything has its origin *arche* in the sacred *hier*. On the other hand, we discover the cosmos is not layered in static levels, but rather one can speak of dynamic "realms" or "domains."[31]

In this view of the world, we encounter three basic realms: the terrestrial or material, the imaginal or the intermediate, and the celestial realm. They correspond respectively to the world of clay out of which the human body is created and where we live, the world of fire where jinn are located, and the world of light where angels dwell. Above the celestial reigns the Infinite or the Divine. These realms are never considered in isolation from each other but rather as a whole. Moreover, the higher realm always impinges upon the one directly below it.

The imaginal realm is essential for our understanding of the jinn's concept because it is believed this is their habitat. It is also a seminal realm in any cosmology. "Without this [imaginal] world which stands between the purely intelligible and the physical world and which possesses its own nonmaterial forms, there is no possibility of a total and complete cosmology nor of the explanations of certain traditional teachings concerning eschatology."[32]

Henry Corbin, French philosopher (d. 1978), used the term "imaginal"[33] after rejecting the term "imaginary" because it means unreal, fantastic, or utopian in the West, yet for Islam, it is a world that *really* exists, "a world as ontologically real as the world of the senses and the world of the intellect, a world that requires a faculty of perception belonging to it, a faculty that is a cognitive function, a noetic value, as fully real as the faculties of sensory perception or intellectual intuition. This faculty is the imaginative power, the one we must avoid confusing with the imagination that modern man identifies with 'fantasy'."[34]

Hence, the "imaginative" faculty of the mind in its highest aspect, the power of framing new and striking intellectual conceptions, is essentially needed to penetrate the realm of the imaginal: the habitat of the jinn. We could speak of space and time there, but it is a different time and space. Forms move in the imaginal realm and interact, albeit in a dissimilar manner because they belong to what could be called "an immaterial materiality."[35] We can't also apply to it the laws of our physical terrestrial domain. It is, as Corbin mentions, "a suprasensory world, insofar as it is not perceptible except by the imaginative perception, and insofar as the events that occur in it cannot be experienced except by the imaginative or imaginant consciousness."[36]

The celestial domain above it affects the imaginal or the "intermediary" realm and, in turn, it affects the material realm below it where we live, to the point one can say we swim in an imaginal liquid; but few of us are aware of it. This domain is also called the "animic" or the "psychic," the habitat of Jung archetypes. We witness the presence of this psychic domain in our dreams when the subtle in us is removed from the coarse. We see forms we assume are physical but are not. We talk to them, and they talk back to us. Dreams might be one of the best means to comprehend imagination, because in dreams, we live a reality that sounds similar to our waking reality but it is not of the same order of corporeality. That is why what we experience in the dreams cannot be interpreted literally. It is a world filled with symbols that need to be decoded.[37]

However, the imaginal realm for Muslims is not limited to the Jungian archetypes. It is much vaster than the conception of Jung in the sense that it is not only a psychic domain, but also a spiritual one rooted in the *tawhid* (Transcendental Unity of God), and ingrained in its hierarchical perspective of the cosmos. Consequently, we necessarily need to view the phenomenon of the jinn and other subtle beings in the context of the Islamic structure of the cosmos, which means they are subtle with regard to corporeal bodies on our Earth, but on the other hand they are opaque with regard to the beings in the celestial realm above them, such as angels.

How could one visit this imaginal realm and meet subtle beings such as the jinn? Corbin refers to Muslim illuminationist philosopher Shihab al-din al-Suhrawardi (d. 1191) who provides us with powerful keys. "As is suggested at the end of Suhrawardi's tale, by the symbol of the drop of balm exposed in the hollow of the hand to the sun, it is a matter of entering, passing into the interior and, in *passing into the interior,* of finding oneself, paradoxically, *outside,* or, in the language of our authors, 'on the convex surface' of the ninth sphere—in other words 'beyond the mountain of Qaf.' The relationship involved is essentially that of the external, the visible, the exoteric (in Arabic *al-zahir*), and the internal, the invisible, the esoteric (in Arabic *batin*), or the natural world and the spiritual world."[38]

Going through the interior to find oneself outside is a way of alluding to the reality of the imaginal, and subsequently the reality of the places described by al-Suhrawardi and others. These places, such as the habitat of the jinn, are not places in the physical sense of the term. They are places *in* the imaginal realm.

The mountain Qaf is of the highest psychic and spiritual height. One accomplishes a long journey to reach it, as al-Suhrawardi tells us. However, one returns always to the point of departure, "like the point of compass returning to the same place."[39] Within this journey, the spirit of the traveler is transformed by what he experienced. One of the most astounding things the traveler discovers is spiritual bodies are not located in a place like material bodies are on our Earth. "It is their world that is *in* them."[40] The words "inside" and "in" should not fool us into believing the imaginal realm where the traveler stayed for a while is only "inside" us. As I have pointed out before, the imaginal realm is part of the hierarchical view of the cosmos for Muslims. It is not inside us only; it is outside us as well, as shall be seen.

Ibn 'Arabi compares the imaginal realm, the dwelling place of the jinn and the locus of the mountain Qaf, of the emerald cities, of Jabalqa and Jabarsa to a *barzakh* (isthmus). "Know that barzakh (isthmus), is something that separates two things. It is never an extreme separation; it is like the line that separates between the sun and its shadow, and like God's Saying: He let forth the two seas that meet together, between them a barzakh they do not overpass" (Qur'an 55:19).[41]

Sensory perception might fail to separate them, and reason stipulates there is a *barzakh* that let them apart.[42] Then he adds, "Imagination is neither existent nor abolished, neither known nor unknown, neither negated nor affirmed. It is like the image that a human sees in the mirror. He knows for sure that he perceives his image in some way, and he knows for sure that he doesn't perceive his image in some way, as he sees it so precise. If the mirror is small he knows that his image is bigger than that in the mirror; and if the mirror is big, he sees his image bigger than it is and he knows for sure that his image is smaller than that in the mirror. In both cases he can't deny that he didn't see his image. He also knows that it is different from what the mirror shows."[43]

Not everyone is capable of undertaking this journey, and not everyone can distinguish between a sensory being and an imaginal one, as ibn 'Arabi warns us, especially that we see both with the same organ of sight, and most people feel the "reality" of things only through their senses. He claims, though, he personally has come to differentiate between an imaginal being and a sensory being. He provides us with some hints on how to recognize an imaginal being from a corporeal one. He explains, for example, if we see beings as static only, we are seeing with the eye of sight, which usually identifies beings from the exterior and doesn't look to what is below them or behind them, like their aura, or their essence. If, on the contrary, we "see" these beings behind their appearance, and if we can capture some of their other aspects, we are witnessing things and beings with the eye of the imagination.

We will find out in the following chapters jinn are essentially shape-shifters.[44] Ibn 'Arabi invites us to be cautious with them and not believe we have seen them because they play tricks on us, and they have many strategies to escape us although we think we are still seeing them.[45] Finally, he cites a very intriguing Qur'anic example of what imagination really means. "And abounding fruit, not picked nor forbidden" (Qur'an 56:32*). He elaborates on this verse, "You look at the fruit and see it not picked and you look at your hand and you see that it is in your hand and you are eating it; and you realize without any doubt that the fruit you are eating is on the tree and hasn't been picked up."[46]

From all of the above, imagination is viewed as a synthesis, a realization of an ambiguous power or a faculty of the mind, a medium that reverses the situation we have on Earth because it "brings about the embodiment of immaterial things, even though they do not gain all the attributes of corporeality, remaining both/and."[47]

In the imaginal world, bodies become subtle shapes, and spirits like jinn don bodies and transform into visible beings. Imagination is like alchemy, a force of change; it is not fantasy. It is mistakenly confused with illusion, defined as a misleading image presented to the mind. Attributing the definition of fantasy or the illusion to imagination or the imaginal is therefore manifestly spurious. We need to stress repeatedly this feature of imagination to grasp the jinn as intelligent beings to whom the Qur'anic message is addressed along with humans. Because of all the qualities mentioned above, imagination is seen by ibn 'Arabi as the most perfect of all human faculties. "There is no intermediary or measure between imagination and meaning, just as there is no intermediary or measure between it and the corporeal object. Hence, imagination is the centerpiece of the collar; meanings go down to it, and the corporeal object is raised up to it, for it comes across the two planes through its quintessence."[48]

THE JINN AND RELATIONSHIPS BETWEEN
MACROCOSM AND MICROCOSM

To grasp how the jinn could impinge upon our physical plane, as classical Islam claims, it is essential to go back to the Islamic cosmological view at that point in time. The texts of Muslim medieval scholars evoke a constant interaction and an incessant communication between the macrocosm (cosmos) and the microcosm (the human being). They maintain there are eternal laws of correspondences and analogies that govern these relations. By correspondences and analogies, they mean the same hierarchical structure is valid for both the cosmos and the human. Indeed, both possess a similar tripartite division that rejects the Cartesian dualistic perspective of soul versus body.[49] "The distinction made between spirit, soul, and body has been applied to the macrocosm as well as to the microcosm. This is hardly surprising if we consider that the constitution of the one is by definition analogous to the constitution of the other, meaning that we are bound to come across elements in either macrocosm or microcosm which correspond exactly to the elements in the other."[50]

Moreover, to each of the three realms in the cosmos, there is an equivalent organ of knowledge in the human. Thus, sense corresponds to the terrestrial, imagination to the imaginal realm, as we have seen, and intellect to the celestial realm.

What is the relevance of these correspondences to the jinn's concept? They indicate the jinn, who are believed in Islam to be part of the Creation, and dwellers of the imaginal, interrelate with us. Like everything in the macrocosm, they infiltrate our world. On the other hand, we too are not isolated beings; we interact with all elements of the cosmos, including the jinn. Together, we nurture the round of energy that is life, and are nurtured by it in return.

The new physics established that the human and the cosmos are significantly interconnected in such a way that the consciousness of the human seems to affect the thing he/she is observing in the cosmos. In such a perspective, obviously, the cosmos is not seen as dead matter that the human controls, as Cartesians willed it. It is rather perceived as a living being that is aware and has its own consciousness. The new physics unraveled a web of interconnections and interdependencies in which humans and everything in the three planes of the cosmos exchange powers. "Their argument ([Albert] Einstein and [Niels] Bohr) had to do with the nature of observation. It seems a quantum mechanical system such as an atom or a subatomic system undergoes a rapid and unpredictable change whenever it is observed. This rapid change cannot be encompassed within the equations that describe quantum systems. It lies embarrassingly outside of the domain of mathematical representation. Somehow the very act of observing something causes an irreversible and uncontrollable change in the system, and this change effects and, for that matter, affects the relationship that exists between the observer and the observed."[51]

The new physics disclosed a new vision of the universe where matter is the exception and the major component is energy, which obviously changes the conventional perception of microcosm (reason) controlling matter (macrocosm). The result is an open field of energy overflowing with infinite potentialities in which we and all the beings of the three realms participate, whether we are aware of it or not.

CONCLUSION

Two points merit consideration toward the end of this chapter:

1. The numerous correlations I have elucidated between the microcosm and the macrocosm entail that the cosmos and the human are inseparable, and that the outside world is also the inside world. With regard to the subject matter of this book, this stipulation implies the jinn belong to the conscience of the natural world as well as to the human conscience. Sufi literature, more than orthodox Islam or popular Islam, eloquently exemplifies this inseparability between the human conscience and the conscience of the hierarchical cosmos with all it contains: "Know that the soul, the devil, the angel are not realities outside of you: you are they."[52]

2. Some western scholars attempt today to reach the spiritual phenomena beyond the paradigm of dualism. James Hillman, for example, a contemporary post-Jungian thinker, considers that the imaginal and the multiple could thrive in a polytheistic perspective of the world. Hillman, who is known for his original and creative contribution to post-Jungian psychology, maintains in this context, "For the 'return to Greece' offers a way of coping when our centers cannot hold and things fall apart. The polytheistic alternative does not set up conflicting opposites between beast and Bethlehem, between chaos and unity; it permits the coexistence of all the psychic fragments and gives them patterns in the imagination of Greek mythology."[53]

In embracing the belief in the intermediate world and its inhabitants, Islam seems to maintain there is no need to return to polytheism or Greek mythology if we wanted the imaginal to thrive. Islam advocates a path called "knowledge by presence" in which knowledge coincides with life itself. One is invited to utterly live one's knowledge. This notion, however, requires that one lifts him/herself to a *different* mode of apprehension, which involves passing beyond the discursive pattern of thinking.

The expression *al-ʿilm al-huduri* (knowledge by presence or presential knowledge), was coined by al-Suhrawardi, who founded the school of *Ishraq* (Illumination), which states intuitive knowledge apprehends reality better than discursive philosophy. The expression "presential knowledge" is in contrast to *al-ʿilm al-husuli* (conceptual knowledge). As contemporary Muslim scholar Seyyed Hossein Nasr expounds, "Man can know through intuition and revelation not because he is a thinking being who imposes the categories of his thought upon what he perceives but because knowledge is being. The nature of reality is none other than consciousness which, needless to say, cannot be limited to only its individual human mode."[54]

Presential knowledge involves unity between knowledge, subject, and object, the three referring to the same reality. Knower relates to known as the created relates to the creator. This resembles the relation established between subject and object in the Quantum physics' perspective, with the exception that the "sacred" dimension or/and the transcendental is not always present in the texts of quantum theorists.

It is possible to understand the multiple worlds and access them if one's life is in agreement and harmony with the existence of these worlds. According to Corbin, "What distinguishes the traditional cosmology of the theosophers in Islam, for example, is that its structure—where the worlds and interworlds beyond the mountain of Qaf, that is, beyond the physical universes, are arranged in levels—is intelligible only for an existence in which the act of being is in accordance with its presence in those worlds, for reciprocally, it is in accordance with this act of being that these worlds are present in it."[55]

Through presential knowledge, one could undertake the journey to the imaginal realm of the jinn without recourse to a polytheist view of things as Hillman suggests. It should be noted here that when Muslim theosophists say knowledge coincides with life, they don't mean one is invited to a literal interpretation of this hierarchical universe with its beings. On the contrary, when one succeeds to *live* the inseparability of natural conscience and human conscience, one experiences the most stunning openness of mind, heart, and spirit, which allows him/her to comprehend these most complex and intriguing correspondences between humans and jinn as classical Islam expounded them, and which I shall explore in the following chapter.

2
Correspondences Between Jinn and Humans

We turned to thee [Muhammad] a company of jinn giving ear to the Qur'an;
and when they were in its presence they said, "Be silent!"
Then, when it was finished, they turned back to their people, warning.
They said, "Our people, we have heard a Book that was sent after Moses,
confirming what was before it, guiding to the Truth and to a Straight Path."
—QUR'AN 46:29–31

*T*he hierarchical Islamic view of the cosmos entails the imaginal realm just above our terrestrial domain impinges unswervingly on us and interferes in our lives in a subtle and hidden manner. Because of the staunch belief in this direct influence on humans, Muslim scholars, poets, and writers found themselves compelled to thoroughly research the link between humans and jinn who originate from the imaginal domain. They mostly relied on the fascinating and intriguing corpus formed by the Qur'an and the Hadith, where both intelligent species are sometimes coupled in this life and in the hereafter, and sometimes opposed.

Chapter 55 of the Qur'an, entitled *al-Rahman* (the All Merciful), embodies at best the correspondence between humans and jinn. Throughout this chapter, written in the dual form to address its message to both jinn and humans, the following sentence is repeated ad infinitum, like a forewarning to jinn and humans: "O which of your Lord's bounties will you [humans] and you [jinn] deny?"

Jinn are addressed in the Qur'an as nations endowed with rational faculties.[1] Jinn and humans have mental faculties that allow them to access knowledge, perceive the truth, and distinguish them from all other living beings in the universe. These two intelligent species are described as discerning the Word of God through reasoning, while the rest of Creation grasps it instinctively.

SHARED FEATURES BETWEEN JINN AND HUMANS

Both Are Responsible

Jinn share with humans an essential *taklif* (religious responsibility). This refers to their knowledge of the Revealed Law. It is believed both species will be accounted for their deeds on the Day of Judgment because they both have received the Revealed Law, and it is implicit they know it. It is maintained God will set up the scales to weigh their good and evil actions. Islam deems both fully capable of making choices that will determine their abode in the afterlife in paradise or hell. If the jinn misuse their rational faculties as humans may, God will equally condemn them on the Day of Judgment. Both are responsible beings in the sense they *shahadah* (bear witness).[2] The Prophet's companion, Abu Sa'id al-Khidri, once advised a shepherd to raise his voice when he performs the call to prayer in the desert, for "whoever of the jinn and men as well as other living things, hears it, even from afar, shall bear witness to it on the Day of Judgment."[3]

Prophets and Messengers of God Sent to Humans and Jinn

The Qur'an and the Hadith argue if the jinn are considered responsible for their deeds, it is because many prophets and messengers were sent to deliver the Divine message to them. The Qur'an, in many instances, reminds both humans and jinn of this prophetic history: "Company of jinn and mankind, did not Messengers come to you from among you, relating to you My signs and warning you of the encounter of this your day? They shall say, 'We bear witness against ourselves'" (Qur'an 6:130).

But were some of these messengers from the side of the jinn, or were all the messengers from the human side alone? What does the Qur'anic expression "from among you" mean? Muslim theologians debated at length whether these verses indicate the messengers of God must have come from among jinn as well as from humans. The majority of Muslim theologians, however, concurred God did not send jinn messengers to the jinn; otherwise, they would have been mentioned in the Holy Book. Prophets were solely sent from humans.

Another question surfaced: If the messengers of God were indeed from the human side alone, how did the jinn gain knowledge of these messages? Muslim theologians argued the jinn seem to have their own communication channels that allow them to receive the Word of God. In one instance, they listened to a recitation of the Qur'an, then went to inform their fellow jinn about the message of God: "We turned to thee a company of jinn giving ear to the Qur'an; and when they were in its presence they said, 'Be silent!' Then, when it was finished, they turned back to their people, warning. They said, 'Our people, we have heard a Book that was sent after Moses, confirming what was before it, guiding to the Truth and to a Straight Path'" (Qur'an 46:29–31).

There are two possible answers to this question. Medievalist compiler and geographer Kamal al-din al-Damiri (d. 1405) claimed the jinn of Nusaybin [now in Turkey] who listened to the Prophet were considered to be messengers because they returned to their people to proclaim to them the coming of the Prophet (Muhammad).[4] Another answer was proposed by Qur'anic scholar Fakhr al-din al-Razi (d. 1210), author of one of the most authoritative commentaries on the Qur'an in the history of Islam, who suggested the encounter of the Prophet Muhammad with the jinn illustrated he was sent to the jinn as well as to humankind. Therefore, this encounter with spiritual entities challenged the pagans of Mecca by notifying them that even the jinn accepted Islam and believed in Muhammad when they heard the Qur'an. Al-Razi added that jinn, like all rational beings, are free to believe or disbelieve in the Word of God because they are responsible *mukallafun* as humans are, and they call their fellows to faith. Finally, he concluded the jinn are among us; they listen to what we say and understand it.[5]

The Qur'an speaks of jinn as having free will like humans. Both species are at liberty to group, to trust or to distrust the Word of God, and to religiously differ. The Islamic notion of responsibility is inseparably related to the notion of free will as in Qur'an 17:84*: "Every one [of jinn and mankind] works according to his manner," and in Qur'an 74:38*: "Every soul will be (held) in pledge for its deeds."

Jinn and Humans Are Formed of Nations

The Qur'an addresses the jinn as *umam* (nations). This Arabic word refers to large groups of people, or communities, which can be made up of either humans or jinn: "Such men are they against whom has been realized the Word concerning nations that passed away before them, men and jinn alike; they were losers" (Qur'an 46:18).

The nations of jinn are formed of tribes, similar to Arab society in pre-Islam. Many of the tribes of jinn are mentioned in the pre-Islamic and Islamic narratives, such as the tribes of Dahrash, Banu Ghazwan and the tribe of 'Asr.[6] Like humans, the jinn are thought to be two groups: sedentary people and those who move around called "the nomads of the jinn." Among those are some who roam by day, and some who roam by night.[7] Although Muslim scholars describe in detail the social organization of the jinn, there is no agreement among them regarding the number of their tribes. Historian al-Husayn ibn 'Ali al-Mas'udi (d. 956), for example, mentions the jinn are distributed among twenty-one tribes.[8] Ibn 'Arabi (d. 1240) claims the jinn are spread among twelve tribes[9] that have their own monarchs and chiefs. Many other scholars acknowledge the number of these tribes is unknown.[10]

Popular Islam in *The Nights* echoes in turn the semblance of the two societies of jinn and humans in many stories. In the story of "Qamar al-Zaman," for example, we are told the jinniyah Maymunah is the daughter of king Dimirat, a renowned monarch of the jinn. "She has giant jinn at her service, like the *marid* (giant jinni) Qashqash." In the story of "Hasan of Basorah," the sister of Hasan discloses to him that the jinniyah he loves is the daughter of a sovereign of the jinn, of one of the most powerful of their kings.[11]

In yet another story of *The Nights* entitled "Sayf al-Muluk and Badi'at al-Jamal," it is said Badi'at al-Jamal is also the daughter of a king of the jinn named "Shayhal ibn Sharukh, a king of the Kings of the true-believing jinn."[12] However, the jinn are not the only spiritual beings whose organization is similar to that of humans, and who have a governing system. Fairies in Celtic and Irish mythology are portrayed as having a king and a queen, and a strong social order as well. It is believed "the small Trooping Fairies and the Little People of Cornwall have a king and a queen and regular government, but are generally rather homelier in their habits."[13]

Islam, however, not only highlights the similarity of the societies of humans and jinn, but also maintains all living beings follow a more or less similar pattern of gathering into neighborhoods, kingships, and the like. The Qur'an often comes to this idea as in Qur'an 6:38: "No creature is there crawling on the earth, no bird flying with its wings, but they are nations like unto yourselves."

Both Have Different Creeds and Beliefs

We are even told in orthodox Islam about the jinn's religious beliefs and that they, like the humans, belong to different sects and different cults. In the Qur'anic chapter entitled "al-Jinn," the jinn themselves admit they follow different paths:

"And some of us are the righteous, and some of us are otherwise; we are sects differing" (Qur'an 72:11).[14] "And some of us have surrendered, and some of us have deviated" (Qur'an 72:14).

Other verses shed light on the creeds of the jinn. In the Qur'anic chapter entitled "al-Ahqaf" (the dunes), Muslim jinn explain to their (apparently Jewish) companions how they converted and what Islam is: "They said, 'Our people, we have heard a Book that was sent after Moses, confirming what was before it, guiding to the Truth and to a Straight Path'" (Qur'an 46:29).

Fourteenth-century jurist Badr al-din al-Shibli (b. 1312) understood these verses refer to the incident when the jinn came to see the Prophet Muhammad, and indicated these jinn were specifically Jews, because they mention Moses.[15] Although the great imam of Basrah, al-Hasan al-Basri (b. 642) concluded some of the jinn who listened to the Prophet are *Qadariyyah* (those who believe they are controllers of their actions and responsible for them), some are *Murji'ah* (those who believe the intention comes first, and all moral assessment is delayed until the Day of Judgment), others are *Rafidah* (broadly, Shi'ite Muslims who reject the caliphate of Muhammad's two successors Abu Bakr and 'Umar), and, finally, those who believe the religious and secular authority over Muslims should remain within the house of the Prophet Muhammad.[16]

In Islamic tradition, one even finds narratives relating the jinn regularly came to meet with the Prophet. Henceforth, the Prophet ordered his cousin 'Ali to teach them. "For among them are believers, heretics, Sabians, Jews, Christians, and Magians."[17]

Jinn and Humans Worship God

There is a strong belief among Muslims all inanimate things and all animate creatures in the universe worship God innately, and unremittingly glorify him, as in Qur'an 17:45*: "The seven heavens and the earth and everyone in them glorify Him. There is nothing which does not glorify Him in praise, but you do not understand their glorification." And as in Qur'an 13:15: "To God bow all who are in the heavens and the earth, willingly or unwillingly, as do their shadows also in the mornings and the evenings." Muslims maintain each heavenly body, mountain, tree, animal, and living being exalts the Divine relentlessly, each in its own language and in its own mode. When the Creation adores intrinsically the

Divine, it is believed it is simultaneously engaging in an act of knowledge of him. This is how the dialogue between God and his creation flows.[18]

Because humans and jinn are intelligent species, they could have knowledge of God through reason and intuition as well as through worship. Through their adoration, each has access in a specific and unique manner to his hidden qualities that become manifest to the faithful among them. As stated in the Qur'an, "I only created jinn and men to worship Me" (Qur'an 51:56*).

Shared Limitations Before the Creator

In many chapters, the Qur'an reminds humankind and jinn of their shared physical and mental limitations with regard to the realm of *al ghayb* (the unseen) as in Qur'an 55:33*: "O people of jinn and men, if you are able to pass through the confines of heaven and earth, pass through them! You shall not pass through except with an authority." Or in verse 17:90*, where God sets a challenge to both intelligent species: "If men and jinn banded together to produce the like of this Qur'an, they would never produce its like, not though they backed one another."

Fakhr al-din al-Razi questioned these shared physical and creative inabilities. He holds that each species has been challenged to accomplish that which corresponds best to its nature.[19] He asks "why God in Qur'an 55:33 puts [the word] 'jinn' before [the word] 'humans,' while in Qur'an 17:90, He puts 'humans' before 'jinn'?" In response, he purports that passing beyond the regions of heavens is more appropriate for jinn who could perform better physical wonders because their bodies are made of fire and air, which allow them to move about through space more easily than humans. In Qur'an 17:90, producing something similar to the Qur'an is more apt for humans, who are closer to the Word of God, than jinn, as the scriptures depict them.

Jinn, Humans, and Evil

Humans and jinn resemble each other with regard to evil as well. This is especially highlighted in the final chapter of the Qur'an (Qur'an 114*): "Say: 'I take refuge with the Lord of Mankind, the King of Mankind, the God of Mankind, from the evil of the slinking whisperer who whispers into the hearts of mankind—[from] among jinn and [from] among Men.'"

It should be noted that Islam distinguishes the following three kinds of spiritual beings: angels, jinn, and demons. This closing verse has inspired various conjectures as to its meaning. Some speculate it is Satan, the evil whisperer and tempter, who entices both humans and jinn. Others maintain there are two demons, one from humans who whispers to them, and one from jinn who whispers to them. It is never pointed out, however, how one could distinguish between the two demons. In any case, these verses explain that evil forces could rise from either or both of the two rational species. It is possible to compare the above interpretation with Qur'an 6:112*, where we read, "so We have appointed to every Prophet an enemy—Satans of men and jinn, revealing cheap speech to each other." This elucidation of evil as originating from both jinn and humans seems plausible within the context of orthodox Islamic tradition, which maintains the two communities of jinn and humans are capable of either good or evil.

Jinn, Humans, and the Afterlife

Jinn and humans are closely associated in matters dealing with the afterlife as well. God will either recompense them or punish them in accordance with their deeds. Both will be judged simultaneously. "On that day none shall be questioned about his sin, neither man nor jinn" (Qur'an 55:39). The same forewarning appears again in Qur'an 7:38: "He will say, 'Enter among nations that passed away before you, jinn and mankind, into the Fire.'"

There is a prolific imagery of the manner in which God will separate good jinn from evil jinn, and good humans from evil humans on the Day of Judgment. To paraphrase Qur'anic commentator Fayd al-Kashani (d. 1680) in his exegesis, God will gather the creatures on one level by calling out to the lowest heaven: "'Descend with the people who dwell in you,' and the people of the lowest heaven will descend with jinn, humans and angels, similar to those who live on earth; then the dwellers of the second heaven will descend in numbers twice as great, and so on, until the dwellers of the seven heavens will go down, and jinn and humans will be in seven pavilions surrounded by seven rings of angels."[20]

The prophetic tradition in turn refers to this association of jinn and humans in the afterlife. According to Abu Hurairah, one of the Prophet's companions, an angel will carry Muhammad on the Day of Judgment and God will ask him:

"What do you want, O Muhammad?" The Prophet will say: "You promised me intercession—let me intercede for Your creation, and then You will judge among them." At that time, the Prophet will return, and stand with the people. While they are standing, they will hear a strong clamor coming from the heavens, and the people of the lower heaven will come down, and the earth will be filled with jinn and humans, and the earth will be illuminated with their light as they approach it. Then God will place His Throne wherever He chooses on the earth, and He will say: "By My Glory and by My Majesty, no one who commits an injustice will go unpunished. O communities of jinn and humans, I have heard what you have said. I have been listening to you from the time I created you until today, watching your actions and hearing your words. Listen! These are your registered deeds inscribed upon you. Those who find good in them, let them thank God Almighty, and those who find other than that, let them blame only themselves."[21]

The Qur'an explicitly states hell will be composed of both humans and jinn.[22] The prophetic tradition expands on this issue, clearly differentiating between the three kinds of intelligent beings according to their dwelling in hell or in paradise: "One kind of beings will dwell in Paradise, and they are the angels; one kind will dwell in Hell, and they are the demons; and another kind will dwell some in Paradise and some in Hell, and those are the jinn and the humans."[23]

The majority of Muslim scholars believe Muslim jinn would enter paradise together with Muslim humans.[24] In his exegesis of the Qur'an, ibn Qayyim al-Jawziyyah, renowned scholar of Islamic tradition (d. 1350), claims believers among the jinn will dwell together in paradise with Muslim humans, and heretics among the jinn will be in hell with the human heretics.[25]

Other Muslim scholars, such as blind Arab poet Abu al-'Ala' al-Ma'arri (d. 1057), simply preferred to find a different location for the Muslim jinn, not far from the paradise where Muslim humans dwell. He argued God has palisades located between hell and paradise where the believers among the jinn will dwell. He imagined a visit from a certain narrator to paradise and hell who carries the news between the two. "The narrator rides on one of the mounts of Paradise, and reaches cities which are similar to the cities of Paradise, from which no shining light is cast; these cities contain narrow straits and dark valleys. So he asks one of the angels: 'What are these, O servant of God?' And the angel replies, 'These are the Paradises of the *'afarit* [a kind of jinn] who believed in Muhammad, the Prophet.'"[26]

Finally, al-Ma'arri's narrator notices the jinni who is accompanying him in the afterlife is not young as are his fellow human inhabitants of paradise. "He swiftly enquires about his old face and gray hair while humans in Paradise are enjoying splendid and eternal youth. The jinni replies that, 'Human beings have been honored by this, and we have been deprived of it, because we have been given the possibility of transforming ourselves in the first abode [referring to their lives on Earth], so that one of us, if he wills, could be a multicolored snake, and if he wills he could also become a bird such as a pigeon, which is why we have been forbidden from changing our shapes in the last abode [the next world], and so we have been left in our shapes, fixed and unchanged, while the children of Adam have been compensated by being allowed to remain in the best of forms.'"[27]

Thus, in the eternal abode, humans transcend their physical and time bound condition and become more prescient and visionary, while jinn turn into a state of decrepitude and ugliness. Moreover, humans become free from any dread of evil jinn, now that they have transcended the terrestrial realm.

Beyond the different dwellings in paradise, many other traits distinguish the two species. For example, Muslim medieval scholarship insisted God would not allow the jinn to see him or come close to him in the afterlife—not even the very pious among them.[28] Furthermore, numerous transformations would occur to both jinn and humans. For example, humans will be able to see jinn in paradise, while jinn will not be able to see them. It is as if the two species exchange qualities now that they dwell in the afterlife. In the same context, Muslim scholarship claimed heretic humans will undergo a demeaning process and will be transformed into jinn in the afterlife as a chastisement for their evil deeds.[29]

Jinn, Humans, and the Antichrist

Because both humans and jinn partake of evil, the Antichrist, prophesied in Islam to come at the end of time, can be either a jinni or a human, and people will not be able to recognize to which intelligent species he belongs. Historian and Qur'an commentator ibn Kathir (d. 1373), for example, tries to answer these questions. However, his interpretation remains ambiguous and indecisive because he once mentions the Antichrist will be a jinni: "Muslims will flee to mount al-Dukhan (smoke) in Syria, and the Antichrist *al-dajjal* will come and besiege them. The siege will intensify, and they will suffer great hardships. Then

Jesus, son of Mary,[30] will descend, and call at dawn: 'O people, what prevented you from coming out to fight this evil liar?' They will answer, 'He is a jinni.'"[31] And another time, he contradicts himself and claims, "The Antichrist will be a man, created by God to be a test for people at the end of time."[32] This last assertion, though, adds even more mystery to this particular issue, because the term *rijal* (men) in the Qur'an, could pertain to both jinn and humans, as expounded by many lexicographers of Arabic.

A MAJOR DIFFERENCE BETWEEN THE HIDDEN JINN AND THE MANIFEST HUMANS

In spite of all the correspondences mentioned above between jinn and humans, a foremost distinction between both remains. Although the subtle jinn can see humans and intervene in their lives, the latter cannot perceive them in the manifest realm, except in rare instances as mentioned in the Qur'an: "Surely, he sees you, he and his tribe, from where you see them not" (Qur'an 7:27).

There is a general agreement among Muslim exegetes that this verse refers to the jinn in general, and Satan in particular. Although Islam differentiates between demons and jinn as two distinct categories of beings, it puts them together when it comes to the issue of invisibility. Muslim thinkers from various backgrounds debated greatly this issue of invisibility. The Asha'ira school of early Muslim philosophy and jurisprudence founded by Abu al-Hasan al-Ash'ari (d. 935), for example, asserted God's acts cannot be discerned and are beyond human understanding, and exalted God's will to the extreme they considered it absolute. The adepts of this school have said jinn can see humans because God created the right preceptors for them to catch sight of them. Humans, on the other hand, cannot see the jinn because God did not create the same preceptors for them.[33] They even added, "Anybody who says that he can see the jinn, we will reject his claim unless he is a prophet."[34] Although the Mu'tazilah school of Islamic theology[35] founded in Basra, Iraq, by Wasil ibn 'Ata' (d. 748) established a doctrine of free will, and introduced rational argumentation in Islamic theology, its position with regard to this issue is not very different from the precedent school. Its adepts stressed, "If human beings do not see the jinn, it is because they have very thin and fine bodies which cannot be seen. If God had increased the power of our sight, we would have seen them as evidently as we see each other, and if God had made their bodies thicker, we would also be able to see them, even with our actual eyes."[36]

As for the Hanafite school of jurisprudence founded by jurist Abu Hanifah (d. 767), it stressed the use of analogy and opinion when dealing with religious or social matters. This school is considered the most liberal among the Islamic schools of jurisprudence. One of its thinkers, jurist Badr al-din al-Shibli (d. 1312), gives the following analogy regarding the invisible and manifest realms: "We don't see the wind as long as it is thin and light but when it gets mixed with dust, we can see it moving."[37]

The Sufi interpretation is exemplary represented by ibn 'Arabi (d. 1240) who wrote extensively on the "channeling" that could take place between the two intelligent species. Ibn 'Arabi's originality is in asserting that one can see with the heart and the faith, and that seeing is not limited to the eye. He writes, "We 'see' them (the jinn) with the eye of the heart rather than with the physical senses, and take it on faith that they are with us."[38]

Al-Suhrawardi (d. 1191), claims jinn themselves have tried to inform humans how to see them. In one of his *Mystical Treatises,* a king of the jinn advises humans to "put a bit of incense on the fire and throw away everything in the house that is made of iron, is comprised of the seven bodies or makes a noise."[39] Because the jinni is an inhabitant of the invisible world, he invites the human to release the environment from all kinds of "weightiness" or substances symbolized by the metal iron, and create instead a space of emptiness for the purpose of "channeling" with him. And finally, to celebrate his "visibility" in front of a human, he asks that incense be thrown on the fire.

Finally, the folkloric medieval interpretation is epitomized in many stories of *The Nights.* In the story of "The Fisherman and the Jinni," for example, the jinni makes himself visible to humans by going into a "smoky" phase: "For a long time, the smoke kept rising from the jar; then it gathered and took shape, and suddenly it shook and there stood a jinni, with his feet on the ground and his head in the clouds."[40] To return back to the jar where he was before, "the jinni shook himself and turned into smoke, which rose, little by little, and began to enter the jar."[41]

The appearance of jinn in the world of humans causes changes to occur, and sometimes disturbs the natural order, as in the story of "The Porter and the Three Ladies" in *The Nights:* "As soon as I kicked the step, there was thunder and lightning, and the earth began to tremble and everything turned dark. I became sober at once and cried out to her, 'What is happening?' She replied, 'The jinni is coming. O my Lord, get up and run for your life!'"[42]

The fact humans are unable to see the jinn sometimes creates problems that could reach dramatic dimensions and even lead to death as in *The Night's* story entitled "The Merchant and the Jinni." It tells the story of a merchant who, after eating his food composed of bread and dates, performed his prayers and was ready to continue his journey when the jinni appears to him:

> The jinni approached until he stood before him and screamed, saying, "Get up, so that I may kill you with this sword, just as you have killed my son." When the merchant saw and heard the jinni, he was terrified and awestricken. He asked, "Master, for what crime do you wish to kill me?" The jinni replied, "I wish to kill you because you have killed my son." The merchant asked, "Who has killed your son?" The jinni replied, "You have killed my son!" The merchant said, "By God, I did not kill your son. When and how could that have been?" The jinni said, "Didn't you sit down, take out some dates from your saddlebag, and eat, throwing the pits right and left?" The merchant replied, "Yes, I did." The jinni said, "You killed my son, for as you were throwing the stones right and left, my son happened to be walking by and was struck and killed by one of them, and I must kill you."[43]

HUMAN SUPERIORITY OVER THE JINN

The numerous instances of the correspondences between jinn and humans do not imply in any sense that both species could ever be equal. In all Muslim sources, humans are depicted as superior to jinn.

Imagination

Although it is true humans are physically unable to access the hidden realm of the jinn, they nevertheless could make their way into it through their imagination, which is a faculty that belongs to humans alone. In many passages of his opus magnum, *al-Futuhat al-makkiyyah,* ibn 'Arabi maintains imagination allows humans to be superior to jinn. He argues the jinn knew of the advent of Islam because they could move easily and quickly. Their swiftness permitted them to investigate the sources of change taking place with the advent of the Revelation:

Note that when they were forbidden from listening [to heaven], and the heavens became inaccessible to them because of the shooting stars,[44] they said, "This is only occurring because something is taking place." So Zawba'ah [one of their known chiefs] gave the order to his friends to roam the earth, its East and its West, to find out what this event was that impeded them from reaching the heavens. When the friends of Zawba'ah arrived at Tihamah, they passed by Nakhlah, where the Prophet was reciting the Qur'an. They listened to it, and said, "This is what prevented us from reaching the news from heaven." If they had not recognized the rank of the Qur'an and its inestimable value, they would not have been able to understand this, and they would not have hurried back to their own people to warn them.[45]

Ibn 'Arabi stresses the jinn were unable to envision the approach of Revelation without freedom from time and space. He claims, "Jinn's use of the imagination is very limited; they employ it to come to the physical world, and they take forms, such as manifesting themselves in animal shapes. But this is all that their imagination can do for them."[46]

Humans, on the other hand, don't need to wander throughout the earth to foresee an event, or a great change. Ibn 'Arabi stresses they are the most developed beings regarding imagination, which allows them access to both 'alam al shahadah (the physical world or the manifest world) and 'alam al ghayb (the hidden world). But despite their imagination,[47] a few among them seem capable of perceiving the jinn because these spirits have many ruses, wiles, and subterfuges they use to hide from human sight. Ibn 'Arabi sketches out some advice to avoid falling prey to their maneuvers: "Whenever the spirit [the jinni] embodies a material form, he can be imprisoned by human sight, and cannot leave this form in which he appeared, nor is there a place where he can hide as long as a human is persistently focusing on him. However, the spirit is able to escape from human sight by creating a shape in front of him, which he can use as a shield, and he will move it to a different place from where he is standing. If the human who is looking at him follows the form created by the spirit, the latter can make his escape."[48]

It is thought some holy and saintly spiritual humans have the ability not only to foresee things through their imagination but also to be in two places at the same time through their extraordinary imagination and their power of concentration. They are called the 'abdal or "spirit guardians." Ibn 'Arabi claims, "They are able to leave an image (or actual form) of their bodies in one place while they simultaneously travel to another place, thus giving people the impression that they have never left the original location. These people have often been 'sighted' in two places at once."[49]

In Sufism, there is a belief that these "spirit guardians" have always looked after humans to keep them allied with the flow of energy and wisdom, which originates from within.[50]

The stories of Sufis seeing jinn are abundant in Sufi literature and popular medieval culture as well. Al-Damiri (d. 1405 CE) tells this story on the Sufi, ʿAbdul Qader al-Gilani (d. 1166), known for his power over the jinn:

> A man from Baghdad came one day to the sheikh ʿAbdul Qader al-Gilani and informed him the jinn abducted his daughter, and asked for his help. So, the sheikh told him to do the following: "Go this night to the ruin of al-Karkh. Sit at the fifth hill and draw a circle on the floor and say while drawing it: 'In the name of God and according to ʿAbdul Qader's intention.' When the night becomes pitch black, you will see tribes of jinn passing by you in different shapes. Don't be afraid! None among them can enter the circle where you sit. When their king comes, he will approach you and enquire about your presence among them. You ought to tell him your story." The man followed exactly the orders of ʿAbdul Qader al-Gilani. As the Sufi sheikh told him, none of the jinn was able to enter the circle where he was sitting until came the king of the jinn who questioned him, and then brought his daughter back to him. She was abducted by one jinni from China! He fell in love with her and carried her away.[51]

Humans Alone Are the Inheritors and the Carriers of the Trust, ʿAmanah

Since the creation of the first man and prophet, Adam, humans are considered, according to the Qurʾan, God's vice-regents on Earth, hence the closest beings to him. It is mentioned in a Hadith *qudsi*, "The earth and the heavens do not contain Me, but the heart of my believing servant contains Me." Humans are created as a sign of God; they are considered noble and fine because their human qualities manifest the Divine Names of God. At the start of creation, the angels understood this unfathomable relationship between humanity and Divinity. This is the reason for the prostration of the angels before Adam, "Since God was manifest in him [Adam], their prostration was not, in reality, to Adam, in the same way today our prostration is not to Mecca or to the Kaʿbah, but rather to the Lord of the House."[52]

The Jinn as Subservient to Humans

It is generally believed those who are enslaved by humans are the heretic jinn who refused to submit to the new religion. In Qur'an 27:39 and 34:12, it is mentioned the evil jinn were at the prophet Solomon's service and performed difficult deeds for him. In some texts of medieval folk literature, especially in *The Nights*, jinn capture humans and force them to work for them. But even in these rare instances, humans manage to escape the servitude of the jinn by virtue of their greater intelligence and cunning.

Elements from Which Humans Are Composed
Give Them Greater Distinction over the Jinn

Although the jinn generally boast about their superiority because they are made of smokeless fire, Muslim scholars believe the element of water, which gives life to everything, and from which humans themselves are created, gives humans actual superiority over the jinn. In this context, ibn 'Arabi mentions a Hadith in which the angels ask: "O God, did you create something stronger than fire?' And God replied, 'Yes, water.' So He made water stronger than fire."[53]

Divinity seems to be associated in Islam and in many other traditions with water. Indeed, the Divine often has been linked to water in many traditions. In the Genesis account of creation, "In the beginning . . . the spirit of God was hovering over the surface of the waters." In the Hindu account of creation, the god Vishnu sleeps on the ocean, like God in the Qur'an who puts his "throne upon the waters." The fountain, in Christianity, represents Christ as a source of immortality, as the Water of Life. According to classical traditions, water and fire are two elements in conflict. They represent all the opposites in the elemental world. Together, they give heat and humidity necessary to the creation of life. In a sense, the burning water becomes the unity of opposites.

Humans as Providers of Knowledge

In pre-Islam, Arabs worshiped jinn. They believed these spirits had easy access to a higher form of knowledge. For example, people believed the jinn possessed the art of working metals. It was a common belief among the pre-Islamic Arabs that jinn craft powerful swords. In a number of pre-Islamic texts, we find detailed comparisons between ordinary swords made by humans and legendary swords made by jinn. Ordinary swords break easily, whereas the swords of the jinn could perform astounding feats. It is alleged that *ma'thur* and *ifranji* are two swords made by these spiritual entities. One of the characteristics of the ifranji is that it is a male sword, and it strikes with greater power, as they have described.[54]

The Arabs were not the only people to hold such viewpoints. Historian Edwyn Bevan (d. 1943), who mostly dealt with the history of the Hellenistic Empire, argues there is "one kind of instruction which the Apocalyptists believed to have been given by supernatural beings in the remote past, and this is just the same kind of knowledge about which the Greeks had a similar belief—the arts of civilized life."[55] The same belief is told about fairies, said to be great musicians and healers.[56]

Another conviction widely spread about the jinn is they were capable of transforming arid lands into fertile ones. Arabs in pre-Islam believed oases full of orchards and palm trees are the work of jinn who jealously defend them; if a human broke into their territories, the jinn would either kill or bring madness upon him. It was also thought the jinn excelled in the science of medicine, and were able to teach humans the secrets of healing diseases. Islam shattered these beliefs, and made humans superior in knowledge to spiritual entities. From providers of knowledge, jinn became seekers of knowledge. From superior to humans in exploring the hidden realm, they became inferior to them.

Jinn are pictured as being particularly interested in Islamic tradition and in the Qur'an, which became their highest source of wisdom and knowledge. Islamic sources reiterate the need for humans to educate these spirits in matters of religion. Well-known jurist and historian Jalal al-din al-Suyuti (d. 1505) recounts on one occasion, he attended the circle of grand jurist ibn al-Jawzi (d. 1200) in Naysabur. Suddenly, ibn al-Jawzi contracted an eye infection and decided to return to his family right away. He had a dream that night, having made the intention to leave, in which a man entered the room and said to him, "O sheikh you cannot go back so soon, for a group of believing jinn attend your circle, and listen to your lectures, and they have just begun to benefit from your teaching. As long as the lessons are not complete, you cannot leave, for God may open their hearts by means of what you say."[57] Thus, ibn al-Jawzi remained and continued teaching the jinn.

Medieval texts dwell at length on the jinn's enthusiasm for studying the Qur'an. A certain Abu al-Fadl al-Jawhari narrated,

> I used to come often visit ['Ali] al-khala'i, the judge, surnamed the jurist of men and jinn. I woke up one night while the moon was at its brightest to the extent that I thought it was already morning, I found at the door of his mosque a beautiful mare, so I went to it and I found near it a handsome young man who was reciting the Qur'an, so I sat beside him, and listened to him until he had read a large part of it. Then he left. I went after him. I saw him ride his mare which flied with him up in the air. I fainted and woke up to the judge's yelling: "Come up, Abu al-Fadl, come up." So I went to him, and he explained to me, "This man is one of the jinn believers who come to me once a week. He recites parts of the Qur'an, and then leaves."[58]

In yet another account, al-Suyuti maintained the jinn would come every Friday night to the mosque to listen to the Sufi al-Hasan al-Basri (b. 642) reading the final section of the Qur'an, and then they would leave.[59] He also claims the jinn were constantly mingling with Muslim humans without the latter noticing it. One quiet night, in the mosque of al-Khayf, a bird landed close to Wahab ibn Munabbih (b. 654), compiler of Islamic tradition, then came and sat in the circle of the attendees: "Wahab greeted the bird, for he knew that he was from the jinn, and said, 'Where is this man from?' The bird answered 'A man from the jinn, from the Muslim jinn.' Wahab said, 'And what do you want?' The jinni replied, 'Do you forbid us from learning from you? Many of us attend your circle, and we always return back to our people reciting what we have heard. We attend your prayers, your *jihad*, we visit your sick, we walk with the mourners in your funerals, and are among you at *'umrah* and at the *hajj*, and we listen to the Qur'an when you recite it.'"[60]

These spirits, in Muslim imagination, seem to be interested not only in theology, but in Arabic language, Arabic grammar, and Arabic poetry as well because they themselves compose poetry. Whatever they study, they seem to excel. The same al-Suyuti mentions the story of a certain Abu al-Hasan ibn al-Kisan, "One night I stayed awake studying grammar, then fell asleep. In my dream I saw a group of jinn studying Islamic law, the Hadith, grammar, and poetry. I asked them, 'Are there any scholars among you?' They answered, 'Yes!' I then asked, 'Whom do they prefer among the grammarians?' They answered, 'Sibawayh.' [d. around 793]"[61]

The imagined pious jinn appear in the prophetic tradition as well, where it is reported the Prophet Muhammad read once *surat al-Rahman* (chapter of The Most Compassionate, Qur'an 55) to his companions, then said to them, "I read it to your brothers the jinn, and they were better listeners than you. Each time I would say, 'So which of your Lord's blessings do you both deny?' They would respond, 'None of Your blessings, O our Lord do we deny.'"[62]

One can certainly see in all these narratives how Islam "invaded" the world of jinn and converted them, and how they became its most ardent disciples and defenders. The first two stories occur in dream, when the unconscious is very active, and the descent into the unknown self is bottomless. The third story takes place at dawn, where obscurity and light, sleep and wakefulness are not yet completely separated. It might well be a blurry vision when the borders of time are still unmarked. In any case, all three stories are definitely located in that sacred hierarchical geography of Islam where jinn and humans interact.

Although official Islam emphasizes the jinn's learning from humans, especially the Qur'an and the Hadith and their submission to the new religion, popular imagination, on the contrary, highlights the notion of the jinn coming to rescue humans. *The Nights* epitomizes these entrenched popular beliefs. It must be noted, however, these folkloric narratives emphasize the jinn's help originates not in the jinn themselves but in God who bestows his support to whomever he chooses from jinn or humans. The jinn themselves acknowledge this Divine source time and again, and contend they are only tools in the hands of the Divine. They intervene in humans' lives to fulfill their destinies. Popular imagination of Islam incessantly makes clear there is no magic whatsoever and no contradiction with the teachings of pure monotheistic Islam.

In the story of "'Ali the Cairene and the haunted house," for example, the jinni literally rains gold on 'Ali who is absorbed in his recitation of the Qur'an. 'Ali is extremely poor and is in dire need of help. As a good Muslim, though, he totally puts his trust in God. While immersed in the Holy Book, the jinni speaks to him. It is as if the prayer addressed to the Divine is finally answered.

A cursory reading of the story would suggest a naive belief in some kind of power that comes to rescue 'Ali from his deadlocked situation, and hints at polytheistic beliefs that are thought to run deeply in some classes of the Islamic medieval society. However, a profound appraisal of this narrative would unravel the complex connections and interdependencies between beliefs, destiny, and the role of the intermediary jinn. 'Ali knows deep inside that this gift is for him and, consequently, is not afraid of the jinni's voice, like the others who preceded him. The jinni in turn understands that, finally, 'Ali is the one he was looking for, and therefore, rains the gold on him.

In two other stories of *The Nights*, the jinn also interfere in humans' lives by introducing two young people and inspiring them to fall in love.[63] Despite the fact each of them lives in a far away country, they are brought together by the jinn while they are asleep. In "Qamar al-Zaman," the young girl, Sitt al-Husun, is a princess whom the jinn carry off from China while asleep and put in the arms of a young man named Qamar al-Zaman who had been refusing to marry any woman. He awakens in the night to find himself sleeping beside a very beautiful woman. He instantly falls deeply in love with her. The same jinni brings Sitt al-Husun back to her palace in China before dawn.[64]

The same pattern is reiterated in the story of "Nur al-din 'Ali and his Brother Shams al-din Muhammad," where one of the characters, Badr al-din Hasan, is brought from Cairo to Basrah by a jinni while sleeping and put in the bed of his cousin.[65] Like the previous story, Badr al-din falls in love with his beautiful cousin.[66] After meddling in the characters' lives, the jinn vanish without leaving any trace, which illustrates their presence was simply tactic and not psychological.

CONCLUSION

One wonders why all these detailed descriptions and explanations? I argue Muslim scholars in classical Islam strived to reconcile two seminal aspects of these correspondences. The first one is the human as the vice-regent of God on Earth, while the second is the strong belief in multiple worlds.

Muslim scholars aimed at preserving the preeminence of humans over all other beings, especially jinn, while keeping open the doors to the wealthy population of the multiple worlds, especially from the imaginal realm. For them this was not an impossible task. On the contrary, they seemed to have believed the originality of Islam lies precisely in this difficult reconciliation, which puts upside down the simplistic definitions of monotheism and polytheism.

3

Beings of Light and of Fire

Angels are souls blown into lights,
jinn are souls blown into winds,
and human beings are souls blown into shapes
—IBN ʿARABI (d. 1240)

*I*slamic teaching, as seen previously, highlights the interaction between humans and jinn, and attempts to interpret every facet that deals with this relationship. It expands much less, however, on the situation of angels and jinn despite the intermediary position of the latter, who are supposed to trade both with humans in the lower level and with angels in the higher level. The reason for this paucity of details seems to lie in the Qur'an, which forbade the jinn from ever approaching the heavens. Islam thus closed the higher realm to jinn who, before its advent, constantly visited angels and engaged in dialogue with them. With the advent of the new religion jinn do not interact with angels any longer. This is why Islam talks about the interaction between jinn and angels in the past; it depicts their historical interaction in the heavens and on Earth and confines itself to comparing their respective compositions and powers.

THE JINN'S COMPOSITION

In many instances, the Qur'an mentions the elements from which the jinn are composed: "Surely, We created mankind of a clay of mud molded, and the jinn created We before of scorching winds" (Qur'an 15:26–27). In addition to the wind, the Qur'an cites the "smokeless fire" mentioned in Qur'an 55:14–15. It is characterized by a brilliant flame of very high intensity mixed with smoldering wind and has a special Arabic name, *marij,* which means "mixed with."[1] It is almost as if the jinn were composed of hell itself or are a living hell, as many Muslim scholars pictured them. They found them fascinating beings but repugnant at the same time because they evoke hell.[2] Muslim medieval scholars asserted the jinn could literally kill because of their dangerous composition. They emphasized heat is an attribute of fire and a vehicle for passions.[3] They ascribed to the jinn strong feelings and immense emotional powers as well as rationality, as we have seen before.

Muslim researchers endeavored to know which of the two elements overcomes the other in their composition. Some believed "fire prevails more than air in their bodies,"[4] while others thought the jinn could not possibly be composed of these two elements alone. Ibn 'Arabi (d. 1240), for example, argued the composition of these spirits includes some moisture as well, because "creatures of fire by themselves could not breathe . . . God Almighty is capable of creating humidity in fire to make life possible in it."[5] The majority concurred, however, that the pure flame in the jinn is lighter than wind itself, which enables them to cross all barriers, walk on water, and twirl in all environments. Wind and fire are, in any case, looked upon as violent forces.

In general, the elements of fire and air of which the jinn are composed appear to be greatly compatible, as Paracelsus the Great (b. 1493), German mystic and alchemist, maintains. "The element of fire is placed in the element of air. For as the water and the earth are comprised in one globe, so the fire and the air are mingled in one, neither injuring the body of the other. They move freely in the air, not leaning or propped up on any foundation."[6]

Despite their apparent compatibility, as Paracelsus has asserted, the two elements that compose the jinn are paradoxically in opposition as well. Although air tends toward heaven, fire pulls down toward Earth, thus creating the intermediary state that distinguishes these spirits half way between the upper realms and the sublunary world.

The jinn are subtle and secret beings whose extremely refined elements veil them from us, fire being a pure energy, and wind being the vital breath of the universe, the vehicle of light par excellence and of the invisible; it is that which we feel around us without being able to touch, almost an intelligent power that appears to direct things. In approximately all traditions across the world, wind represents the ineffable; a force we cannot apprehend by the senses alone, but still has an undeniable existence. It is a spiritual power that dwells in the human and outside of him as well. Fire often has been pictured as a fierce beast. The

Egyptians, for example, said it is a voracious, ravenous animal that gulps down everything in its way.[7]

Across traditions fire is linked to the dragon known to be a fire-breathing beast. It also was thought every hundred years the phoenix smeared its wings with myrrh and burst into flames, only to rejuvenate itself from the ashes of the fire to live anew. Hence, fire is an ambiguous symbol of birth and destruction, a manifest element to the eye, while wind remains ineffable, unseen, and subtle. In Hinduism, fire is the power of annihilation exerted by the Indian god, Shiva. In Pythagorean thought, it is the first element in creation. In Zoroastrianism, fire symbolizes the energy of the Creator, which is glowing, unpolluted, and life supporting; Zoroastrians usually pray in front of some form of fire or light. As a religion of synthesis, Islam integrated in its concept of the jinn the many ancient symbols of air and fire that existed in the traditions before it.

ANGELS, GODS, AND JINN IN THE PRE-ISLAMIC PERIOD

The term jinn in Arabic refers to all invisible spiritual entities. As already mentioned, each time the two Arabic letters jim and nun occur together, they carry the meaning of invisible, hidden, and mysterious. Hence, the term jinn in Arabic encompasses jinn, demons, and angels, because all three are invisible. This use of the term jinn was prevalent in pre-Islam, and remained in use during Islam, at least in the beginning.[8]

The blurring of definitions between angels and jinn persuaded some historians of pre-Islam that Arabs were ignorant of the existence of angels; they claimed they only had notions of the jinn. Thus, Toufic Fahd, contemporary French anthropologist and historian of religions, makes the point that pre-Islamic Arabs were entirely ignorant of the concept of angels. He insists, "Angelology penetrated Arabia only with the birth of Islam,"[9] while French ethnographer Joseph Chelhod (d. 1994), whose work focuses on the religions and customs of South Arabia, disagrees with this point of view. He maintains that the concept of angels as distinct from jinn already existed in pre-Islamic Arabia: "Although the term 'angels' *mala'ikah* has probably a foreign origin (it might be Ethiopian or Aramaic), it must have penetrated into the Hijaz [in West Arabia] very early, to the point that at the eve of the Hijrah [the Prophet's migration to Madinah], it was already part of their religious vocabulary."[10]

Fahd's assumption is erroneous because it ignores four things. First, the two letters jim and nun refer to all kinds of spirits, including jinn and angels. If the Arabs at that point in time used the term "jinn" to refer to both angels and jinn, that simply means they knew of the existence of angels. Second, pre-Islamic Arabia was composed not only of pagan Arabs, but also of Arab Jews, Arab Christians, and Zoroastrians who spoke of the existence of angels in their books. As the study of Arabs before Islam shows, there was a constant and lively exchange between these religious communities.[11] Arabs knew of the existence of angels from them. Third, the Qur'an, in turn, asserts that the pre-Islamic Arabs were familiar with the concept of angels, and that they knew angels were sent to certain chosen individuals, such as prophets. Some of the pagan chieftains of Mecca mockingly asked the Prophet Muhammad to show them his "angel" to prove his prophethood to them, whereupon the following Qur'anic verses were revealed: "Perchance thou art leaving part of what is revealed to thee, and thy breast is straitened by it, because they say, 'Why has a treasure not been sent down upon him, or an angel not come with him?'" (Qur'an 11:15).

Fourth, pagan Arabs spoke about fallen angels, which again testifies to their knowledge of this concept. They thought, for example, that fallen angels were among them, that they interacted with humans, and even had sexual relations with them. They believed God sends a fallen angel to Earth in the image of a man.[12] One of the most well-known examples is that of the Arab tribe of Jurhum. The Arabs of pre-Islam claimed Jurhum, founder of the tribe by his name, was the result of a union between a fallen angel and a human woman. This legend took on excessive importance for the Arabs at that point in time, because this tribe controlled the ancient sanctuary of Mecca for a considerable period of time.[13] Arab historians and commentators exalted this story, and claimed that Ismael, the son of Abraham and the father of Arabs, married a women from Jurhum.[14]

In addition to their knowledge of angels and jinn, the pre-Islamic Arabs revered many gods and goddesses, especially the goddess al-Lat. It is said that "Her temple in Ta'if was as venerated as the Ka'bah is today."[15] Another goddess, al-'Uzza, was worshiped at Nakhlah near Mecca and Madinah, especially by the tribe of Quraysh. As for the goddess Manat, she had a shrine between Mecca and Madinah and was primarily worshiped by the Arabs of Madinah. The pagan Arabs flocked in pilgrimage to the shrines of these three goddesses and performed religious ceremonies there.[16]

In fact, each tribe in the Arabian Peninsula had its own god or goddess. Quraysh (the tribe of the Prophet) acquired the property of the god Hubal, who was the chief deity of the Ka'bah. It was painted red and had the shape of a human. It is claimed Hubal was brought from Syria, and "his hand was broken, so Quraysh provided him a hand of gold instead."[17] The tribe of Hudhayl obtained the god Suwa', the tribe of Rabi'ah worshiped the god Nasr, and the tribe of Himyar had the goddesses al-Lat and al-'Uzza.

The two gods Suwa' and Nasr began as simple, naively carved idols; then they were gradually transformed into gods bearing a relationship to heaven, particularly in the religion of Southern Arabia, which orbited around a worship of the celestial triad of the sun, the moon, and the planet Venus.[18] The three goddesses, al-Lat, al-'Uzza, and Manat, were worshipped as angels, which once again testifies to the spread of the concept of angels among pagan Arabs.[19] They were occasionally referred to as daughters of Allah. "Those who do not believe in the world to come name the angels with the names of females. They have not any knowledge thereof; they follow only surmise, and surmise avails naught against truth" (Qur'an 53:27–28).

Arabs at that point in time even held the belief God kept angels for himself because they were female. The Qur'an strongly condemns this belief: "What, has your Lord favored you with sons and taken to Himself from the angels females? Surely it is a monstrous thing you are saying!" (Qur'an 17:41).[20] Moreover, they believed these goddesses were veiled because of their close similarity to women. The sun, for example, which was worshiped, is a feminine word in Arabic because its brilliant flame makes it difficult to see.

In fact, a belief in gods possessing the characteristics of angels was not limited to pagan Arabs, but was rather common to many peoples of the Near East, specifically in the Canaanite and Mesopotamian religions, which had many winged gods. Thus, the god El in the Canaanite religion is himself explicitly pictured with four wings upon his shoulders, two for flying and two folded. His allies are similarly pictured: "But to the rest of the gods two wings for each on the shoulders in order that they might fly with Kronos."[21] The banquet text from Ugarit (RS 24, 252; Ug. V.2), for example, reveals the goddess Anat herself could fly: "And verily Anat flies swiftly, she soars like an eagle."[22]

The idea of worshiping angels as goddesses and female sub-deities is one of the most perplexing ideas in the religion of polytheistic Arabia. It is known that a few Arab tribes of pre-Islamic Arabia had great contempt for female offspring. One of their most barbaric customs, which the Qur'an forcefully denounces in many places,[23] was the live burial of infant girls.

Arabs in pre-Islam believed as well these female sub-deities interceded on their behalf before God. Furthermore, and now more astonishing to us, they maintained angels were the children of unions between God and the daughters of the jinn. In the Qur'an, we find numerous allusions to the fact that the pre-Islamic Arabs, especially of the Hijaz region, believed Allah and the jinn were relatives. Some of them went so far as to worship the jinn because of their relationship to God. "Yet they ascribe to God, as associates, the jinn, though He created them; and they impute to Him sons and daughters without any knowledge. Glory be to Him!" (Qur'an 6:100). The proper name of 'Abdul-jinn (servant of the jinn) was spread before the advent of Islam, which indicates that the adoration of the jinn was common.[24] The Qur'an repeatedly refers to this worship: "Upon the day when He shall muster them all together, then He shall say to the angels, 'Was it you these people were [worshiping?]' They shall say, 'Glory be to Thee! Thou art our Protector, apart from them, nay rather, No, they were worshiping the jinn; most of them believed in them'" (Qur'an 34:40).

The worship of the jinn is also attested to in Arab Safaitic inscriptions from Northern Arabia. The Arabs, to cite historian of Near Eastern religions Jean Starcky (b. 1910), brought these deities with them when the Syrian steppe was arabized as a result of Arab invasions during the second half of the first millennium.[25]

The jinn-deities were especially conspicuous in the ancient Syrian city of Palmyra. A similarity in beliefs between different areas of the ancient Near East is only natural when we remember that since time immemorial, the Near East was never an inaccessible area, and the Arabs were never as isolated as has been commonly asserted. Trade and consecutive migration, as well as invasions and wars, connected them to other people in the area. Palmyra, for example, was a major crossroad of peoples and cultures. Many peoples settled in it: first, the Amorites, then the Aramaeans, the Arabs, and finally the Romans.

Some archeologists and historians of religion speak of the worship of jinn as gods in Palmyra, asserting these jinn-deities used to be called "gene" by the Aramaeans (which also means invisible in Aramaic) at that time. These names appear on inscriptions from the third century CE at Dura in the Jabal al-Sha'r, northwest of Palmyra.[26] W. F. Albright, a biblical archaeologist and Middle Eastern scholar noted especially for his excavations of biblical sites (d. 1971), relates that these deities were exactly the same as the jinn who were worshiped by the pre-Islamic Arabs. He also believes these same deities were worshiped in Babylonia and other areas of the Near East under different names.[27]

In 1933 and 1935, French archeologist and historian Daniel Schlumberger (d. 1972) unearthed the area northwest of Palmyra and uncovered a great number of inscriptions that were, for the most part, votive. They often mention the *ginaya* as the tutelary deities of villages, settlements, encampments, orchards, tribes, and so forth.

Under Tiberius Augustus (14–38), Palmyra became a city tributary to the Roman Empire, and was named Palmyra (in Arabic Tadmur). Under Antonius (96–193) and the house of Severan (193–222), it was transformed into one of the chief cities of the East that thrived until the middle of the third century CE. Gradually, the civilization of Palmyra became a mixture. There was great tendency to syncretism. It is thought that "The Arab goddess al-Lat, for example, was worshiped with the features of Athena."[28] Some even surmise that the jinn-gods of Arab Palmyra gave birth to the Latin term "genie."[29]

Contemporary archeologist and historian of the Middle East Javier Teixidor (b. 1930) maintained, for example, there are many similarities between the two concepts of genie and jinn. Teixidor refers at length to the classical scholars who acknowledged the existence of tutelary deities for persons as well as places, exactly like the pre-Islamic Arabs. He writes: "These innate (the jinn) were comparable to the Roman 'genii': they were deities who were tutelary of persons and places believed to take care of human lives and enterprises. They protected flocks and caravans and also those who had settled or were in process of sedentarization. Shrines erected for such gods occurred especially in the semi-nomadic surroundings of Palmyra in places that were centers of settled life and halts for passing caravans."[30]

THE JINN INHABITED THE EARTH LONG BEFORE HUMANS

The idea that spiritual beings or gods were created before humans and inhabited the Earth long before them is found in many ancient religions. In general, world mythologies speak of proximity and relationships between humans and gods or supernatural beings. Primordially, Earth was closer to heaven. Humans and gods of all kinds mingled. Humans could climb to heaven through the axis mundi. World mythologies speak even of a marriage between heaven and Earth. An example of this is found in the Sumerian Epic tradition between the god Dumuzi and Inanna.

Hesiod, Greek philosopher and poet who lived around 700 BCE, painted in his work *Theogony* the Greek myth of creation and the marriage between *Ouranos* (heaven) and *Gaia* (Earth). Ouranos embodies the Mountain of Heaven, which literally falls upon Gaia. The result of this union is the birth of the mountains and the sea, etc. It is also thought the fairies of the Irish and Celtic mythologies are the children of the goddess Dana or Danann. They were later called the Fairy Folk or the Sidhe. It is believed, "Wise men do not know the origin of the Tuatha De Danann, but that it seems likely to them that they came from heaven, on account of their intelligence and for the excellence of their knowledge."[31]

It is believed the jinn, before Islam, used to climb up to the heavens to overhear the angels. However, the advent of Islam smothered their Promethean nature. If they attempt to approach the heavens, the fire of meteorites will burn them instantly. Beings of fire are vulnerable to fire, and because jinn kill by fire, they are killed by it. Only angels are allowed to dwell in heaven.

In Islam, the relationship between jinn and angels started at the beginning of time, when the jinn were sent to Earth by the Creator to build and prosper. The story of their creation before humans is mentioned in the Qur'an, "whereas the jinn We have created, long before that, out of the fire of scorching winds" (Qur'an 15:27*).

When 'Ali ibn abi Taleb, the Prophet's son-in-law and the fourth caliph (d. 661), was once asked whether there were people dwelling on Earth before Adam, he replied: "Yes. God created the earth and created in it nations of jinn who praised Him and glorified Him without interruption. They often used to fly to heavens, and meet with the angels and salute them, and learn from them good things as well as the events that were occurring there. Then they were expelled from the earth because they rebelled and shed blood and ignored God."[32] In fact, in medieval Muslim narratives, the jinn are named "the Pre-Adamites." The same pattern is repeated in all these sources time and again: the jinn rebelled, spread corruption on Earth, and rejected the laws of the prophets who came to them. Then God sent his army of angels to expel them from Earth and fierce and violent struggles occurred between jinn and angels. A legion of angels equipped with swords or spears, with an angel named al-Harith[33] at their head, came down to Earth to fight the jinn. They attacked them with fire billowing out of their mouths and the jinn resisted vigorously. Finally, after intense fighting, the angels won, and the jinn were defeated. God Almighty hurled on them a fire that burned them, and a wind that blew them away, banishing them to the seas.[34]

But who were these spiritual entities that came to Earth to combat the bad jinn? Were they themselves angels or jinn?[35] The confusion between the two entities resurfaces in these battles and many different versions exist. The first one maintains the angels were helped by a lower category of jinn, called *hinn*[36]; while a second version represented by the Ikhwan al-Safa', or the Brethren of Purity (who lived in Basra, Iraq, during the 10th century), as noted in one of their *Epistles,* contends God sent angels to chase away the evil among the jinn to the far extremities of the Earth. The angels, according to Ikhwan al-Safa', took some of the jinn to heaven as prisoners, and among them was Iblis (Satan). He was then still a young jinni, and he was raised with the angels. When God created Adam, He said to the angels: "I am creating a vice-regent on earth, [other than you, and I will raise you to heavens]." The angels who were living on Earth abhorred the idea of leaving their familiar homeland, and answered God, "Are you going to put in it [the earth] people who will shed blood and do corruption, [as did the jinn], while we glorify You and praise You?"[37]

In a third variation on these dramatic events, it is mentioned the battles occurred between two categories of jinn: angels and *jann,* suggesting angels were also named jinn since the term "jinn" refers to both spiritual entities. According to this account, God sent them an army of angels who were dwelling in the lower heavens. "This army was called the jinn. Among those angels was Iblis. He came down with four thousands. He chased the jann away from the earth with his army, and expelled them into the islands of the sea. Then Iblis and his army inhabited the earth."[38] It looks like Iblis was the chief of the angels in the lower heavens before God commanded him to come down to Earth and combat the bad jinn.[39]

Ibn 'Arabi also confirms the dwelling of a pious Iblis on Earth before the creation of Adam. He thinks that "God (exalted be He) had appointed him as a vice-regent therein, along with a body of angels, and he had been there for quite a long time faithfully worshiping God."[40]

The jinn in all of these accounts disobey the Divine command. What is the meaning of their disobedience, if not that they are the first to create a pattern humans will imitate? Indeed, humans will rebel and reject heavenly messengers. They will shed blood, spread corruption, and exploit the environment, as if the earth were to become the locus par excellence of defiance to the Divine and waywardness.

Muslim writers raised these intriguing questions: Were all the jinn killed in these battles? If some of them did survive the fierce battles with the angels, where did they hide? How long? There exists a popular belief that many of those who ran away have continued to roam the earth, even building giant constructions and famous monuments. One finds frequent allusions to this belief in Arab poetry as well. In an ode by pre-Islamic poet al-Nabighah (d. 604), we read: "Exploit the jinn, for I have permitted them/to build Tadmur [Palmyra] with iron and columns."[41]

Folk Islam claims these "Pre-Adamites" jinn are still on Earth; they prefer to dwell far from humankind, and choose the wild, deserted, and desolate places where wasteland swarms with unknown perils. The expression "someone was hosted by a jinni" means he or she stayed in a wild place, where no friendly person dwells, except the jinn.[42]

Some sources suggest that Iblis remained on Earth only until the time of Adam,[43] while others maintain many jinn were still present when Adam was created.[44] Ibn Kathir (d. 1373) concurred with the common acceptation of the idea the jinn remained on Earth in the company of humans, and still do.[45]

ANGELS IN ISLAM

Because jinn were forbidden to bear news from heaven to Earth, according to the Qur'an, angels became the only transmitters of the Revelation. The angel Jibril (Gabriel), in particular, called *al-ruh al-qudus* (the Holy Spirit), as well as *al-ruh al-amin* (the Faithful Spirit) (Qur'an 26:192) and the "Entrusted Powerful One" (Qur'an 53:3–6) is the Revelatory angel to prophets. In the prophetic tradition, Muhammad describes how Gabriel first brought the Revelation "down upon his heart." "He came to him and said, 'Read!' He said, 'I cannot read.' Then the Prophet said, 'He seized me and squeezed me until all the strength went out of me, and then released me and said, 'Read!' I said, 'I cannot read.' Then he said: '[Read]: In the name of thy Lord who created, created Man of a blood-clot. [Read]:

And thy Lord is the Most Generous, who taught by the pen, taught Man that he knew not'" (Qur'an 96).[46]

Islamic philosophy debated at length the role of angels as messengers from the divine to humans. The Ishraqi (illuminationist) School of philosophy in particular distinguished itself by its original discussion of angels in Islam. Founded by al-Suhrawardi, the key argument was that humans could obtain knowledge by intuition, through the heart more than through reason. The angel Gabriel is represented in this mystical philosophy as the source of intellect and the messenger of knowledge, not only to the Prophet Muhammad, but also to the prophets Abraham, Zachariah, and the Virgin Mary as well. The Qur'an recounts how the angel Gabriel came to Mary in the form of a handsome man to announce she will bear Jesus. Gabriel, in the view of al-Suhrawardi and all Ishraqi philosophers, is "the angel of knowledge."[47]

Revelation in Islam is not limited to the Qur'an. The Hadith Qudsi (the Holy Tradition) is one example because it is believed God directly spoke to the Prophet without the intermediacy of the angel Gabriel.[48] Moreover, in one singular instance, the Prophet is reported to have penetrated the domain of the unseen in the night of the Ascension when a removal of the veils occurred, and no intermediary was present, as stated in the Qur'an: "He revealed to His servant what He revealed. His heart didn't lie about what he saw . . . He saw Him again another time" (Qur'an 53:10–13*).

Many other angels are described in the Qur'an, as well as in other works, though not all of these are messengers. There are, for example, the Guardian Angels who are entrusted with the protection of each person, as mentioned in Qur'an 13:10–11 and 6:61. There are *al-hafazah* (the Keeper Angels) (Qur'an 82:10 and 85:4), who keep records for each person as mentioned in the Qur'an and the traditions of the Prophet. There are messengers of good and protectors of humans from the assaults of the Devil as mentioned in Qur'an 13:11. There are the angels Munkar and Nakir who question humans in the grave while others are custodians of paradise and hell. There is the angel Israfil who will sound the trumpet to call the dead from their graves, as in Qur'an 61:73; 18:99; 20:99; and 34:51. He is described in the *Wonders of the Creatures* by geographer al-Qazwini (d. 1283) as being colossal in size, his feet reaching below the seventh earth, and his head reaching to the pillars of the Throne of God. Some angels bear the Throne of God on the Last Day, as described in Qur'an 59:17. For the most part, the

Qur'an distinguishes angels from humans and jinn by their inherent goodness. In Qur'an 66:6 God praises them because they unquestioningly abide by what he commands. They are also praised in Qur'an 21:20 because they never fail to worship him by night and by day. For Muslim medieval scholarship, being unconditionally obedient to God doesn't imply angels are ignorant. In fact, one of the seminal questions discussed by Muslim scholars revolved around the following: Are angels more knowledgeable than humans, or less? These debates took as their main point of departure the Qur'anic passage Qur'an 2:28, where the angels seem to know that humans will bring havoc to the earth. Angelic superiority, however, is superseded by that of human consciousness in the person of the first prophet, Adam. God taught him all the names and, by that supreme knowledge, enabled his mind to penetrate every possible detail of the universe: "And He taught Adam the names, all of them; then he presented them unto the angels and said, 'Now tell Me the names of these, if you speak truly.' They said, 'Glory be to Thee! We know not save what Thou hast taught us'" (Qur'an 2:29–31).

The question of how the angels were able to know Adam's descendants would corrupt the earth has been argued frequently in Muslim theology. Historian and exegete ibn Jarir al-Tabari (d. 923), in his exegesis of the Qur'an, suggests they might have seen it in heaven's *al-lawh al mahfuz* (Secured Records) where it is believed all knowledge from all time has been recorded. However, in Qur'an 2:31, it appears Adam has greater knowledge than the angels, and it is Adam alone who is shown to possess the ability to think conceptually. It is Adam who is taught the supreme knowledge (the secret of all names) by God, and not the angels who acknowledge their ignorance and submit themselves to his will.

Islamic philosophy constantly emphasizes the idea humans should strive to return to their original "angelic" state. The treatises of Ikhwan al-Safa' state this is the goal of philosophy. They believe it is through philosophy that humans realize the virtual characteristics of their humanness. They affirm, "Man attains the form of humanity, and progresses in the hierarchy of beings until in crossing the straight way (bridge) and the correct path he becomes an angel."[49] In the same context, one should mention also al-Suhrawardi, who maintains in his visionary narratives that humans who purify themselves could reach again their angelic state where they belong. Al-Suhrawardi particularly expands this commentary in *The Rustling of Gabriel's Wings,* which is a tale of exodus and a meeting with the angel Gabriel.[50] Finally, angels are always depicted as totally submitted to

God and existing only to fulfill his commands. 'Abdul-Qader al-Gilani (d. 1166), founder of the Qaderi Order in Baghdad, believed, "Angels have no will, while prophets have no passion, and the rest of humans and jinn have both will and passion, except for certain saints who are free of passion."[51]

THE CASE OF IBLIS (SATAN)

One of the crucial issues related to the mythical battles waged between the angels and the jinn on Earth at the beginning of time concerned the nature of Iblis: was he a jinni made out of fire or an angel made out of light? Muslim scholars differ as to whether Iblis was the chief of the angels who led the battles against the jinn on Earth, or whether he was a repentant jinni who disagreed with the evil jinn and who decided at a certain time to join the angels. The Qur'an is not very clear about it. In what follows, I will attempt to explain the two positions.

Iblis as Angel

In Qur'an 17:61, we are shown that Iblis is among the angels. When God asked the angels to bow to Adam, they all bowed, except Iblis who is described in some Muslim sources as a four-winged angel.[52] It is believed Iblis, of all the angels, was the most afraid of Adam. Whenever he passed by him in paradise he would strike him, and Adam's body would make an echoing sound like clay.[53] Some Muslim scholars stated Iblis was one of the guardians of paradise.[54] They claimed, "Iblis was the chief of the angels of heaven and their ruler, as well as ruler over the earth. He was one of the most studious angels and the most knowledgeable. He ruled between heaven and earth. He took great pride and honor in it. But he became arrogant and haughty. He rebelled and was ungrateful to God who transformed him into a cursed devil, *shaytan*."[55]

Al-Mu'tazilah school of theology and Islamic thought (eighth–tenth century), which introduced the categories and methods of Hellenistic philosophy, tended to view Iblis as depicted in Qur'an 18:50 as an angel rather than a jinni.[56] Many Sufis were inclined to consider him a faithful worshiper, if not the most faithful. In their eyes, Iblis rebelled because he refused to bow to anyone other than God. From this standpoint, he was an example of the sincere monotheist. Iblis did not envy humanity in the least, but was instead an enthusiastic lover of

God's unity. However, Persian Sufi Najm al-din al-Razi (d. 1256) makes an exception among Sufis. He claims Iblis rebelled because he had insight into the future of Adam before the other angels. Najm al-din al-Razi tells how Iblis stole the news Adam would be appointed the vice-regent of God on Earth: "Iblis, that arrogant, black-fortuned one, who in his inquisitiveness had once made stealthy and illicit entry into Adam's frame, gazed with the eye of contempt upon the domain of his vice-regency, and desired in vain to make a breach in the treasure house of his heart, was therefore seized on the charge of robbery and bound with the rope of wretchedness. When it was time for all the angels to prostrate themselves, Iblis was unable to do so, for he had in reality been bound with the rope of wretchedness on the day he entered the workshop of the unseen without permission."[57]

In Najm al-din al-Razi's opinion then, Iblis was punished not because he refused to bow to Adam, but because he stole the news from the Divine Records without God's permission. This is rather unconvincing because several Muslim sources maintained the angels might have read the future of Adam in the Secure Records as well, which didn't prompt them in the least to rebel against God as did Iblis. In any case, if Iblis were an angel, one cannot find in this Islamic explanation of his "fall" any traces of the Christian consensus that the Devil had fallen because of his envy of God or his desire to usurp God's place of power. In the eyes of strictly monotheistic Islamic exegesis, it was unthinkable Iblis could envy God.

In Christianity, the duel between Satan and God is very conspicuous. The concept of the Devil is central to The New Testament, where he appears as a counter principle to Christ. From the Christian point of view, there is a continuous conflict between good and evil and the mission of Christ is precisely to fight the Devil and to save humans from his evil. Such a battle parallels other battles found in Zoroaster's teachings: the battle of Ahura Mazda, the Wise Lord and the ultimate God against the arch-demon Angra Mainyu, who lives in darkness in the north, the home of all demons. In Islam, the concept of the Devil is different. Muslims do not believe in the original sin. The utmost of God's blessings to humans are the free will and the intellectual and moral abilities that allow him/her to know and distinguish between good and evil. The human is accountable for his/her use of all these blessings of God, and he/she ought to keep in mind this accountability and take part in the fight against Devil. Thus, when Iblis asked, "My Lord, grant me a reprieve until the day they [the humans] are raised again," God answered, "You are among the reprieved until the day whose time is known" (Qur'an 15:36–37*).[58]

Iblis as Jinni

We find in Qur'an 7:12–13 Iblis is created of fire, and therefore is a jinni. God, in these verses, asked Iblis what prevented him from bowing to Adam, and what permitted him to disobey the Divine command, and Iblis answered arrogantly: "I am better than he; You created me of fire, and him You created of clay." The jinn nature of Iblis becomes unquestionably certain in Qur'an 17:50. This verse unmistakably states Iblis was one of the jinn, and committed ungodliness against his Lord's command.

Those who reject Iblis' angelic nature argue if he were an angel, he couldn't have disobeyed God's command when he refused to prostrate before Adam. Angels act in accordance with God's will as stated in Qur'an 2:33–34. Ibn Arabi expands on the reasons that made Iblis the jinni so haughty before Adam. He mentions the original and everlasting enmity between jinn and humans. This hostility was shown even before the creation of Adam, when the Angel of Death took a handful from all parts of the Earth for God's creation of Adam. When the clay for Adam was kneaded to dough, and his form was shaped in that clay, it came about that "[Adam's] soul was formed from that dust on which Iblis had trampled with his foot, whereas his heart was created from dust on which Iblis had not trampled with his foot. Thus the soul acquired the evil and blamable qualities it possesses from the touch of Iblis' trampling. This is why the psyche *al-nafs* has been appointed to be the abode of lusts, and Satan's living in it and his authority over it is because his footprints are in it. This is also why Iblis thought himself superior to Adam, because he found him to be from the dust that had been under his feet. Looking into the essence of his own constituent element, which was fire, he then laid claim to the potter, and inclined to overweening pride."[59]

To resolve the incoherence between the two interpretations on the nature of Iblis, Muslim scholarship came up with some ingenious ideas. Al-Tabari, for example, argued it is possible God created one part of his angels from light and another part from fire; Iblis possibly could belong to that group of angels who were created from the scorching winds. Al-Baydawi (d. 1286), meanwhile, had a more plausible explanation. He argued Iblis, a jinni made out of fire, was carried off as a captive by the angels during one of the combats between jinn and angels that took place on Earth. Because Iblis was still a child, he grew up among angels. When God ordered the angels to bow before Adam, Iblis refused, and thus revealed his true jinni nature.[60]

Both Are Invisible

In his analysis of the common characteristics between jinn and angels, ibn Arabi maintains God meant them to be invisible. "When God created the luminous spirits and the fiery ones, I mean angels and jinn, He gave them a common feature which was to be veiled from human eyes."[61]

Although jinn and angels are beings of the invisible realm, they don't belong to the same degree or quality of invisibility in the sense that light is stronger than fire. It has a deeper spiritual meaning. Light, out of which angels are made, reaches farther in space. Indeed, angels belong to the celestial realm, which occupies a higher place in the Muslim hierarchical cosmology. It is situated above the imaginal or intermediary realm from where jinn come to visit our Earth.

Both Are Disembodied Spirits

Both jinn and angels are disembodied spirits. It is not possible to attribute to any creature the word "spirit" except to souls that don't have bodies, such as jinn, angels, demons, and whatever resembles them. Spirits are in this sense incorporeal and eerie, and can't be seen. They have a power, a life force, or an energy that could be called "spiritual agency" believed to affect the course of events on Earth. In contrast, humans are corporeal, solid, and visible, and they have souls. Despite this sharp distinction, ibn 'Arabi seems to see commonalities between spirits and humans rather than differences. He writes this intriguing and complex assertion, "Angels are souls blown into lights, jinn are souls blown into winds, and human beings are souls blown into shapes *'ashbah*."[62] In this statement, ibn Arabi appears to be underscoring two things: one is the "artistic" act of creation referred to as "blown into"; and second is the term "soul" that these three beings share. Ibn 'Arabi uses the term *'arwah* in Arabic. Humans are thus seen only through what is the most sublime in them—the soul; they emerge as being essentially incorporeal.

They are blown into "shapes!" He doesn't use the term "bodies," as if to make them lighter, less attached to Earth. By the same token, he causes the three kinds of beings to come closer to each other.

Both Are Luminous Beings

Both jinn and angels are luminous beings; fire and light are akin. All kinds of spiritual entities, whether they are called peris, daevas, fairies, daemons, jinn, or angels, shine and are described in most traditions across the world as shining apparitions. It is believed light emanates even from Lucifer, the fallen angel, and the prince of darkness.

Both Are Shape Shifters

It is believed angels and jinn can take different shapes. Although jinn can embody any possible shape, including animals, angels can appear only in beautiful forms. For example, it is told Gabriel came once to the Prophet Muhammad in the appearance of a very beautiful man wearing a robe of white cloth and having very dark hair. He also manifested himself to the Virgin Mary as a very handsome man, as in Qur'an 19:16–21*: "Then We sent Our Spirit to her and it took on for her the form of a handsome, well-built man."[63]

Both Are Noncompounded Beings

Both angel and jinn are not composed of the four elements. Angels are pure light, as we just mentioned. As for jinn, it is difficult to consider the fire and air of which they are composed are akin to the fire and air we know in our manifest world. The jinn's fire is a pure, smokeless fire of a very soaring intensity. The jinn's wind is scorching and of the highest possible strength.

Both Came to Earth

I have already expounded on the belief jinn inhabited the earth before humans. Medieval Muslim sources mention also angels came to Earth several times to fight the evil jinn who spread corruption. They came later to humans, and delivered heavenly messages to prophets. In one version of the mythical battles that occurred between the two spiritual entities, it is said angels stayed on Earth for a while after chasing the evil jinn. More interesting, Sufis speak of angels circumambulating the Ka'bah thousands of years before Adam.

Some accounts maintained that not only jinn are among us but angels as well. In an intriguing text narrated by 'Abdullah ibn 'Abbas (d. 688), one of the companions of the Prophet Muhammad and one of the compilers who told many stories on him, we read: "God has angels on earth called al-hafazah [the keepers]. They write down every leaf that falls from the trees. If any among you needed help, when in a desert, or when in necessity, let him say, 'O worshipers of God [meaning the angels], may God have mercy upon you, help me!' Then, you will be helped!"[64]

THE ISLAMIC CORRESPONDENCES
BETWEEN JINN AND ANGELS: DIFFERENCES

Different Geographies

Despite the fact angels visited Earth several times and many of them might still be on our planet as claimed by some medieval compilers, the majority dwell in *al-malakut,* the celestial realm, while jinn live in the sublunary realm. The differences between them do not become manifest by their acts and functions alone, but also by the place they occupy in Islamic cosmology.[65] In his philosophical narrative entitled *Hayy ibn Yaqzan,* Muslim philosopher ibn Sina (Avicenna, 980–1037) envisages the "terrestrial" angels who visit Earth in the following terms: "He who succeeds in leaving this clime enters the climes of the Angels, among which is one that marches with the earth, a clime in which the terrestrial angels dwell. These angels form two groups. One occupies the right side: they are the angels who know and order. Opposite them is a group that occupies the left side: they are the angels who obey and act. Sometimes the two groups of angels descend to the climes of men and jinn, and sometimes they mount to heaven."[66]

Most important, because jinn belong to the intermediary realm, they remain essentially threshold beings, hesitant beings, so to speak, while angels are bound to be of only one nature because their domain is the starry heavens.

Wings

It is known angels have wings. However, jinn are represented only in folk tales as flying, especially in the stories of *The Nights*. Interesting enough, we find many demons in the old Sumerian and Babylonian mythologies are also pictured with wings, such as Lamashtu. The Hebrew demons that borrowed their features from these mythologies have wings as well. Lilith, for example, is in the Bible as a winged female demon who strangles children.

In the prophetic tradition, angels are described as "spreading their wings for the seeker of knowledge out of pleasure for what he is doing. Everyone in heaven and everyone on earth asks forgiveness for a man of knowledge, even the fish in the water."[67]

Muslim tradition maintained wings denote transcendence, freedom, and speed in time and space. Angels have a mission, which is to inform humans of God's commands. Their wings denote their pure spiritual undertaking and hierarchy.

Different Powers

Angels and jinn possess different powers in various ways, which can be accessed differently by humans. Because they are thought to dwell in the sublunary world, it could be easier for humans to contact jinn than it is for them to contact angels in heavens. The power derived from getting in touch with each is different, jinn being incapable of giving humans the power that angels are thought able to provide.[68] Ibn Arabi argues, "Only this much is different—the spirits of the jinn are lower spirits, while the spirits of angels are heavenly spirits."[69]

Immortality Versus Mortality

Angels are immortal; their food and drink consist of praising God, while fiery jinn eat, drink, sleep, procreate, and die, after having lived extremely long lives that can extend for thousands of years.[70] In this context, it is significant to draw some parallels with the concept of daemons in Greek philosophy that are represented as growing old and, finally, dying, like the jinn. Greek epic poet Hesiod (who lived around 700 BCE) thinks, "The sum total of a daemon's life span is nine-thousand seven-hundred and twenty years!"[71]

To illustrate the jinn's extended life span, *The Tales of the Prophets* include many stories in which some of the jinn encountered a number of the prophets long before Muhammad. In these tales, it is claimed jinn met with many prophets since time immemorial, like Noah, Moses, Jesus and, finally, Muhammad who taught them the Qur'an.[72] Muslim writers even discussed the food the jinn eat, while angels have no need for it.[73] When the angels, the guests of Ibrahim (Abraham), came to announce his wife would bear him a son (Qur'an 15:51 and 11:72–74), Ibrahim, with the usual Arabian hospitality, invites them to eat. When he sees their hands do not reach out for the food, he becomes afraid and understands they are heavenly messengers.

Again, we can find a parallel here between the jinn and the daemons of Greek philosophy, because unlike the angels, but like the jinn, the daemons also eat food. Perhaps the most interesting aspect of this fact is both daemons and jinn do not manifest themselves physically while eating. Greek philosopher of the third century Philostratus, in *The Life of Apollonius,* tells the story of the ghost of an Ethiopian satyr who was very enamored and pursued the women of a village. Appollonius set up a trap, a container full of wine, and though the ghost remained invisible, the wine was seen to disappear from the container.[74] Similarly, when a jinni married a girl from the tribe of the great Kufic jurist al-A'mash (d. 765), he asked the jinni: "What is your favorite food?" "Rice," answered the jinni. So he brought him some rice and watched the rice disappearing, but no hands were taking it.[75] Muslim sources, however, indicate jinn prefer bones to any other food. As for the jinni who preferred rice, he seemed to have had in fact an exotic taste. The Prophet once said, "Bones are the food of your brothers the jinn. They sniff them in the manner of animals."[76]

The jinn mate and procreate as well. However, when we talk about their biological functions, we have to bear in mind these are not similar to humans. Jinn mating, as ibn Arabi puts it, "is a curvature, the way you see smoke coming out of a furnace or from a clay oven, smoke mixing with smoke, and each of the two entities gaining pleasure from this meshing. As for the seed they eject, it is similar to the pollen of a palm tree."[77]

When renowned compiler of prophetic tradition Wahb ibn Munabbih (d. 654) was asked whether the jinn eat, drink, or mate, he replied: "Genuine jinn are like winds; they do not eat, drink, sleep, or procreate in this world. Other species among them eat, however, drink and mate, such as the *si'lats,* the ghouls and the *qutrubs,* as well as those who resemble them."[78]

Different Abilities

Although angels know God innately and praise him incessantly, jinn, like humans, know God through their reflection and reason as well as through their intuition. Finally, if it is possible to describe an angel, it is almost impossible to give a full depiction of a jinni. Jinn being intermediary beings, the way they have been described has always been elusive. It is as if the imagination can endlessly play with their representation, while it remains confined to the realm of purity and certainty when it depicts the world of angels. And, although angels epitomize the heavenly realm, jinn suggest the multifarious sublunary plane of transience and transgression, of antipodes and fragmentation. Jinn are tricksters par excellence, ambiguous, and indefinite. Angels belong to "the immutable spiritual verities and the heavenly entities like the Pen, the Preserved Tablet, the Balance, and the Throne."[79]

CONCLUSION

By prohibiting the jinn from climbing to heavens, Islam consecrated the severance of beings of light from beings of fire, highlighted the hierarchical structure of the cosmos, and stressed that jinn are not allowed to trespass the celestial domain of the angels above them. Islam, thus, emphasized the sublunary position of the jinn and stressed the immortal and pure light of the angels. By degrading the jinn, Islam didn't, however, demonize them or oppose them to angels because it clarified jinn could be good or bad like humans.

The most significant consequence of this new repartition of spiritual beings was Muslims should mainly understand the jinn through the lens of cosmology, which opened wide the doors to a deep interpretation of things beyond the simple contrast of evil versus good.

4

Divination, Revelation, and the Jinn

When he invited Satan to his Call,

His own Satan turned Muslim on his account.

He made the call likewise, with the consent of the Creator,

Clear to the jinn on the Night of the jinn.

—FARID AL-DIN AL-'ATTAR (d. 1230)

*W*ith the advent of Islam, jinn were transformed from kings of the unseen to servants of the new religion. Islam retained their power, but made it subservient to the One God. They could still change the course of human events if God willed them to do so. Those who didn't join Islam, the evil ones, were told in the Qur'an they would be accountable for their bad deeds on the Day of Judgment.

To comprehend the complex and difficult relationship of the jinn to the Islamic revelation, we need to place it in the overall Islamic standpoint, which stipulates all beings, everything in the universe, whether animate or inanimate, receive the Word of God and worship him. The Qur'an repeatedly maintains this assertion. The jinn who accepted the Qur'an are part of this general Islamic picture.

"The seven heavens and the earth, and whosoever in them is, extol Him; nothing is, that does not proclaim His praise, but you do not understand their extolling" (Qur'an 17:44).

DIVINATION IN ANCIENT NEAR EASTERN TRADITIONS AND IN PRE-ISLAMIC ARABIA

Near Eastern Traditions

Divination is a worldwide cultural phenomenon anthropologists ascertain still exists in most traditions across our planet. It is believed diviners search to obtain

53

information from supernatural and invisible powers with whom they enter into contact. They then attempt to decode the signs they received from these authorities. Diviners claim the future they predict could be prevented through repentance, prayer, and proper apotropic rituals.

In the ancient Near East, diviners from different countries influenced each other through conquests, wars, religions, trades, and travels. Divination was central to the peoples of the ancient Near East, regardless of its origin in pre-Islamic Arabia, Mesopotamia, Greece, Rome, or Persia where divination reached its peak at the time of emperor Khosro I Anoshirvan (531–578 BCE). Divination through the stars was especially important to Sassanian Imperial ideology. The stars ruled the destiny of humans, and the kings anticipated receiving special protection from their diviners. It is said the Magi interpreted the eclipse of the sun as the declining of the Greeks, against whom the Persians were fighting. References about divination in Persia can be found especially in the famous epic, *Shah-namah* (Book of Kings) of al-Firdawsi, abu al-Qasim (d. 1020). This work is bursting with stories where the destiny of the heroes is determined in the astronomical charts read at the time of their birth. In the story of Alexander, for example, the sages discerned the downfall of the king from the birth of a monstrous child.

In Babylon, divination was a basic feature of life. Senior practitioners had influence and were held in high esteem. Both individuals and officers of state consulted them on important occasions. Around 2000 BCE, a variety of omens were written down and collected. They are considered the largest surviving type of Akkadian literature. In the Assyro-Babylonian civilization, the seers, or *baru* (which literally means "an inspector of the divine," or "one who sees the divine"), were a special class of priests whose main job was to ascertain the will of the gods through dreams and visions, which they were then supposed to decipher. The *baru* had a collective lexicon of symbolic and significant events that formed the basis of his opinions.[1]

The object of divination was to determine the future and will of the deities by watching the behavior of an animal's sacrifice. Such reactions as a change in color, appearance of the entrails, and activity of the smoke from a burnt offering would help the *baru* to forecast the future. It was believed reading the signs in such a way, particularly from observing the shapes of a liver, was the invention of the Assyrian god Shamash. This remained the main means of consulting the will of gods, even as divination from celestial bodies was gaining importance, as late as in the reign of King Nabonidus (555–539 BCE).

Divination in Pre-Islamic Arabia

Divination, *kihanah*, or the action of the seers, was extensively spread among the pre-Islamic Arabs. It is defined as "the art of predicting the future."[2] It was believed seers often entered into contact with the jinn from whom they obtained their knowledge that they then communicated to their kin. Arabs at that point in time imagined the jinn, because of their swift motion, were able to go up to the gods and quickly snatch the gods' news and communicate it to the seer. In the pre-Islamic period, seers were considered spiritual and intellectual guides, capable of attaining the highest degrees of clairvoyance regarding the most important matters of life and death. Their work was far from being limited to individual requests and religious matters. They were consulted on practical daily matters, such as wars and quarrels between tribes, finding lost animals, transferring blessings or curses, removing curses cast by others, and settling disputes between individuals.

Seers were highly respected in Arabia. Each tribe had its own seer, its own poet, and its own preacher. Sometimes the seer was altogether an orator and kind of poet, because his prose consisted of sophisticated rhymed prose[3], which was condemned by the Prophet Muhammad at the advent of Islam, mainly because of its connection to the seers of the pre-Islamic period, and particularly because "none knows the Unseen in the heavens and earth except God" (Qur'an 27:65). In one of his sayings, the Prophet is reported to have said: "Beware the rhymed prose of the seers."[4] Sometimes, seers were also asked to guard the sanctuaries and offer sacrifices to the gods.[5] Very few seers, however, bore these responsibilities simultaneously. A different person Arabs called *sadin*, meaning "custodian" of a sanctuary, fulfilled these obligations.[6] Many sanctuaries had their guardians. In Mecca, for example, the Ka'bah had its own custodian. He was often called the servant 'abd al Ka'bah. The reverence for the servant of the sanctuary was derived from the importance of the sanctuary he guarded. For example, the custodian of the Ka'bah was more respected than the custodian of the shrines of the goddesses. The rank of custodian of a sanctuary generally remained within the same family for generations.[7]

Despite the reverence accorded to the seers in general, they were never looked upon as a priestly caste. The seer of pre-Islamic Arabia was more a diviner rather than a priest of the hallowed altar. He was not an official serving a centralized state because many Arab tribes during that time were essentially nomads. In fact, the question of the seer's relation to a temple or specific ritual was insignificant to the pre-Islamic Arabs who were mostly engrossed in the seer's relationship to the jinn. People thought the seer was under the sway of his personal jinni who was also called *tabi'* (follower) and sometimes *ra'i* (visionary). They also believed he received news from heavens through his own jinni.[8] One legend of pre-Islam tells how the seer 'Amr ibn Luhayy (reputed to have lived in the third century CE) was ordered by his own jinni to travel to Syria to bring back idols.[9]

In pre-Islam, it was imagined the jinni would convey the "stolen" data from the sky to the seer, as follows; "He would empty the secret heard from heaven into the ear of the soothsayer the way you empty a bottle of its contents."[10] The jinn, it was thought, had many different ways of getting the "heavenly" information. Sometimes "they would climb to the heavens, one on top of another, until the one on top could hear the deity. He would then transmit what he heard to the one under him, and so on, until it reached the first jinni who would then cast it into the ear of the seer. The latter would take it and embellish it."[11] Arabs at that point in time believed some seers themselves were the offspring of unions between humans and jinn, such as a seer named Shiqq. They envisioned "his mother was one of the jinn, and that she was from the town of Maryul where the jinn dwell."[12] They described him as half a person with one hand, one leg, and one eye. Another legendary seer of Banu Dhi'b by the name of Satih was represented as made of such soft flesh that you would fold him up as you would fold a robe. He had no bones except for his skull. His face was in his chest. It was believed these seers lived for many centuries.[13]

But divination was not limited to men in the pre-Islamic period. Many narratives of that time reveal the names of many women seers who had their own jinni, like Tarifah al-Khayr, Salma al-Hamadaniyyah, Fatimah bint al-Nu'man, and Zarqa' al-Yamamah. Arab priestesses were considered very powerful. People believed the jinni working with a female seer takes possession of her body more easily than does the one working with a male seer. They thought something other than the priestess herself, an intervening agent from outside, entered her body and spoke through her lips.

In one legend, the priestess Tarifah advised her tribe of al-Ghasasinah to conquer the tribe of 'Akk. But a jinni by the name of Jaza' ibn Sinan intervened, and fought beside the people of 'Akk. In spite of this, the al-Ghasasinah won the war.[14] This is the same Tarifah who predicted the collapse of the dam of Ma'rib.[15] We are also told Quraysh in pre-Islam wanted to control the well of Zamazam after Abd al-Muttaleb (the grandfather of Muhammad) found it. To solve this dispute, Quraysh suggested a priestess from Banu Sa'd be the judge between them and Abd al-Muttaleb.[16] Another Muslim historian tells the story of a woman seer by the name of 'Ufayra from Himyar, who succeeded in interpreting the dream of the king Murtadd ibn 'Abdul-Kilal when all the other male seers failed. The king wanted to marry her, but she refused because her jinni/lover would have been jealous.[17]

It is alleged the jinni would always require from his seer a *hulwan* (sweet reward). The jinni sometimes refused even to transmit the knowledge to the seer if he was not rewarded. It is possible to read this act as a minor sacrifice the seer offers to his jinni. To obtain the jinni's divine knowledge and prompt its "descent" on him, the seer was compelled to always obey the request of his jinni.[18]

Divination in Greece and Rome

The same belief seems to have prevailed among the ancient Greeks. In Greek tradition, the power of the seers was also derived from spiritual entities called daemons, capable of foretelling the future. The Greeks considered daemons mediators between humans and gods, interpreters of symbols, and the mouthpiece of destiny at the oracular shrines. Divination had its public representatives in the priestesses of the oracles, particularly in the Pythia of Delphi. Historians of Antiquity tell "the oracle of Delphi was written in an incomprehensible manner. The client would take the written piece to a professional interpreter who would explain it to him. Around the temple of Delphi, many seers were consulted to 'explain' the etymological origins of the oracle's words."[19] Interesting enough, it seems there was a reward or a fee to be given, like the oracle of pre-Islamic Arabia. It is not, however, specified if this reward was offered to the seer or to the daemon. "Anybody who wanted to consult the oracle, whether in a private capacity or as delegate from a city, had first to pay a fee, known as the *pelanos* (sacred cake). In Euripides' *Ion,* the young servant of the temple says to the Athenian women who have come to Delphi with their queen, Creusa, 'If you have offered the sacred cake in the temple and wish to consult Apollo, draw near these altars.'"[20]

Many Greek philosophers spoke with pious respect of the Delphic oracle. Heraclitus, who lived in the late sixth century BCE and whose philosophy focused on the unity of opposites in everything, believed in the power of the sibyls. Socrates (d. 399 BCE) wanted religious questions to be treated by revealed decisions from the *Pythia* of Delphi. He often expressed his belief in a kind of irrational intuition, in what he called the inner voice of the "daemon." Plato (d. 347 BCE) himself is reputed to have said, "Every daemon is something in between a god and a mortal."[21] He emphasized the importance of rationality, but asserted, however, that divine intentions might be unveiled through utterances that are not due to reason, but to a psychic state of adulation. "Plato considers the daemons, whom we can call genii [jinn] and *lares,* to be ministers of the gods, guardians of humans, and interpreters for humans should the latter wish anything from the gods."[22]

In doing so, Plato went beyond the limits of fifth century rationalism. In fact, Plato enriched the tradition of Greek rationality with some emotional elements and some occult religious ideas as scholar E. R. Dodds (b. 1893) stresses: "In the *Timaeus,* where he is trying to reformulate his earlier vision of man's destiny in terms compatible with his later psychology and cosmology, we meet again the unitary soul of the *Phaedo;* and it is significant that Plato applies to it the old religious term that Empedocles had used for the self—he calls it the daemon."[23]

Greek philosopher Plutarch (d. 125)—who served as one of the two priests at the temple of Apollo at Delphi, site of the renowned Delphic prophecy—went a step further by arguing, "Daemons are spiritual beings that think so intensely that they produce vibrations in the air which enable other spiritual beings (i.e., other daemons) as well as highly sensitive men and women, to 'receive' their thoughts, as through antennae. Thus the phenomena of clairvoyance, prophecy, and the like can be explained."[24]

In Roman divination, daemons were not as important as they were in Greek divination. The inspection of a slaughtered animal, especially the liver, was among the most important kinds of predicting the future. Romans believed the liver was a mirror image of the macrocosm, especially when pulled out hot. The most important works of divination in ancient Rome were *The Sibylline Books* that were put down by the Sibyls of Cuma; the title Sibyl referred to the position and not to an individual. The Sibyls were the prophetesses of Apollo, who wrote their answers to questions on palm leaves; they were kept for centuries and consulted on special occasions only by order of the senate before battle or when in danger of attack.

There were many generations of Sibyls over the centuries.[25] The Roman scholar Varro listed ten of them in the first century BCE. A famous Sibyl emerges in both epic and tragic poetry: it was the figure of the young Trojan woman, Cassandra, daughter of Priam and beloved of Apollo.[26]

In all these civilizations of the ancient Middle East, it was believed spiritual entities, be it jinn or daemons, snatched away the news from heavens and delivered it to seers. Ancient Greece, however, distinguished itself by stressing not only seers but also enlightened people like philosophers and poets could themselves communicate with the invisible through daemons. Socrates' example illustrates perfectly this view. Greek thought during this time highlighted the necessity of according significance to both reason and intuition. Islam, as shall be seen later in this book, stressed equally these two aspects. However, as already stated, Islam prohibited the jinn from climbing up to the heavens. By doing so, it limited the access to the invisible to prophets who receive the Word of God through angels, thereby causing Revelation to supersede divination.

THE DESCENT OF THE REVELATION

It is in this ancient Near Eastern environment where divination was prevailing that the Qur'anic revelation came down upon the Prophet Muhammad. Immediately, pagan Arabs initiated a brutal battle against it. They disbelieved in it and ferociously rejected Islam's condemnation of their way of life, especially pre-Islamic divination and its association with the jinn. The Qur'an utterly rebukes the assistance many pagan Arabs sought from seers and jinn. To stop the proliferation of "news" from above, Islam secluded the divine in "secured" heaven and forbade jinn from approaching it. The Qur'an states that the jinn soon discovered this new reality, "and we stretched toward heaven, but we found it filled with terrible guards and meteors. We would sit there on seats to hear; but any listening now finds a meteor in wait for him" (Qur'an 72:8–9).

The Prophet himself is reported to have passed negative judgments on divination in general, and on the use of the jinn in particular, such as, "He who practices evil omens is not of us [Muslim community]. He who soothsays or listens to divination is not of us."[27] Or, "He who resorts to a seer or a fortune-teller is a heretic who does not believe in what has been sent down upon Muhammad."[28]

Muslim scholars discredited the value of messages transmitted by seers. The roles of prophets and seers became diametrically opposed because prophets were devoted to God, while seers served spiritual entities, such as the jinn. More important, although a seer was viewed as simply someone who had psychic powers, and who employed the jinn to unveil the hidden world, the Prophet Muhammad was chosen by God to pass on his message to humans, as the Qur'an expresses it: "He discloses not His Unseen to anyone, save only to such a messenger as He is well-pleased with" (Qur'an 72:25–26) or "God will not inform you of the Unseen; but God chooses out of His Messengers whom He will" (Qur'an 3:174).

Islamic scholarship commented at length on the choice of the prophets by God. It underscored the election by God from among the purest and most moral of his humans. It stated, "Prophecy is not a qualification by the Prophet himself, nor a degree that can be attained and acquired. It is not an internal preparation that enables a prophet to be in contact with the spiritual realm. It is a mercy sent by God to whomever he elects among His servants."[29] Although the jinni delivered data from the unseen to the seer, the Prophet Muhammad is reported to have received revelation through the intermediacy of Gabriel. As ibn 'Arabi (d. 1240) sums it up, "Revelation in the most specific sense is the descent of the angel upon the hearing and heart of the messenger or prophet, and it no longer occurs, since there is no prophet after Muhammad."[30]

Finally, although seers in pre-Islam were devoted to presage the future to kings and chiefs of tribes, revelation according to Islam manifested itself as universal—a "mercy unto all beings" (Qur'an 21:107), and Muhammad as "the seal of all prophets" (Qur'an 33:40). However, some Sufis unfoundedly believed Muhammad was elected as "the seal of all prophets" since the beginning of time. They repeatedly quote this Hadith, "I was a prophet when Adam was still between water and clay."[31]

From the outset of Muhammad's prophethood, Meccans deemed the revelation a form of divination. They projected the image of their seers upon Muhammad and decoded the early chapters of the Qur'an in the light of their pre-Islamic beliefs. For example, the fact after the initial revelation in the Cave of Hira' Muhammad went to his wife Khadijah and had her wrap him in a cloak (Qur'an

73): "O thou enwrapped in thy robes," was understood by Meccans as a sign the Prophet was a seer, because seers in the pre-Islamic period wrapped themselves up in a similar way.[32]

In the prose rhymes of the Qur'an, many Meccans found resemblances to the utterances of pre-Islam's seers who spoke in a similar form of rhymed discourse. They thought the Qur'an was communicated to Muhammad by one of the jinn who usually dictate their words to seers, or that he might be possessed by a jinni, like the pre-Islamic diviners. The Qur'an, however, responds to this in Qur'an 52:29: "Therefore remind! By thy Lord's blessings thou art not a soothsayer neither possessed." The Meccans also claimed the Qur'an was the work of a poet. They are represented as saying: "What, shall we forsake our gods for a poet possessed?" (Qur'an 37:36), or in Qur'an 36:69, "We have not taught him poetry; it is not seemly for him. It is only a remembrance and a Clear Qur'an."[33]

These verses generated lengthy discussions on *ilham* (poetical inspiration) and *wahi* (revelation) among Muslim scholars, in which they analyzed the relationship of meaning to rhyme in the Holy Book as compared to that in Arabic poetry in general. To distinguish between revelation and inspiration, Muslim scholars reckoned inspiration as being inferior to revelation because it doesn't refer to a dream vision or to the encounter with the angel. It is an act of the imagination, and not a transmission of the Divine to other men.[34] In general, Meccans were divided with regard to the truth of the revelation as al-Walid ibn al-Mughirah, one of the notable chiefs of Mecca, stated after listening to Muhammad: "The nearest thing to the truth is your saying that he is a sorcerer who has brought a message, by which he separates a man from his father, or from his brother, or from his wife, or from his family."[35]

The Prophet is described as having an eloquent and powerful speech as well as a beautiful voice when reciting the Qur'an. The same aforementioned person heard him reciting the Qur'an one day at the Ka'bah. He returned to the people of Quraysh and said to them, "By God, I heard from Muhammad a speech that does not belong to human speech nor to the speech of the jinn."[36]

News about the Prophet's physiological and emotional condition during the descent of the revelation bewildered Meccans even more. Muhammad himself described it in these terms: "Sometimes, it is revealed like the ringing of a bell—this form of revelation is the hardest of all—and then this state passes away after I have grasped what is revealed. Sometimes the Angel Gabriel comes in the form of a man and talks to me, and I comprehend all what he says. ['A'ishah, the Prophet's wife, added], 'Once I saw the Prophet receive the revelation on a very cold day, and observed sweat dropping from his forehead as the revelation was fulfilled.'"[37]

The Qur'an sustained its discussion of revelation as coming from the Divine and underscored the futility of Meccans' arguments. To differentiate between revelation and the seers' possession by jinn, the Qur'an reminded pagan Arabs that the Word of God has such power, energy, and absoluteness that it could destroy mountains as in Qur'an 59:21: "If We had sent this Qur'an down upon a mountain, thou wouldst have seen it humbled, split asunder out of the fear of God."[38]

However, the battle between those who joined the new religion and pagan Arabs continued for a while. Toward the end of the Prophet's life, and during the first Caliphate of Abu Bakr (d. 634), many soothsayers tried to impose again their seership on the Arabs. Some of them even proclaimed themselves prophets, and entered into war against the new religion. One of the most well-known leaders of these battles was Musaylimah al-kadhdhab (d. 632) (Musyalimah the liar), who proclaimed himself the prophet of Yamamah in the Arabian Peninsula. Another "false" prophet arose in Yemen, just after the death of Muhammad in 632. He was surnamed Dhu al-Khimar (the man of the veil) and also al-Aswad (the black one). He revolted against Islam (claiming revelations for himself), seized control of the Yemen, and made San'a his capital until he was assassinated in 632 CE. His death marked the end of the soothsayers' rebellion in Arabia.[39]

MUHAMMAD AND THE JINN IN THE QUR'AN

It is from the Qur'an we essentially learn of the encounters of the Prophet Muhammad with the jinn. The Qur'an, however, does not give the origin, the number, and the names of these jinn. According to it, there seem to be two encounters.[40] In Qur'an 46:29–32, the jinn listening to the Prophet seem to be Jewish jinn because they mention they already believed in the revelation of Moses, while in Qur'an 72:2–7, the jinn who heard the Qur'an and accepted the revelation seem to be pagans who formerly aided soothsayers. Therefore, the two chapters relate two separate events that took place during two separate journeys.[41]

Scholars in Islamic tradition agree the event mentioned in Qur'an 46:29–32 took place during the Prophet's return journey from Ta'if in the tenth year of his prophethood around 619. It is said to have taken place in the small oasis of Nakhlah, on the way leading from Mecca to Ta'if, as al-Tabari (d. 923) maintains. In these verses, we read:

> And when We turned to thee a company of jinn giving ear to the Qur'an; and when they were in its presence they said, "Be silent!" Then, when it was finished, they turned back to their people, warning. They said, "Our people, we have heard a Book that was sent down after Moses, confirming what was before it, guiding to the truth and to a straight path."

Ibn Ishaq (d. 768), one of the first biographers of the Prophet, asserted these jinn came from the region of Nusaybin in Syria (now in Turkey). They listened to Muhammad and ran to their fellow jinn to warn them.[42] Al-Kashani (d. 1680) argued the jinn who came to listen to the Prophet were nine, and only one was from Nusaybin, while the other eight were from the jinn tribe of Banu 'Amru ibn 'Amir.[43]

A careful reading of Qur'an 8–20 clearly shows the second encounter of the jinn with the Prophet could only have happened during the early years of the prophethood. The jinn used to listen to the news of heaven. In these verses, it is stated that with the advent of Islam, every time they reached out toward heaven they found it filled with mighty guards and comets. Some of them began roaming around looking for the cause, and on such a raid, a company of them heard the Qur'an being recited, and went to warn the rest of the jinn about it.

Ibn Mas'ud, one of the closest companions to the Prophet, maintains there was no one with the Prophet during his second encounter with the jinn. They saw him coming from afar and asked him where he had been, and he replied, "the jinn's emissary came to me, and I went to recite the Qur'an to them." Ibn Mas'ud continued, "He took us and showed us their traces and the traces of their fire."[44] Another commentator of this specific Qur'anic chapter claims, "Seventy-one jinn came and pledged allegiance to the Prophet for fasting, performing the prayers, the *zakat* (alms), the jihad and giving advice to Muslims. They apologized because they had said 'outrageous things about God.' As for their pledge, it is asserted in their saying at the beginning of the chapter: 'When we heard the guidance, we believed in it' [Qur'an 72:14]. As to how they perform all their obligations, we do not know."[45]

According to Zubayr ibn al-'Awwam, one of the ten companions who were personally promised paradise by the Prophet, the Prophet on this particular night sat all the time inside a circle reciting the Qur'an to the crowds of jinn who met him. He tells that the Prophet, after performing the prayer in the mosque of al-Madinah, asked his companions:

> "Which of you will follow me to a delegation of the jinn tonight?" But the people kept silent and no one said a word. He asked it three times, then he walked past me and took me by the hand, and I walked with him until all the mountains of Madinah were distant from us and we had reached open country. And there we encountered men, tall as lances, completely wrapped in their mantles from their feet up. When I saw them, a great quivering seized me, until my feet would hardly support me from fear. When we came close to them, the Prophet drew a line for me on the ground with his big toe and said: "Sit in the middle of that." When I sat down, all the fear I had felt before left me. The Prophet passed between them and me, and recited the Qur'an in a loud voice until dawn. Then he walked past me and said: "Take hold of me." So I walked with him, and we went a little distance. Then he said to me: "Turn and look. Do you see anyone where these were?" I turned and said: "O Apostle of God, all I see is blackness!"[46]

This encounter of the Prophet with the jinn remains shrouded with mystery. The beings described as jinn are tall and "completely wrapped in black from their feet up," which makes it impossible to distinguish any detail of these disembodied beings. They are represented as mere shapes, kind of "black ghosts" that move. They are not perceived as individuals, or separate entities, but rather as a compact mass, as "blackness." This lack of precision raises doubts about the possibility of perceiving them. It was already mentioned in this book that jinn are imaginal beings, which means they manifest themselves within the parameters of an immaterial corporeality. Moreover, ibn al-'Awwam was in a terrible state of anxiety and dread, which held back any possible objectivity.

There is a double inscrutability here: the darkness of the night and the fact the jinn were enveloped in the murkiness of their black mantles that disguised them. It is as if this double obscurity acknowledged their belonging to the hidden world. They seem to be out there for ibn al-'Awwam only because they move in the open country. Their shrouded march is a possible indication of their reality.

The Prophet alone appears to discern them. He read the Qur'an to them all night long in "a loud voice" and in all quietude. Al-'Awwam becomes serene in turn when he sat in the circle Muhammad drew for him with his big toe. Muhammad himself remained all night in another circle reciting the Qur'an. The Prophet seems to be knowledgeable of the protective and sacred power of the circle, which hinders evil from entering it, and impinges tranquility on the one who dwells inside it. The circle is known in many traditions across the world "as having no beginning or end, and spacelessness as having no above or below; as circular and spherical it is the abolition of time and space."[47] As such, it is an eternal and a "shielding" space that is delivered from contingencies.

Finally, this story exemplifies the notion Muhammad was sent to both humans and jinn as the majority of Muslim theologians argued during this time.

Although the Qur'an mentions only two encounters between the Prophet and the jinn, Muslim literature invented a number of additional encounters. In most of these narrations, it is claimed the jinn came several times to the Prophet to ask for guidance and wisdom in settling their disputes.[48] For popular Islam, it seemed only natural the Prophet interacted with these spiritual entities more than twice, as the Qur'an reveals. Popular Islam emphasized the notion that a face-to-face encounter was necessary, inasmuch as the jinn were beginning to learn about the new religion and constantly needed elucidations and advice.

Some authors even indicated the exact locations of these encounters between the jinn and the Prophet. Needless to say, mentioning a real place where these meetings are thought to have occurred makes them all the more gripping and enthralling in the eyes of Muslims. Compiler Muhammad ibn 'Abdallah al-Azraqi (d. 1582), for example, maintains, "In the upper areas of Mecca there is a mosque called the Mosque of the Jinn. It is also called the Mosque of the Allegiance."[49] It is claimed the jinn proclaimed their allegiance to the Prophet in this mosque. In yet another account, Malik ibn Anas, one of the Prophet's companions, narrates the following intriguing encounter of the Prophet with a very old jinni. Anas alleges he was with Muhammad, leaving the mountains of Mecca, when an old sheikh came by.

> The Prophet said to the jinni: "This is the stride of a jinni, as well as the tone of his voice!" The jinni replied: "My name is Hamah ibn Laqqis ibn Iblis." The Prophet said: "Only two generations separate you from him [Iblis]." He replied:

"True." The Prophet asked: "How long have you lived?" The jinni replied: "Almost all of time. I was a small boy when Abel was killed. I believed in Noah and repented at his hands after I stubbornly refused to submit to his call, until he wept and wept. I am indeed a repentant—God keep me from being among the ignorant! I met the prophet Hud and believed in his call. I met Abraham, and I was with him when he was thrown in the fire. I was with Joseph, too, when his brothers hurled him into the well—I preceded him to its bottom. I met the prophet Shu'ayb, and Moses and Jesus the son of Mary, who told me: 'If you meet Muhammad, tell him Jesus salutes thee!' Now I've delivered his message to you, and I believe in you." The Prophet said: "What is your desire, O Hamah?" He said: "Moses taught me the Torah, Jesus the Gospels, can you teach me the Qur'an?" So the Prophet taught him the Qur'an.[50]

This dialogue attributed to a jinni and the Prophet seems a lesson in religion rather than a conversation between a spiritual entity that manifested itself and the Prophet of Islam. It is meant to encapsulate beliefs regarding Islam in general, and the jinn in particular. First, it reminds Muslim listeners and/or readers spiritual entities could be as pious as humans, and even better, and they seek to learn about the world of the Spirit in general, and about Islam in particular. Second, jinn seem to know about all past revelations because they live very long lives, which allow them, like this jinni, to have contact with past prophets. Third, Islam is indeed a religion of synthesis that accepted all the prophets who came before Muhammad.[51] The jinni specifically underscores a greeting from Jesus to the Prophet, which shows how the figure of Christ is cherished in popular Islam. Finally, it highlights a popular belief that Muhammad did engage in dialogue with the jinn.

One could, however, wonder about the truth of these accounts ascribed to the Prophet, especially the last one. It is impossible not to discern a popular voice that added material to satisfy popular demands. It goes without saying the figure of the Prophet in the Qur'an is different from his figure in these accounts.

CONCLUSION

With respect to the relation of the jinn to the Prophet, there are still some details that continue to elude scholars, such as how many times the Prophet encountered the jinn during his prophethood. Moreover, Muslim scholars have never agreed on the names of the jinn who came to him, or on the places where these encounters took place.[52]

But the most important controversy involves the question of whether the Prophet actually saw the jinn, or only heard them. In reality, this question is linked to the concept of revelation. The majority of Muslim scholars seem to believe that the Prophet did not see the jinn, contrary to what the popular accounts mention. A tradition of the Prophet indicates he was not aware of their presence when he recited the Qur'an—as documented by Muslim (d. 875), ibn Hanbal (d. 855), and al-Tirmidhi (d. 892)—but that it was God who apprised him of their words and acts.[53]

In the Qur'an, it is clear it is God who informed the Prophet of what happened in the invisible realm beyond human perception—*ghayb*. The first verse of the Qur'anic chapter al-jinn opens with "It has been revealed to me" (Qur'an 72:1). The expression "it has been revealed to me" indicates the Prophet did not see the jinn, for if he had, we would not have this expression. What we know through direct seeing cannot belong to the revelation.

Other Muslim scholars hold the opinion the Prophet was able to see jinn and demons because of the nature of his prophethood. These scholars maintained prophets and saints could see that which the rest of humans are incapable of seeing. In their view, seeing jinn is a miracle that belongs to prophethood alone. They emphasized prophets could see all kinds of spiritual entities in the shapes in which God created them.[54]

An important question was also raised regarding the jinn listening to the Qur'an: How do the jinn comprehend the recitation of the Qur'an? How do they translate its message into their own language(s) when "they returned to their people as warners?" (Qur'an 46:29).

While visiting the paradise of *'afarit*, the narrator of *Risalat al-Ghufran* (The Epistle of Forgiveness) written by al-Ma'arri (d. 1057) asks the jinni Abu Hadrash about communication between humans and jinn, what is the language of the jinn, are they Arabs who do not know Greek, or Greeks who do not understand Arabs? The jinni answers: "We are folk of clairvoyance and cleverness. We know all human beings' languages and beyond, and we have a language that men do not know."[55]

It should be mentioned here that seeing or hearing spiritual entities is a subject matter debated by other traditions as well. For example, Greek philosophers discussed at length whether or not one could see or hear the daemons. Socrates' personal daemon was central to this consideration. Plutarch, for example, asserted Socrates often heard his daemon speak, but not once did he assert he saw him. Plutarch in a chapter entitled "On Socrates' personal deity" discusses at length with friends and disciples of Socrates the instances in which this "deity" appeared to Socrates and how the philosopher interacted with it.[56]

Neo-Platonism, however, claimed seeing daemons is not impossible for humans. On this seminal aspect of the communication between the invisible realm of spirits and the visible realm of humans, contemporary scholar of Greek culture Georg Luck maintains, "The belief in the existence of daemons seems to have been an essential part of Neo-Platonism, but the ability to actually see one's own guardian spirit was a privilege granted to only a few. Those who, like Plotinus, were granted the gift, apparently encouraged their disciples to study hard, work on themselves, and achieve the spiritual progress that would lead them to a higher level of awareness."[57]

Scholars of classical Islam also raised the question of seeing the angels and hearing them. Can a prophet see his angel or only hear him? Did the Prophet Muhammad see or only hear the angel Gabriel? During the second and third centuries of Islam, this debate was called "the externality" of the revelation, that is, Revelation as coming to Muhammad through the angel Gabriel, as in Qur'an 26:19 and 2:97.

In Qur'an 75:16–19, God addresses the Prophet, "Move not thy tongue with it to hasten it; Ours it is to gather it, and to recite it. So, when We recite it, follow thou its recitation. Then Ours it is to explain it." The same meaning occurs again in Qur'an 20:114: "And hasten not with the Qur'an ere its revelation is accomplished unto thee; and say, 'O my Lord, increase me in knowledge.'" This verse was interpreted by the scholars to mean the Prophet heard Gabriel physically and, in his anxiousness to retain what was said, hurried to repeat it. It is not mentioned, however, that he saw the angel. Avicenna (d. 1037) considered the means of transmission of revelation from the angel to the Prophet as follows:

Angels have real and absolute being, but also a being relative to humans. Their real being is in the transcendental realm, and is contacted only by the holy human spirits. When the two meet, the human's both senses—internal and external—are attracted upwards, and the angel is presented to them in accordance with the power of the man who sees the angel not in the absolute but in the relative form. He hears the latter's speech as a voice, even though it is intrinsically a spiritual communication, wahi. Spiritual communication is the indication of the mind of the angel to the human spirit in a direct manner, and this is the real "speech." For speech is only that which brings home the meaning of the addresser's mind (to the addressee's mind) so that the later becomes like the former.[58]

The communication that took place between the Prophet and the angel is not an ordinary one. We cannot apply to it the rules that govern any ordinary conversation between two ordinary humans. It takes place at the intersection of two realms: the manifest one and the invisible one. Both the relative and the absolute intermingle for a very short lapse of time during which a message from the unseen is sent. It is at the origin a kind of telepathy the Prophet grasps, and is then conveyed to him through a voice he hears, as Avicenna mentions.

As we have seen in this chapter, divination was then brought to a standstill, and the jinn ceased to steal news from heavens. Along with humans, believers among the jinn embraced Islam, and shared with their humans' co-religionists the Revelation. The Prophet himself treasured the jinn's recognition of the Revelation.

It is in this context the Qur'anic chapter "al-jinn" occupies a special place in the heart of Islam, inasmuch as it asserts the submission of spiritual entities, the jinn, to God. This Qur'anic chapter is the prime example of how the "Word of God" is spread in a multiplicity of realms and is understood among intelligences beyond our human sphere. The Prophet mentioned its importance in these terms, "He who reads surat al-Jinn (the Qur'anic chapter of the jinn), his reward from God will be as large as if he had freed a number of slaves equal to the number of jinn who believed in me as well as to the number of the jinn who disbelieved in me."[59]

5

Magic, Possession, Diseases, and the Jinn

They carried Jiran al-'Awd and put him back in
a high place where the jinn play music.

—JIRAN AL-'AWD (pre-Islamic poet)

*M*edieval Islamic literature on the jinn maintains Muslims had little apprehension of the jinn who converted to Islam. They dreaded, however, the heretic
jinn who rejected Islam. Muslims claimed these malevolent spirits could attack
them at any time and in any place. They considered them harmful, and they
endeavored to fend off their evil. Scholars, theologians, magicians, and healers
worked together to record a list of legal procedures for Muslims to use to protect
themselves from the evil of these spirits.

MAGIC, DISEASES, POSSESSION, AND HEALING

IN THE ANCIENT NEAR EAST

Merriam Webster's Dictionary explains the term "magic" is derived from the
Greek "magus," which describes a sorcerer. The Greeks seem to have taken this
word from Persia where it referred to a member of the priestly class, which indicates magic was officially part of the religion of the ancient Persian Empire. This
pinpoints the intricate relationship between magic and religion. Magical beliefs
and practices were a primary and acknowledged part of the daily life of the peoples of the Near East. It was neither inferior to religion nor superior to it. People
always believed unseen spiritual entities, such as gods, daemons, demons, or
jinn, went into the bodies of humans to injure them, bring madness upon them,
or even kill them. They envisaged all diseases major and minor, from plague to
fever and even headache, to be brought about by male and female demons against
whom the magician battled as a fighter. In the religious and magical texts of the

ancient Near East, people pictured the human body as the locus of fights between good and bad spirits.

Egypt

Magic has always been omnipresent in Egypt, called "the mother of magicians" by Clement of Alexandria (d. about 215). It was there one could find a wealthy variety of amulets written or painted on gigantic temple walls as well as on papyrus scrolls intended to act against all kinds of bites and stings of noxious creatures. Some gods were considered more protectors than others, such as the bull-man and the god dwarf Bes or Bisu, also known as a kind of savior deity. Bes was often pictured with an ugly face to drive away the evil forces that resided in the body and were bringing about sickness or madness. It is thought that Bes "fulfilled the same function as the hideous and sometimes obscene gargoyles found on many Christian churches."[1]

Magicians were respected in ancient Egypt and often worked hand in hand with priests and official doctors whose medical procedures were accompanied by incantations and hymns. It is believed the god Thoth, who was altogether a magician and a healer, wrote the majority of the books on magic in ancient Egypt.[2] Many of these books were found in temples. They include spells, incantations to drive away the evil spirits, hymns, and rituals to perform to exorcize the spirit dwelling in a human. It is worthy to note the magical parts of the surviving Egyptian papyri mix rational cures and spells. This led some contemporary scholars of ancient Egypt, such as Geraldine Pinch, to assert, "It is even doubtful whether there ever was a time in Egyptian history when medicine and magic were not complementary parts of a doctor's skills."[3]

Babylon and Assyria

Mesopotamia left incredible riches of occult sciences that influenced the whole ancient Near East, especially Greece and Persia.[4] It is believed that Persian magicians who settled in Mesopotamia combined their clandestine traditions with the rites and formulas codified by the Chaldean sorcerers.

In Babylon's ancient civilizations, magic and healing were prominently represented in the incantation literature found in cuneiform and baked clay tablets. This intriguing literature describes the offensive work of unseen spiritual entities against the human body. The magician in Babylon used instruments often compared to weapons; for each human illness there was a different weapon and a corresponding spirit. The exorcist was responsible for chasing away the spirits. It was vital to identify the god or the demon that sent the illness and to call him or her by name, and to search for a matching healing. The demon Utukku, for example, was extremely vicious and, with several fever-demons, assailed the throat; there were other demons associated with fever too, such as the demon Asag/Asakku, whose name is connected to fever in the poetical enumerations of diseases. The demon Alu assaulted the chest; the demon Gallu-the hand; Rabisu-the skin. To guard themselves from the diseases brought by these classes of demons and to drive them away, Babylonians used incantation bowls as well as the ringing of bells.[5] Some gods were known to heal the sick, if the patient prayed to them and promised to offer them a gift, such as the gods Ea and Marduk who were portrayed as coming to the rescue of the diseased after receiving their sacrifices.[6]

In one early Assyrian incantation, the priest enumerated all the kinds of diseases evil spirits had imposed on a person:

> Unto the side of the wanderer have drawn nigh,
> Casting a woeful fever upon his body.
> A ban (*manit*) of evil hath settled on his body,
> An evil disease on his body they have cast,
> An evil plague hath settled on his body,
> Evil venom on his body they have cast,
> An evil curse hath settled on his body,
> Evil (and) sin on his body they have cast,
> Venom (and) wickedness have settled upon him.[7]

Greece

The idea of illness, possession, and madness as coming from gods or daemons was widespread in ancient Greece as well. Homer, in *The Odyssey*, speaks of the penetration of a hostile daemon that obsessed the body in a miserable and excruciating manner. Ulysses is depicted as assaulted by a fuming power.[8] During his hunt with the sons of Autolycus, he is wounded in the leg by a wild boar. His friends circle him, and dexterously tie up his wound, and use an *epaoide*—specific charm—to stanch the flow of dark blood. They try to pacify the power stirring up the hemorrhage by binding his wound in a magical way.[9] Greeks thought that even the plague was caused by the intervention of evil spirits: "The disease visited by Apollo upon the Acheans thus consists of a defiling object, a material reality 'divinely' super-induced upon the body of the sufferer, in short a physical stain. The relationship between this conception of the disease state and the idea of the magical intrusion of a foreign and harmful object cannot be denied."[10]

The Greeks took many healing procedures from Mesopotamians, Chaldeans, and Egyptians. It is maintained that naturalist philosopher Democritus (d. 370 BCE), best known for his atomic theory, traveled to Mesopotamia where he was exposed to the corpus accumulated by the priests of Babylon. It is thought Democritus procured some elements of this inconsistent material, especially regarding properties of plants and minerals, and maybe some experiments of physics. Toward the end of the Alexandrine period, many Babylonian books on magic were already translated into Greek.

Philosopher Pythagoras of Samos (b. 569 BCE), surnamed the great healer, also traveled to Egypt, Mesopotamia, Persia, and India where he learned magic; then he came back to Samos, founded his own school, and taught his disciples how to apply magic and incantations in their cures. It is believed Pythagoras was able by his magical skills to beckon to animals and birds, and to foresee the future. The Greeks strongly believed gods or daemons were the cause of diseases, possession, and madness. "Most of the gods specified by professional purifiers had special associations with disease, especially skin disease, and madness."[11]

Pre-Islamic Arabia

The Arabs before Islam had similar beliefs to their neighbors regarding magic, spirits, and healing. Like them, they were preoccupied with how to ward off disease and ill fortune. They believed, for example, like the Greeks, the plague is brought upon humans by spiritual entities. They described it as "the spears of the jinn."[12] Fear of the plague led them to some strange and intriguing behaviors. "They would imitate the braying of a donkey before entering a village, for fear that the jinn would attack them. Some of them would even hang on them the heel of a rabbit, to protect themselves."[13]

Pre-Islamic Arabs believed evil jinn bring madness upon people as well. In fact, the term *majnun* (possessed/mad/insane in Arabic) literally means "to be possessed by a jinni." The terms jinn and *majnun* both are derived from the same linguistic root *j-n-n*.

How do the jinn bring madness upon a person? In some narratives from pre-Islam, one can find a relationship between the sounds uttered by the jinn and the loss of reason. The jinn avenge their dead by inflicting upon humans strange sounds, resembling the sirens' songs, which bewitch sailors. The sounds produced by the jinn could be similar to the pounding of a drum, the buzzing of certain flies, a twitter, or simply a loud voice coming from an invisible source the Arabs called *hatif* (a call from the unseen).[14] Sometimes, the jinn simulate the sounds of the winds in the sands, or a thin murmur. This jinn's music is also called *'azif*.[15]

The music of the jinn by which they possess humans has been immortalized by the poets of pre-Islam, as in this verse of Jiran al-'Awd (his exact date of birth or death is unknown) where he described himself carried away by the jinn: "They carried Jiran al-'Awd and put him back in a high place where the jinn play music."[16] Another anonymous poet of pre-Islam chanted the following verse: "You hear in it the jinn saying zizi zima."[17]

The Arabs of pre-Islam invented a whole set of exorcism procedures to protect themselves from the evil actions of the jinn on their bodies and minds, such as the use of beads, incense, bones, salt, and charms written in Arabic, Hebrew, and Syriac, or the hanging around their necks of a dead animal's teeth such as a fox or a cat to frighten the jinn, and keep them away.[18] Others would give their children names they thought could scare off the jinn, especially names of animals. Pre-Islamic Arabs bonded with animals to acquire strength against evil jinn. They imagined the power of animals would terrify these evil spirits. The idea of getting help from animals seems, however, paradoxical at first glance. As shall be seen in the following chapter of this book, pre-Islamic Arabs believed the jinn sometimes take the shape of animals to hide their identity from humans. One wonders then how is it possible to ascertain an evil jinni is not dwelling in one of these animals. One could read this behavior, though, as the pre-Islamic Arabs wanting to utilize the "animal power" before the jinn did. In any case, it is interesting to see how both humans and jinn exploit the animal strength and mystery to gain power. The animal realm seems to mediate in a way between the human realm and the intermediary realm of the jinn.

However, not all pre-Islamic Arabs were afraid of the jinn. Many of them befriended them, as we have already seen, and even sought their aid. They believed the jinn do not respond to the person calling them unless he/she becomes wild and dwells in barren and ruined places, and unless this person quits the society of humans.[19]

DEFINING "ISLAMIC" MAGIC

Through Arab conquests, Islam assimilated many magical procedures from the religions of the conquered peoples. The *Fihrist* (catalogue) of the compiler Muhammad ibn Ishaq ibn al-Nadim (d. 849) mentions the old sources such as Greek, Mesopotamian, Egyptian, Chaldean, and Hindu, which inspired Muslim magic. He indicates Arabs translated the Indian books on magic, as well as those in Chinese and Turkish. He also acknowledges Arabs borrowed from Persians and Jews.[20] Islam was not in fact different from other religions that appropriated elements from the preceding religions. There is no totally autonomous religion, independent of what occurred before it, as Dutch historian of religion and Christian theologian Gerardus van der Leeuw (d. 1950) maintains: "Every religion, therefore, has its own previous history and is to a certain extent a 'syncretism.' Then comes the time when, from being a summation, it becomes a whole and obeys its own laws."[21]

The conviction the jinn somehow could intervene in Muslims' lives is still part of their general belief in the simultaneous existence of the invisible and the visible realms. In medieval times, Muslims thought jinn could enter their houses, run in the streets, and even make their way into food and drink. They claimed they have felt their presence; that is why some Muslims searched for ways to neutralize them through magic. It is reported the Prophet Muhammad himself once said, "Cover your utensils and tie your water skins, and close your door and keep your children close to you at night, as the jinn come out at that time and snatch things away."[22]

At the time of the Prophet, there were some *nushrahs* (a kind of charm, some say a certain kind of incantation used to chase away the evil of heretic jinn) known as non-Arabic, such as the *nushra* using the Hebrew language. People flocked to the Jews who would put together magical spells for them. Muhammad forbade the use of incantations containing Hebrew or even Syriac words as well as any spell not in agreement with the teachings of Islam.[23] What made Muslims strongly reckon evil could intrude in their lives was the account telling Muhammad himself was once bewitched. The complete story is told in the prophetic tradition:

> 'A'isha [the Prophet's wife] recounted magic was worked on the Prophet so he began to imagine he was doing an action which he was not actually doing. One day he appealed to God for a long period and then said: "I feel that God has inspired me as to how to heal myself. Two persons came to me (in my dream) and sat, one by my head and the other by my feet. One of them asked the other: 'What is the illness of this man?' The other replied: 'Magic was worked on him.' The first asked: 'Who has bewitched him?' The other replied: 'Labid ibn al-'awwam.' The first one asked: 'What material has he used?' The other replied: 'A comb, the hair gathered on it, and the outer skin of the pollen of the male date-palm.' The first asked: 'Where is that?' The other replied: 'It is in the well of Dharwan.'" So the Prophet went to the well and then came back and said to me: "Its date-palms [the date-palms near the well] resemble the heads of the devils." I asked: "Did you remove these things with which the magic was worked?" He said: "No, for I have been cured by God, and I am afraid that this action may spread evil amongst the people." Later on, the well was filled up with earth.[24]

The Prophet in this story not only does not dwell on details when asked about the well and refuses to bring up from it the material that bewitched him, but he also orders the well with its contents be "filled up with earth," buried forever, as if not to leave any trace or any witness of this act of bewitching. By doing so, he certainly doesn't want to leave any magical material someone from the community might use. But beyond that, the Prophet is also implicitly asking people to take for granted what he told them without any manifest proof.

The prophetic tradition is not the only source that points to the act of bewitching through knots. The Qur'an itself brings up this prominent act of sorcery. Indeed, the act of tying or binding knots is stated in Qur'an 113:3*: "And I seek refuge from the chanters over the knots."

In the opinion of many Qur'an commentators, chapter 113 of the Qur'an refers to the practice of witches and sorcerers who tied a string into a number of knots while blowing or puffing upon them, and muttering magical incantations. This act of tying and binding is not the invention of Islam, but rather is found in many texts of the ancient Near East. As previously mentioned, Islam, like most religions, acknowledges borrowings from preceding religions.[25] The ancient Greeks, for example, believed undoing knots on board a ship could bring up the wind. And in the Roman Empire, the poet Virgil (b. 70 BCE), who was considered in medieval times a kind of magician and whose *Aeneid* was used for divination, also sang of the impact of knots to bewitch someone: "Knot, Amaryllis, tie! Of colors three/Then say, 'These bonds I knit for Venus be.'"[26]

In the ancient Babylonian religion, prayers were offered to Shamash, the god of the sun, to liberate the ensnared ones. And in *Enuma Elish,* the Babylonian epic of Creation, the god Marduk fights the ferocious Tiamat who was plotting the gods' destruction. He finally subdues her and her helpers with a net; "In the net they were caught and in the snare they sat down. They received punishment from him, they were held in bondage."[27]

The sorcerer's knots hold back or "bind" the person he would like to harm. Knotting fetters the other in its snares, and ties or fixes him in a specific state. Evil comes from the sorcerer's concentration on this person while he/she is tying his/her threads as well as from the power of the ritual and the incantations that accompany it, be it chanting or puffing. Exorcism could be the literal and spiritual act of extracting the victim from the shackles of this devilish bond by untying or loosening the sorcerer's knots.

The Vedic texts of Ancient India illustrate it is not sorcerers who devilishly tie humans, but rather gods, such as Varuna, Indra, Yama, and Vritra, etc., which points to the multiple meanings of knotting in Hinduism. It is a mixture of religion and magic. During this era, gods had in them some demonic attributes, as Mircea Eliade elucidates, "But on the one hand, here we often have to do with religious beings who are ambivalent (Tvashtri, Maruts) in the sense that a demonic element coexists in them with the divine elements; and, on the other hand, the attribute 'magician' is not specific, but is only attached to the divine personalities as an additional honor."[28]

Despite assimilations and appropriations from the ancient religious traditions of the Near East, Islam distinguished itself by emphasizing the difference between magic and sorcery. Magic is considered a divine gift that can heal sickness and possession in the name of God, while sorcery resorts to the evil of heretic jinn and demons, and is condemned by Islam. Ibn al-Nadim elucidates the difference between Islamic magic and sorcery as follows:

The exorcists, who pretend to observe the sacred laws, claim that this "power" is because of obedience to God . . . Thus invocation is addressed to Him, and oaths by the spirits and devils are by His help, with the abandoning of lusts and by consequence of religious practices. Moreover, [they claim] the jinn and the devils obey them, either because of obedience to God, may His name be magnified, or on account of [their making] oaths by Him, or else for fear of Him, uplifted and glorious is He. The sorcerers assert that they enslave the devils by offerings and prohibitive acts. They maintain the devils are pleased by the committing of acts which are forbidden and which God, may His name be magnified, has prohibited.[29]

Ibn al-Nadim adds further in the same passage, "The sorcerers declare that they bind the devils by sacrifices and prohibitive acts. They assert that the devils are satisfied by the committing of such acts that God has prohibited, may His name be sanctified."[30]

HEALING TECHNIQUES IN CLASSICAL ISLAM

The Qur'an as Healing Energy

Although God as a healer is not one of the 99 Divine Names, He is mentioned six times in the Qur'an as such. Moreover, the Holy text itself is represented as having a therapeutic value as in Qur'an 17:82, "And we cause to descend of the Qur'an what is a healing and a mercy to the believers." In Qur'an 26:80, God is said to cure ailments: "and, whenever I am sick, He heals me." One prophetic tradition mentions, "The best medicines are: honey and the Qur'an."[31]

Since its advent, Islam made it clear nothing other than the Words of God, or his names, or the Arabic letters with which the Qur'an was conveyed could be brought into a spell, a charm, an incantation, or the like and Muslims endeavored to comply with the rules. Theologians, Qur'an commentators, and Sufis strived to use the Qur'anic text in ingenious ways, as to write down the six verses that mention healing in the Qur'an on a piece of paper, erase them in a cup full of water, and then drink the contents. They claimed this would heal the drinker from his sickness.[32]

"Drinking" the Words of God seems to involve the whole body in the process of change. This is viewed as an almost alchemical process where the swallowing of this liquid transmutes the sick person into a new healed being.

Similar beliefs were held by different traditions across the ancient Near East. It is reported that a certain pious Egyptian by the name of Naneferkaptah heard that the god Thoth had written books of magic with his own hand. So he undertook a voyage to find it. Once in possession of the book, Naneferkaptah, "a good scribe and very wise man, had a sheet of new papyrus brought to him. He wrote on it every word that was in the book before him. He soaked it in beer, then he dissolved it in water. When he knew it had dissolved, he drank it and knew what had been in it."[33]

In this last example, drinking the sacred text is not so much for purposes of healing but rather for knowledge. It assumes knowledge is not located in the mind alone, but circulates throughout the whole body which digests it in its own way. As Garth Fowden, contemporary scholar of Greek and Roman Antiquity, mentions, "This practice gave special point to the Gnostic *topos* of 'drinking down knowledge.'"[34]

In the Old Testament, one also finds this procedure of "drinking" written sacred words, but in a different context. If the ancient Israelites, for example, wanted to try a woman accused of adultery, they would make her drink water into which a written curse had been dissolved, then the woman swore an oath of innocence or "made a solemn declaration of innocence" (Numbers 5:16–31). If she swore falsely, the curse in the water would convict her through a physical manifestation, making her infertile:

> The priest is to have the woman stand at my altar, where he will pour sacred water into a clay jar and stir in some dust from the floor of the sacred tent. Next, he will remove her veil, then hand her the barley offering, and say, "If you have been faithful to your husband, this water won't harm you. But if you have been unfaithful, it will bring down the Lord's curse—you will never be able to give birth to a child, and everyone will curse your name."
>
> Then the woman will answer, "If I am guilty, let it happen just as you say."
>
> The priest will write these curses on special paper and wash them off into the bitter water, so that when the woman drinks this water, the curses will enter her body. He will take the barley offering from her and lift it up in dedication to me, the Lord. Then he will place it on my altar and burn part of it as a sacrifice. After that, the woman must drink the bitter water. If the woman has been unfaithful, the water will immediately make her unable to have children, and she will be a curse among her people. But if she is innocent, her body will not be harmed, and she will still be able to have children.

> This is the ceremony that must take place at my altar when a husband sus-
> pects his wife has been unfaithful. The priest must have the woman stand in my
> presence and carefully follow these instructions. If the husband is wrong, he
> will not be punished; but if his wife is guilty, she will be punished.[35]

"Drinking the Qur'an" has never replaced reciting it for protection from evil.
In medieval times, just as today, Muslims believe the recitation of Qur'an 2:255,
called "the Verse of the Throne," could expel evil jinn. They recite it to protect
themselves and entrust themselves to God's care. In addition to "the verse of the
Throne," there are many other verses believed to protect from evil jinn. First are
the verses of protection or safeguard, *ayat al-hifz,* usually used as talismans. Some
of these verses are Qur'an 12:64, 13:11, 3:7, 33:3, 33:48, 4:81, and 15:17. Second is the
Qur'anic chapter entitled *Yasin,* surnamed the heart of the Book, and considered to
be of capital importance for all kinds of diseases. Third, the opening chapter of the
Qur'an, *al-fatihah,* as well as the *basmalah: bism-il-lahi al-rahman al-rahim* (In the
Name of God, the Merciful, the Compassionate) Muslims recite in the event of any
distress, sickness, or to protect themselves from evil jinn. Finally, the two Qur'anic
chapters 113 and 114 of refuge, called *al-muʿawwidhatan,* are of particular value for
protecting the believers from evil jinn and demons.

Qur'anic verses were sometimes written on amulets, which were conserved
in a leather case, and worn around the neck or on the body as another way to be
protected from evil jinn. Occasionally, it was not enough to carry the Qur'anic
verses in amulets. Some authors of popular medicine advised even writing the
verses directly on the body of the possessed or the diseased, especially on the
patient's palms and his forehead. The changes claimed to have taken place, as
we are told in these texts of Islamic magic, are a result of the fervent belief of the
faithful in the strength of the divine word, which is thought to be inimitable.

The power of the Holy text also comes from the belief the earthly Qur'an
is, for Muslims, a copy of the Divine Qur'an that is preserved since eternity in
heaven as in Qur'an 85:22. Henceforth, reciting it, writing it, wearing it, or drinking it is an unswerving act of participation in the Divine source itself. One could
say the believer at that time was literally "living" in the Qur'an to the point he
became one with it. In fact, the Qur'anic verses themselves were considered living beings. Scholars of classical Islam maintained they would act as witnesses on
behalf of humans on the Day of Judgment.

The Divine Names and the Protection from Evil

Besides the Qur'an, it was common practice in medieval times to recite and write down the Most Beautiful Names of God to be protected from wicked jinn. It also was thought the repetition of the Mystical Divine Name, *ism allah al-'a'zam* (the Greatest Name of God), which is above all the others, could heal the person possessed by jinn. Among all his names, Allah is the most perfect. It is composed of four Arabic letters, which is believed to correspond to the four elements, the four cardinal points, the four seasons. We are reminded here of the supreme oath of the Pythagorean philosophical community: "By him who gave the fourness to our soul."

In turn, folk Islam brings into play the greatest name of God to defeat sorcery. In the "Porter and the Three Ladies" from *The Nights,* the pious Muslim princess fights a sorcerer jinni who transformed a man into an ape. She succeeds after an atrocious struggle and the unremitting recitation of the greatest name of God to bring back the ape to his original human form. However, at the end of the battle, both princess and jinni die, worn out by the ruthlessness of the attacks and the efforts wielded to achieve their respective goals: "The speaker was the princess who had burnt the ifrit, and he was become a heap of ashes. Then she came to us and said: 'reach me a cup of water.' They brought it to her, and she spoke over it words we understood not, and sprinkling me with it cried, 'By virtue of the Truth, and by the most Great Name of God, I charge thee to return to thy former shape.' And behold, I shook, and became a man as before, save that I had utterly lost an eye."[36]

Some authors found it indispensable to indicate which names of God should be recited to dispel the wicked jinn, and in which sequence, as did al-Suyuti (d. 1505). He advises the recitation of the following Divine Names in this order: "Oh God, the Vigilant, the Preserver, the Merciful. Oh God, the Living, the Gentle, the Great, the Gracious, the Generous. Oh God, the Living, the Everlasting, the Steadfast by whom one gains freedom from his enemies."[37]

Others claimed it was not enough to recite or write down the names of God. They came up with resourceful procedures to drive away the malevolent spirits. In this context, Ahmad ibn 'Ali al-Buni (d. 1225), a prominent mathematician, wrote on the esoteric denomination of Arabic letters in his magnum opus, *shams al-ma'arif.* Al-Buni maintained one could detain an evil jinni or even burn him by writing the Sufi invocation of God *huwa* (He) on a blue cloth and by inciting the jinni to smell it.[38]

The author here assumes the jinni is embodying a visible shape in front of the human and he is close enough to sniff the cloth on which the Divine Name is written. Moreover, we are not told why the author suggests the use of a blue cloth, over a red or green one, nor why the act of smelling the cloth would burn the evil jinni.[39]

The Magical Power of Arabic Letters

Medieval Islamic magic also resorted to Arabic letters for chasing away the jinn believed to dwell in a human body. Arabic letters were written disconnected in most talismans and amulets, which is thought to increase their potency because each separate letter manifests its intrinsic force, and behaves as a unique and living field of energy. Al-Buni maintained Arabic letters have their kingdoms, their traditions, and their secrets. Each letter has its own servants and its own ruler. He deemed them "a nation among nations."[40] He alleged one should not use them in magic if he/she is not aware they are like living beings. Each letter of the Arabic script has its particular power derived from being linked to one of the four elements, to a certain number, to heavens, or to the lower world, and to either light or darkness. The letters of light, for example, produce love and unity, while the letters of darkness generate hatred and war. Hence, each letter is used for a specific disease or a specific relation with the jinn. Muslim alchemists and magicians indicated in medieval times the letter *aleph,* for example, is connected to the beginnings of creation. Its supremacy has no equal because its origin is in the Divine Name itself.[41]

Ibn 'Arabi attributed an even greater role to the Arabic letters because he considered them not only a nation among other nations, but also "the *imams* [leaders] of words,"[42] which points to their role as guides to humans in the realm of knowledge and spiritual awakening. He distributed them on four levels. The first level is the Divine one, composed of letters such as aleph and *lam.* The second level is the human one to which belong letters such as *nun, sad,* and *dad.* The third level is that of the jinn to which belong letters such as *ayn, ghayn, sin, shin,* and *qaf.* Finally, the fourth level is that of angelic letters.[43] Ibn 'Arabi also claimed each letter has two meanings because it could manifest itself either in the visible or invisible realm.[44]

Moreover, a number of Arabic letters open some Qur'anic chapters, and are thus considered of particular sacredness. There is no consensus among scholars on the exact meaning of these separate letters. Some highlight the numeric values of these letters and stress their esoteric meaning, while others simply maintain they are an intrinsic part of the Revelation that is mysterious, inimitable, and wondrous. Some Muslims believed these opening letters have more power than others, and have the ability to chase away evil jinn, in particular the *qaf*. It is told that al-Shibli (d. 1368) visited once a man who was possessed by an evil jinni, so al-Shibli wrote a letter *qaf* on the possessed man's palm, then drew seven circles around it. He then asked the possessed to lick it. Al-Shibli claims the man was instantly healed.[45]

One can surmise the choice of the letter *qaf* over other letters appears to spring from its being the first letter in the following Divine Names: al-Qadir (the all-powerful), al Qahhar (the omnipotent), al-Qawiyy (the mighty), al-Qayyum (the everlasting), which express the omnipotence of God over his creation, including evil jinn.

Like al-Shibli, al-Buni reiterates the power of the letter *qaf* regarding chasing away evil jinn. He invites his disciples to do the following: "Write the letter *qaf* and place it in half a circle. Sit in this semi circle where no flying or diving jinn can ever harm you."[46] It was often asserted the letter *qaf* also refers to *qalb* (heart), to the Holy Book, al-Qur'an, or to *qalam* (the Pen). All of these words bear an undeniable symbolic meaning.[47]

Both al-Shibli and al-Buni draw the letter *qaf* in a circle or semi-circle. In a preceding chapter, al-Gilani (d. 1166) also asked a person—who was looking for his abducted daughter—to sit in a circle when the jinn pass by him to protect him. Muhammad himself commanded one of his companions to stay within the limits of a circle as well, while he went and recited the Qur'an to some jinn.[48]

The notion of circles as sacred symbols of eternity is spread across traditions. The Divine itself has been compared to a circle in the words of Hermes Trismegistus, "God is a circle whose center is everywhere and circumference is nowhere."[49] It is in this spirit circles were used in classical Islam; they were considered a field of holy energy that could save the person sitting within its boundaries from any harm.

POSSESSION, EPILEPSY, AND HEALING

The Qur'an mentions the word *majnun* eleven times in relation to madness and epilepsy. In seven instances, it refers to the Prophet directly. Muhammad's opponents believed he was jinn-possessed, or epileptic, and a jinni was dictating to him the words. In three instances, God replies to these accusations.[50]

The Prophet's tradition includes stories regarding possession and epilepsy. Although the Prophet is not mentioned in the Qur'an as an exorcist, one finds a different portrait in the prophetic tradition, where he exercises fully his healer's powers. For example, there is a story of a woman who brought her epileptic son to him: he opened his mouth, and puffed three times into it reciting the following: "In the Name of God the Compassionate, the Merciful, go away enemy of God for I am the Servant of God!" He told the woman to bring the boy after a while. She returned and told the Prophet he was completely healed.[51]

The prophetic tradition mentions that often the Prophet would repeat the words cited above, especially: "Depart, enemy of God, I am His Messenger." It is alleged the evil spirit would leave the person instantly.[52]

Here, Muhammad just commands the evil spirit to leave the body of the possessed—no persuasion of any kind—simply the injunction of a prophet connected to the "invisible" world. Other accounts portray sheikhs as entering into dialogue with the evil spirit. They argue with it, and they claim that the invisible entity talks back as in this story told by al-Jawziyyah (d. 1350) in his book, *The Medicine of the Prophet,* where he relates the following procedure of exorcism performed by a sheikh:

> The sheikh told me that he once recited this verse [verse of the Throne, Qur'an 2:255] into the ear of an epileptic, and the spirit said: "Yes." And its voice reached him. He said: "So I took a stick to hit, and I beat the patient with it on the veins of his neck until my hands grew tired from the beating. The people present had no doubt that he would die from the blows. During this beating the spirit said: 'I love him.' So I said to it: 'He does not love you.' Then it said: 'I wish to accompany him.' I replied: 'He does not want your company.' It said then, 'I will leave him out of respect for you.' I replied: 'No, rather in obedience to God and his Messenger.' And it said: 'I am departing from him.' Then, the epileptic sat up, looked around him, right and left, and asked: 'What brought me to the sheikh?'"[53]

It is possible to find parallel beliefs in possession by evil spirits in other religions, as in Taoism, for example. Huston Smith, contemporary historian of religion, evokes a similar case of possession to the one depicted by ibn al-Qayyim. It is an eyewitness account of a man possessed by an evil spirit and a Taoist priest trying to exorcise him. "The energumen, a rather emaciated man of about twenty-five, lay on an iron bedstead on a rush mat. He was very pale and his look was a wild, roving look in his fevered eyes. The Taoist priest, holding an elongated ivory tablet held ceremonially in both hands in front of his chest, approached the bed slowly. There was a visible transformation on the energumen's face. His eyes were filled with malice as he watched the priest's measured advance with a sly cunning and hatred. Suddenly he gave a bestial whoop and jumped up in his bed, the four attendants rushing to hold him."[54]

Like the sheikh in the story of ibn al-Qayyim, the Taoist priest cured the possessed man who finally woke up to reality and recognized his family. He was indeed present yet absent in a realm between the tangible and the intangible, which made everything around him look eerie, yet not totally unfamiliar. In both accounts, there seems to be a violent interaction between the two realms of the invisible (the evil spirit thought to hide in the body) and the manifest (the possessed human who seems to have lost his free will). The evil spirit plays tricks until he exits the human body. Until the last minute, he attempts to hide in the man. The nature of evil is believed to endlessly play with humans as a cat does with a mouse. Theologians warned Muslims to exercise caution, for evil jinn are capable of luring them time and again. It is in this context that ibn Taymiyah (d. 1328) alerted people to the fact jinn could make them believe they departed from the body they possessed, while in reality they lie. Ibn Taymiyah maintained jinn often imitate human voices; for example if a human calls a friend to help him, the jinni would simulate the voice of this friend and mislead the human.[55] Again, it was advised to recite "the verse of the Throne" (Qur'an 2:255) in the ear of the possessed if one wanted to swiftly deliver this person from evil jinn.

Some people in classical Islam also believed one could become either sick or possessed if he/she stays a long time at a threshold. They claimed thresholds in general are somehow connected to jinn, and it would be better not to linger in these particular locales. They alleged, if someone pours water over the threshold of a house, or if a parent beats a child at this place, both could become mad or sick.[56]

One wonders why people linked the jinn to the threshold. What is specific about a threshold? "As a boundary symbol it is the line of meeting of the natural and supernatural."[57] Therefore, one could surmise if one lingers there, one almost risks stumbling into the other side, into the invisible realm where jinn lurk. We often see in popular Islam the jinn guard jealously their domains and don't welcome humans who trespass their boundaries. The symbols embedded in a threshold seem to reflect the human anxiety of leaving the granted for the conjectural. As for pouring water over a threshold, people thought it could be dangerous because they believed water might mix in its flow imaginal and physical realms, and hence, brings forth the jinn.

Beating a child on a threshold was seen as an act of exorcism in many traditions. Beating, flogging, or whipping were used as means to cast away the evil spirits. This act might trigger the manifestation of evil jinn and, consequently, bring forward the madness of both parent and child at the sight of these evil entities.[58]

Frontiers like thresholds where imaginal and terrestrial realms might interpenetrate are located not only in space but also in time. If thresholds were viewed in classical Islam as locales where the intermediary realm might surface, sunrises were looked upon by fairies as stations in time when these spirits pass by humans without the latter noticing them.

In a story collected by Irish poet, W. B. Yeats (d. 1939), entitled "Paddy Corcoran's Wife," we are told a woman fell sick, until one day, after seven years of continuous sickness, a fairy visited her while she was lying in bed and informed her the fairies caused her sickness because she threw her trash at sunrise each day, exactly when the fairies were passing by her door. They requested she do it at different times and they would heal her; she obeyed, and was healed.[59]

It is worthy to note the fairies impose their rule on the sick woman rather than changing their time of passage. It might be that, for these spirits, passing by human habitations at sunrise is a kind of ritual not up for discussion. Sunrise is seen in old Irish mythology as "the eye of the day." The same word *sul* refers to eye and sun in Gaelic language.[60]

CONCLUSION

Finding ways to ward off evil jinn thought to cause madness, possession, or epilepsy was not considered superstitious by Muslims in medieval times. It didn't mean in any sense to be less Muslim because these procedures were inspired from Islam and sanctioned by Muslim theologians. All these kinds of spiritual healing—sometimes called "Islamic magic"—were indeed inspired from certain verses of the Qur'an, the Most Beautiful Names of God, and the Arabic alphabet by which the Word of God was revealed to Muhammad.

In classical Islam, both orthodox religion and spiritual healing considered the human being as the microcosm and the universe as the macrocosm. Both spoke of the constant interaction and resemblances between macrocosm and microcosm. Both stressed everything bears the sign of the Creator, and should be dealt with as such. Muslim theologians asserted the exorcist needed to respect certain religious conditions for his "help" to act. From their writings, one concludes the exorcist is almost a kind of saint who must lead a life of perfect piety in solitude and abstinence, and totally devoted to prayers and meditations. Classical Islam didn't consider the exorcist a Promethean man working against the religion, but rather a pontifical man whose success was bestowed upon him by no one else but God.

Furthermore, warding off evil jinn was not an act of rejection of medicine. Islamic magic has never hampered Muslims from probing scientific cures for sick and epileptic people. Because medicine was engrained in the religion itself, it couldn't get in the way of scientific progress. The prophetic tradition orders Muslims, "Take medicine, o servants of God. For every illness He gave medicine."[61] Classical Islam stressed that Muslims should strive to find cures for diseases. Islamic physicians built up a huge and intricate medical corpus. This all-embracing literature was not confined to strict medical knowledge in the sense that modern medical literature is. Rather, it was blended with philosophy, natural science, mathematics, astrology, alchemy, biology, spirit healers, charms, and religion. In this sense, it was what we call today "interdisciplinary." In addition, there were abundant books on *al-tibb al-ruhi* (spiritual medicine), like the books written by Zakariya al-Razi (d. 923) and ibn Qayyim al-Jawziyyah (d. 1350) in which they discussed issues dealing with moods and emotions affecting the body as well as the influence of the spiritual life on the physical one. Physicians were themselves an embodiment of this synthesis. They were equally interested in issues of medical progress and in mysticism. Avicenna (d. 1037) was one of their most inventive and prominent physicians who wrote medical treatises as well as mystical allegories. He was altogether a mathematician, a physician, a poet, an astronomer, and a mystic. He was especially interested in the effect of the mind on the body, and wrote a great deal on psychology as well.

Engrossed by Islamic teachings, "Islamic magic" and medicine worked hand in hand. Illness was perceived as a discordance, a disharmony between man, nature, and the intermediary realm. Classical Islam strived to create concord between nature and culture, being and thought, rather than seeing things through the lenses of a dualism based on the opposition of sacred versus profane.

Still today, it is difficult for many westerners to comprehend how classical Islam blended in religion, medicine, and spiritual healing. Most of the West still views the progress of humanity as evolving from magic to religion and, finally, to science in spite of the assertion of many contemporary anthropologists who reject the ideas of their predecessors and maintain they don't see this linear progress in every culture they study.[62]

6
Jinn in Animal Shapes

The jinn are of three kinds: one has wings and flies,
serpents and dogs are another, and the third keeps roaming.
—Prophetic tradition[1]

*H*umans seem always to have spiritualized animals, and keenly associated the spiritual realm with the animal one. This correlation might have its origin in the enduring human belief animals are mysterious beings, somehow related to the invisible domain. People believe animals could feel the approach of disasters; for example, they sense the approach of a storm, an earthquake, or a flood. Scientists nowadays, like contemporary American biologist Rupert Sheldrake, suppose both wild and domesticated animals have a kind of sixth sense regarding impending natural catastrophes. Sheldrake maintains, "premonitions occur among many species of animals. They are natural, not supernatural."[2] He seems to think those animals that have a sharper sense of premonition than others are better privileged by biological choice. In this sense, animals are conscious beings, and not mere automata, as Cartesians would have it.

In general, animals seem to strongly interact with humans, nature, and all things in the universe. It is to this "animal energy" Eliade (d. 1986) alludes when he writes, "Animal language is only a variant of spiritual language."[3] Eliade's assertion opens the door to all kinds of speculations regarding the relationships between spirits and animals. It also hints at the fact animals make us discover a different consciousness, and return us to the rhythms of nature, not intellectually, but rather intuitively.

SPIRITS IN ANIMALS FORMS ACROSS TRADITIONS

The great ancient civilizations presented a vision of the world in which natural and supernatural were constantly combined. The delineations between gods, demons, spirits, and animals were not always very clear—wild animals were often thought of as demons, or vaguely as "spirits." Gods were represented as taking their energy from specific animals, which made them sacred.

In Egypt, for example, almost all Egyptian gods were associated with certain animal aspects, and some gods were never represented except with the head of their appropriate animal, although their bodies were human. The scorpion-goddess Serqet, or Selqet, was associated with the powers of an evil spirit in some of her aspects. Horus, the sky god, had the head of a hawk and the body of a man. Anubis, the god of mummies who guided the souls of the dead into the underworld, was often represented as a man with the head of a jackal.

Some Egyptologists, such as E. A. Wallis Budge (d. 1934), firmly believed, "The Egyptians developed the idea that individual animals were the abodes of the gods, and they believed that certain deities were incarnate in them."[4]

However, this opinion is exaggerated. It is true the ancient Egyptians worshiped at an early stage some animals, or at least considered them sacred, like the cat at Bubastis, the wolf Ophois who was a god of war, and the Ibis Thoth who was a god of knowledge. However, Thoth was also identified with the baboon. When one carefully surveys the Egyptian myths, one notices gods were not becoming animals, or at least dwelling in the bodies of animals. Throughout Egyptian history, we see gods always accompanied by animals, even when their heads were those of animals.

The Babylonian pantheon, parallel to the Egyptian one in time, was one of the richest in gods and demons having animal forms. Thus, the demon Gallu was often portrayed in the form of a bull, while Alu was represented in a composite form, half human and half animal. The demon Pazuzu was represented as a five-footed monster, half bird, half lion and scorpion. The demon Mukil-Resh-Lemutti had the head of a bird, but the feet and hands of a human. The demon Samanum had the head of a lion, the claws of an eagle, and the tail of a crayfish. The demon Lamastu had the head of a woman who holds a serpent in each hand, while a dog and a pig are suckling at her breasts.

Besides demons in the Babylonian religion, there were the good genies—protectors of humans—who also took on animal forms, especially that of huge bulls and lions.[5] These good genies sat at the entrance of the underworld to protect humans from attacks by demons that manifested themselves in animal forms. Good genies and bad demons bellowed, roared, barked, and vociferated at each other. The ancient Babylonians firmly believed anyone who did not have a genie protecting him or her was exposed to a demon's attacks.[6] Generally speaking, the world for the Babylonians during this time was filled with good and bad spirits fighting each other in animal shapes.

Gods and spiritual entities were not the only ones to be close to the animal realm. The *Enuma Elish* informs us that humans and animals were created out of earth mingled with the life-blood of a god. Thus, the source of life for gods, humans, and animals was perceived as one and divine by the Babylonians, which led them to consider all forms of life as sacred.[7]

Beyond the Near East, one finds the same recurrence of gods or spirits appearing in animal forms. Thus, in Indian mythology, for example, the Naig-amesa, the messenger of Indra and the chief of devas, has the head of a goat and rides on a peacock cart.[8] There are also the Gandharvas, often described as men with birds' legs and wings. The Rakshasas usually appear in the shape of a dog or a bird with a fat body. They are believed to distract yogis in their meditation. In Hindu mythology, the first three avatars (incarnations) of the god Vishnu were Kurma the tortoise, Varaha the boar, and Nr-simha the man-lion.[9]

In the rich Celtic and Irish traditions, spiritual entities could also appear in animal shapes. It is alleged when the fairies embody animal forms, they keep changing their forms and sizes until they vanish from sight, as in the following account: "There exists a kind of fairy called *The Bugganes,* who can appear in any shape they please—as ogresses with huge heads and great fiery eyes, or without any heads at all; as small dogs who grow larger and larger as you watch them until they are larger than elephants, when perhaps they turn into the shape of men or disappear into nothing; as horned monsters, or anything they choose."[10]

None other than poets can seize this constant metamorphosis of these enti-ties, as this poem from Irish lore where some kind of spiritual entities describe their constant metamorphosis: "Who now like knight and lady seem/And now like dwarf and ape."[11]

Native American culture is crammed with animals' spirits that preside over important aspects of life.[12] These spirits often manifest themselves as ravens who speak, or coyotes who control humans. In these old traditions, the shaman often captures his visions from an animal spirit who guides him into the unseen world. The shaman is known to contact his animal spirit regularly and to talk to him. Native Americans call this kind of communication "dancing the animal."

Within an altered state of consciousness, in which he performs his duties, the shaman recourses to his animal spirit, which assists him in accomplishing his task. The latter is never hurtful to the shaman but accompanies him through the underworld or guides him on his mystical climb to the sky.

JINN/ANIMALS IN THE ARAB & MUSLIM TRADITION

Along with other nations, Arabs in pre-Islam acknowledged animals could be the dwelling places for spiritual entities. They depicted jinn as taking animal shapes to hide from humans, or trick them, or deliver a message to them. They first thought the jinn chose to dwell in deer because of their beauty and fragility. The deer was looked at as a magical animal. People often alleged "deer are the cattle of the jinn."[13] Then, they described ostriches as mounts for the jinn. The alliance of evil jinn and ostriches seems to be a mostly Semitic belief because we find it in profusion in Arabic literature as well as in Hebrew literature, which describe them as voracious creatures. Scholar of Jewish and Christian demonology Edward Langton (b. 1886) claims, "By the Arabs, ostriches are definitely connected with demons, which are said to ride upon them or to assume their form."[14] However, one correction needs to be made here. It is important to clarify it is evil jinn that take the shape of ostriches and not demons, as Langton asserts. We know evil jinn are not equated with demons in Islam because we have discussed three distinct categories: angels, jinn, and demons. Interesting enough, the same ostrich becomes in Zoroastrianism and Ancient Egypt "a divine storm bird."[15] Symbols, despite their universality, keep at the same time some patchy local elements.

These beliefs continued in Islam. Muslims particularly stressed the malevolence of black dogs. They thought they were an abode for evil jinn. They lavished on them lunar and negative connotations. Muslim compilers like al-Jahiz (d. 868) pictured black dogs as "digging out graves and eating the dead."[16] The prophetic tradition offers, however, an ambivalent picture of jinn/dogs. Thus, in one saying, "Angels do not enter a house in which there is a dog or [worshiped] pictures,"[17] while in another, the Prophet invites Muslims to help all kinds of animals, including dogs.

In general, it seems it is mostly black dogs that were rejected and cursed because of their association with sorcery and witchcraft. The idea of black dogs as embodiment of malevolence might be borrowed from or shared with neighboring civilizations where dogs were always connected with the underworld. In Greek mythology, for example, "The dogs of Hades represent the gloom of dawn and dusk which contain hostile powers and are dangerous and demonic times."[18]

In some narratives, jinn embody strange dogs' shapes to deliver a message to humans, as in the intriguing story narrated by the theologian 'Abd al-Wahab ibn Ahmad al-Sha'rani (d. 1563) in which he claims a group of Muslim jinn sent him some questions regarding metaphysical issues. These queries were written on a piece of paper and delivered to him by a yellow dog who informed him he is a jinni taking a dog form to bring him this note in secret. Al-Sha'rani's guardian chased him away. But he came back, this time from the window, carrying in his mouth the letter of Muslim jinn philosophers to the author.[19]

The choice of the dog's color merits a quick note. We have seen that black dogs were considered impure and evil, while white dogs were not forbidden. The color yellow here is rather unusual. It refers to the magical aspect of this dog. Whenever an animal appears in a bizarre color or shape or produces unusual sounds, it is believed throughout traditions it is not of this physical dimension in which we live.

Stories abound about the animal manifestation of jinn in classical Islam. It is related that a man was in charge of guarding a basket filled with dates. He noticed the quantity of dates kept decreasing. He doubled his efforts to find the thief. Finally, he found "a beast as small as a young boy. He caught it, and asked it: 'Are you a jinni or a human?' To which it replied: 'I am a jinni.' The man shook hands with it, and, to his great surprise, discovered that it had the hands and the feet of a dog!"[20] It is noteworthy the human is not frightened at all of this strange being. His question implied he expected to encounter a non-human. This seems to be a common assumption during this time. It underscores the wide belief in jinn's presence among people.

In addition to dogs, deer, and ostriches, jinn are described as embodying the forms of many other animals such as foxes and porcupines[21] as well as "the raven, the dove, the hedgehog, and the rabbit."[22] This is exemplified in the many stories that classical Islam weaved on the prophet Solomon. According to Qur'an 17:27, God made the jinn subservient to him. It is said a huge number of evil jinn in animal appearances were brought in front of him by order of God. The strangest description is the one written by geographer Zakaria ibn Muhammad al-Qazwini

(d. 1283). It illustrates with rich and vivid details how Gabriel called the jinn and the demons by command of God to obey his prophet Solomon, and how the jinn and satans streamed out of the caverns, mountains, hills, valleys, and deserts, saying: "Here we are at your service!" They were guided by the angels as cattle are guided by a shepherd, until they arrived in front of Solomon, obedient and humble. Solomon looked at their strange figures: some of them were white, others black, others yellow, and others blond. They had the forms of horses, mules, and lions with trunks, tails, claws, and horns.[23]

Al-Mas'udi (d. 956) in turn added picturesque details to this sight. He offered an entire scenery of eerie beings with two faces, one in front and one in the rear, with their heads similar to birds' heads. Some spoke like thunder; still others cried like birds, and had their mouths in their chests. There was a nation among them that resembled insects, but had bulky bodies and horns on their heads. Others resembled flying snakes and yet had many feet and hands. It was believed these beings worked day and night at Solomon's court.[24]

In these two popular accounts, jinn appear as hideous, atrocious, and hybrid beings that lack symmetry. It is assumed the hard labor these entities perform for their master, Solomon, is a punishment they deserve for having rebelled against him. Evil jinn in general are characterized by their infinite shape shifting, which has a goal of luring humans and enticing them. It is exemplified by the following story recited by a jinni called Abu-Hadraj:

The children of Adam were evil to me, and I likewise treated them. Once I entered their world wanting to sleep with one of their maids. I changed my shape into the form of a field rat, and the cats chased me. And when they got me, I shape-shifted into a striped serpent and slinked into a tree stump there. But they uncovered me, and at that moment I feared death and made a dim hissing, and followed along the timber's plank, and one broke open a place in the wood but didn't see me. And they said in their bewilderment, "There is no place here where it could hide," and while they were wondering where I was, I went to the virgin who was under a mosquito net, and when she saw me the fear of falling hit her. Then her family gathered around her from all sides and brought exorcists, and called doctors, and they made every effort to revive her, and did not omit amulets to charm me away from her, but I did not respond. And the doctors continued to administer medicines to heal her, but I clutched to her tightly. When death hit her, I sought to replace her by another, then another, until God aided me with repentance and great reward, so I incessantly praised Him: "I praise the One who took my burden away, and now my sins are forgiven."[25]

This story is worthy of note because it sums up many aspects of the interaction between jinn and humans, as people imagined it in classical Islam. The narrative pertains first to the ensnaring maneuvers of the jinni, and to his speed that enabled him to quickly vanish without being caught.

Second, Abu-Hadraj desired a human woman and didn't hesitate to come to her while doctors and members of her family were still looking for him. As we shall see in the next chapter, it is alleged jinn sometimes fall in love with humans. They could harm them or even bring their death if they don't respond to their love. Third, this story depicts humans' recourse to magic to drive out evil jinn. They attempted to dispel malevolence by using amulets and charms. But it was in vain. Finally, and most important, this jinni converts to Islam, and hence, becomes a good jinni devoted to the worship of God. Be that as it may, this text illustrates the elusive nature of the jinn and their trickster character. It also reiterates the Islamic belief evil jinn could be redeemed by the Word of God anywhere and anytime.

It is important to mention Abu al-'Ala' al-Ma'arri (d. 1057), author of this story, was an agnostic. However, he brings in this narrative to underscore the beliefs of people during that time. One could surmise, though, he is being sarcastic as well because he is known for his rationality and his sharp criticism of religion.

SERPENTS AS THE EMBODIMENTS OF SPIRITS
IN VARIOUS RELIGIOUS TRADITIONS

Our first reading of Arab/Muslim narratives seems to convey jinn could embody any animal shape. However, this is not a comprehensive picture of the jinn's capabilities. The majority of accounts in classical Islam notify us jinn prefer to dwell in serpents. Interesting enough, this appears to hold true for most spirits across the world. The serpent, simply put, is a central figure in all mythologies. It is also perceived as an ambiguous being. On one hand, it is looked at as a lowly animal because it cannot leave the ground. But on the other hand, it is considered a supernatural being because it lives very long, sheds its skin, and is thus reborn. One of the most recognizable serpent symbols is the *Ouroboros*. It is found in alchemy and in ancient Egyptian, Greek, and Gnostic religions. It is a serpent that is swallowing its own tail, and usually makes a circle that is itself a symbol of perfection, rebirth, and eternity. Across cultures, humans look at this slinking power under the moon as a psychic and telepathic creature. The repulsion a serpent causes through its size and strength, and the mysterious action of its silent and slithering movements make it an embodiment of mythical force. The serpent is thus a creature to be envied as well as feared, a being of immeasurable slyness, intricacy, and perhaps evil.

Before embarking in an analysis of the serpent's relation to the jinn in classical Islam, I would like to underscore the universal connection between serpents and spirits across traditions to highlight this universal belief. Serpents were closely associated with spirits throughout the ancient Near East. The idea of spiritual entities in serpent form was a familiar one from Egypt to Persia and from Babylon to Canaan. In Egypt, the serpent was a multifaceted symbol of deity and evil altogether. On one hand, it was worshiped as a goddess of good and kept in large numbers in temples. It often appears as a personal or house protecting amulet throughout Egyptian history. Egyptians venerated many varieties of serpents. The pharaoh himself wore a serpent emblem on his headdress to show his divinity. But on the other hand, the serpent was considered a dark power to be feared because "the great enemy of Horus, Ra, Osiris, and also of the deceased in the underworld, was the monster serpent Apep, or Apophys, which directed the attacks on gods and men of numbers of serpent broods, and which was held to be the personification of all evil."[26]

In Babylon, serpents were also perceived as malevolent beings, primarily associated with the netherworld. In the Sumerian Enuma Elish, the god Marduk fights the goddess Tiamat identified with the "evil serpent" or the "serpent of darkness." It is also said the city of Babylon was built above the "Gate of *Apsu,*" the serpent present before Creation. The demonic aspect of the serpent is also seen in the myths of *Labbu,* and in the serpent that stole the plant of immortality from king Gilgamesh (about 2700 BCE), thus depriving him of the sole opportunity to acquire immortality. However, like in Egypt, serpents were worshiped as well because of their secret knowledge. The Babylonian goddess Astarte is often shown with serpents in her hands.

In Palmyra's religion, in Syria, the myth of the serpent as a demon of the underworld is overwhelmingly present as well. Furthermore, there was the idea that the river of the Orontes that flows nearby contained a jinni in serpentine form.[27]

As for Persian mythology, the serpent Dahaka is the incarnation of the evil spirit Angra Mainyu. And in Greek mythology, many battles took place between gods and dragons, or monsters with a serpentine form, such as the battle of Zeus with Typhon, a horrible creature with a hundred burning snake heads, who swam among sea serpents, or the battle between the hero Perseus and the Medusa, who had snakes for hair. There was a widespread belief in Greece that serpents and dragons lived in the world of the deep, maybe protecting humans from the polluting darkness of earth. As for the Romans, they used to keep a large number of tame snakes in their temples and houses for protection.[28]

The Hebrew too had their own representations of serpents as ambivalent creatures. One encounters the serpent as an evil being in several passages of the Old Testament that refer to demonic creatures of serpentine form. The myth of the chaos-dragon, for example, is found in the writings of the post-exilic prophets. In Isaiah 27:1 we read that "On that day, Leviathan, the sea monster, will squirm and try to escape, but the Lord will kill him with a cruel, sharp sword."[29]

In this context, one should note historians, theologians, and archeologists have been working together in the last decades to offer a comprehensive picture of the duality and complexity of the serpent myth in the Old Testament. It is in this context that S. H. Hooke, British specialist of Middle Eastern mythology (d. 1968), looked upon the archeological unearthing in the Middle East. Hooke believed certain features of the discoveries at the Canaanite city *Beth-Shan* (Arabic: *Beisan*)—situated above the Jordan Valley in the vicinity of the Plain of *Esdraelon* (Arabic *Marj ibn 'Amer*)—are crucial in the sense they help us unravel the ambivalence of the serpent in the Old Testament. "The name of the place, as well as various objects found there, indicates that it was a center of serpent worship, a cult which survived in Jerusalem as late as the time of Hezekiah."[30] Therefore, it seems the inhabitants of Beth-Shan, like many other people of the ancient Middle East, were divided between worshiping the serpent for its powers and abhorring it for its embodiment of evil.

Indian mythology in turn perceived the serpent as a twofold symbol. The *Nagas* are supernatural entities, kind of genies. They dwell in waters, and manifest themselves in serpent or dragon forms with human faces. *Nagas* are a primordial race of divine serpent-people that play an important part in religion. On one hand, they are looked upon as the guardians of rain and fertility, and on the other hand they are thought to bring disasters such as floods and drought. They are also the protectors of springs, wells, and rivers. The god Varuna, a kind of Indian Poseidon, who assumes the role of the regent of water, rules over them; he is called Naga Raja. Interesting enough, *Nagas* seem to still be venerated in India today, and their cult is popular, especially in the region of Deccan. Every August 5th, after the new moon, there is a big celebration called the feast of *Naga-Panchami*, when children and women sculpt images of cobras and venerate them, and offer flowers, food, and water to them.[31]

Indian myths speak also of a battle that occurred at a certain point in time between the god Indra and a gigantic serpent that entrapped the waters and kept them from gushing. Indra defeated it, though, and made the waters stream again. By killing the serpent, the god mastered the powers of chaos that threatened to destroy the world, and reinstated order. The serpent was also believed to be a cosmic force, like the *kundalini,* which is a feminine noun meaning serpent. *Kundalini* is essential spiritual energy pictured as a twisting serpent slumbering in each of us.

SERPENTS AS THE EMBODIMENTS OF JINN

Classical Islam in turn perceived jinn as assuming serpentine form. Already in pre-Islam, serpents were associated with jinn because, like them, they wandered around ruins, graves, and barren places, strangely manifesting themselves, then vanishing. Both jinn and serpents were imagined in pre-Islam as living close to the invisible realm, gliding into obscure and deserted caverns and haunted clefts. It was alleged both move promptly, in a flowing and puzzling manner, without feet or wings. Both were considered psychic and telepathic beings. Furthermore, serpents were also considered the daughters of the jinn in pre-Islam.[32]

Classical Islam inherited from pre-Islamic times and from the ancient civilizations of the Near East the complex belief in serpents representing good and evil. This ambivalence is particularly found in the prophetic tradition. On one hand, Muhammad stresses the necessity of eliminating these animals. Thus, he is reported to have said, "He who kills a serpent kills an unbeliever in God, and he who leaves alive a serpent out of fear, does not belong to us."[33] But on the other hand, he maintained Muslim jinn usually embody white serpents, and should not be killed. They were called *'ummar,* and often lived in houses. If one is in doubt about the true nature of the serpent, one should recite the call to prayer three times before killing it. If the serpent leaves, then it could mean a Muslim jinni is embodied in it; if it stays, however, it should be killed. The call to prayer seems to be the ultimate test.[34]

In this context, Mecca occupies a place of first importance regarding the representation of jinn in serpent shapes, both before Islam and in classical Islam as well. Thus, it was alleged in pre-Islam that *shaytan* was a serpent nothing resisted.[35] It used to come to the Ka'bah (the holy shrine in Mecca) before Islam, and hit the ground with its body. Anything that came close to it was doomed to perish.[36] In classical Islam, battles raged between heretic jinn and Muslim jinn, both embodying serpents. For example, we are told, "When a jinni, on the seventh day of his marriage, wanted to circumambulate the Ka'bah seven times and complete his pilgrimage, he left his family in the shape of a white serpent. While he was on his way back, passing by the encampment of the jinn tribe of Banu Sahm, a youth from their tribe killed him. Consequently, a Trojan-style war broke out between the tribe of Banu Sahm and the tribe of the serpent/jinn who was assassinated. A great dust-cloud entered Mecca, so thick the mountains could no longer be seen."[37]

IBLIS AND THE SERPENT

Although the Qur'anic representation of evil is concise, and although there is no mention of the serpent whatsoever, Qur'anic commentaries as well as the *Tales of the Prophets* invented a mythology of the serpent that is simply nonexistent in the Holy Book. Those texts added supernatural elements borrowed from ancient Near-Eastern beliefs, and mostly from oral Jewish accounts circulating in the Arabian Peninsula at that point in time. In the Qur'an, Iblis is described only as an evildoer, but not as a serpent. In Qur'an 20:120*, Iblis whispers to Adam: "Adam, shall I show you the way to the Tree of Everlasting Life and to a kingdom which will never fade away?"

Popular commentators on these verses, however, suggested that Iblis couldn't perform his evil act without the assistance of the serpent that hid him in its mouth, and thus enabled him to slither into paradise. These works claimed Iblis spoke to Adam from inside the mouth of the serpent. They added he asked all the animals to carry him into paradise, but they refused, except the serpent. Some of the commentators even alleged God spoke to the serpent and cursed it for carrying

Iblis into paradise. These narratives were reiterating the biblical malediction God imposed on it, compelling this being to seek its sustenance in the earth, and making it the eternal enemy of man.[38]

Popular imagination added further fanciful details to the original and unfinished story. Some commentators went so far as to contend "Iblis married the serpent."[39] They even maintained Iblis transformed himself into a wind to enter into the mouth of the serpent.[40] The exuberant imagination of ibn Kathir (d. 1373), for example, concocted a whole new scenario for the serpent based on his own fantastic reading of the Qur'an. He claimed the serpent was really mentioned in the Qur'an when God expelled Adam and Eve from paradise, and God really cursed not only Iblis and the serpent, but also Adam and Eve.

In the Qur'anic story of the creation, however, Adam and Eve are expelled from paradise, but the curse falls only upon Iblis. God did not curse Adam or Eve. That is perhaps one of the reasons why the original sin does not exist in Islam, and why Man is considered gloriously free, created with original purity and innocence (*fitrah*); he is responsible only for his own deeds. "No soul laden bears the load of another" (Qur'an 6:164).

CONCLUSION

Despite hiding in animal shapes to trick humans, people believed evil jinn could forsake their wickedness at any time and become good Muslims, as in the story of Abu-Hadraj. This freedom of choice means, from an Islamic perspective, there is no evil jinni steeped forever in his evil, although a demon will always be evil. Even ghouls (kinds of jinn) could turn into worshipers of God at any moment.[41] Islamic medieval literature reports many stories of malevolent ghouls that were subdued and pacified by the Word of God.[42]

In fact, Satan and his descendants, the demons, are perhaps the only exception of chaos in the Islamic cosmos where every being, every thing is submitted to the Divine and glorifies it manifestly or in an invisible way. In this context, Islam offers a specific conception of chaos brought about by demons and evil jinn versus order established by the Divine. Indeed, although Timothy K. Beal, contemporary writer on religion and professor of biblical literature at Case Western Reserve University could mention "by demonizing our monsters, we keep God on our side,"[43] Islam could say by converting monsters and evil beings, we bring them to our side. It should be noted, however, Islam did send away some eerie beings to places far away from the Muslim Empire, like the *nasnas* that was believed to thrive in China or unknown parts of the planet. But even from these distant places outside the Muslim arena, the *nasnas* could turn to Islam anytime, if he chooses to do so, and, therefore, join the realm of order and harmony.[44]

Beal does not mention the possibility of convincing the monstrous to forsake chaos and evil. The only solution is to just send it away from us. "Often we demonize the monster as a threat not only to 'our' order but also to the order of the gods or God. In this way the monstrous other who threatens 'us' and 'our world' is represented as an enemy of God and then is exorcized from the right order of things and sent to some sort of hell. 'Our' order is identified with the sacred order against a diabolically monstrous chaos."[45]

By making jinn responsible and with free choice, Islam granted them a spiritual power that not only affects their destinies, but also reminds humans of their duties, when they err. It is in this Muslim perspective of responsibility toward their own communities on one hand, and toward the cosmos and its beings on the other hand, that a group of Muslim scholars, *Ikhwan al-Safa' wa khillan al-wafa'* (The Brethren of Purity and Loyal Friends), formed a secret Arab organization of neo-Platonic and Gnostic philosophers in al-Basrah, Iraq, around 970. The organization is best known for having produced a philosophical and religious encyclopedia, *Epistles of the Brethren of Purity and Loyal Friends,* whose purpose was to provide enlightenment that would purify the soul and provide happiness in the next life.

One of these remarkable Epistles that concerns our study is entitled *The Case of the Animals Versus Man before the King of the Jinn.* It is a fable that narrates how a group of humans one day landed on an island after their ship was wrecked. They immediately began to exploit the nature and the animals living in harmony with the jinn, their rulers. One day, the animals bring their case before the king of the jinn, and ask for help to escape the tyranny of the humans. The work is formed of a series of speeches, where several animals explain how humans abuse them. The latter in turn expound their views, and bring about Qur'anic ideas that stress how God gave the animals to Adam to serve him and obey him. At the end, an enlightening discussion between some jinn philosophers and some intelligent humans lead to the idea of compassion. Yes, humans could use the animals, but they also have to respect them, and treat them kindly and justly.[46] The key word of this work is the three realms of humans, jinn, and animals are interconnected and form a whole.

To survive, humans need to be aware of all forms of life in the cosmos, respect them, protect them, and more important, think about their own human nature through them. After all, are not humans the vice-regents of God on Earth, as Islam stipulates? As such, they are supposed to be just and empathetic toward every living being as well as toward nature that should not be exploited and destroyed.

The interconnectedness of all living beings is epitomized in the Arabic term *al-hayawan,* which refers to animals as well as to all forms of energy, all living beings. Arabic lexicography defines it as "all the created species. It is life itself."[47]

The Qur'an uses the term *al-hayawan* only once, "Surely the Last Abode is [the true] Life [al-hayawan], did they but know" (Qur'an 29:64). The Qur'an elucidates the true *al-hayawan* is not the human life on Earth, which is an illusion of life. The true life exists only in paradise. It loads this term with so much meaning that *al-hayawan* becomes the immortality that humans have always desired and searched for since the dawn of their history. In this sense, one could surmise from the perspective of Islam, the life or energy humans and jinn experience in this world becomes an everlasting vigor in the last abode.

7
Love Between Humans and Jinn

O doctor of the jinn, woe unto you, find me a cure, for
the doctor of humans is helpless against my ill.
— MAJNUN LAILA, seventh-century Arab poet [1]

$\mathcal{L}$ove between humans and jinn could be considered one of the most extravagant and intriguing aspects in the two species' interaction. This particular theme
fascinated Muslims in medieval times. Aberrant love affairs between jinn and
humans circulated, creating fear, and flaring the curiosity of all classes of the
society. Writers from the three layers of Islam—Orthodox, popular, and Sufi—
were equally drawn toward this topic. All of them extensively wrote on it. The
corpus they generated is one of the most original and captivating materials written on human/spirit love affairs across cultures. It was, though, the most difficult
thing to deal with. Religious leaders strove to put down laws to control these
alleged and dangerous relations. But the public remained immensely entranced
by these strange narratives.

LOVE STORIES BETWEEN JINN AND HUMANS IN PRE-ISLAM

In pre-Islam, a jinni who loved a woman or a jinniyah who loved a man would
take on a human form, and sometimes an animal form. They were called *tabi'*,
"follower," masculine, or *tabi'ah*, feminine, from the Arabic root *t.b'*, meaning
"to follow." It was alleged these spiritual entities would always follow the human
they loved, whether the latter was aware of their presence or not. People thought
if the jinn were pleased with humans they, in return, would teach them the arts of
medicine and the art of war, especially how to make fine swords. For example, in
one account, we are told "a certain jinni, called Manzur, loved a woman from the
humans, called Habbah. He befriended her and taught her the arts of healing." [2]

The notion jinn would offer humans their knowledge in return is notewor-thy. Before Islam, people supposed knowledge came from gods or spirits; that humans had to seek it outside of themselves. Two branches of knowledge specifi-cally interested them: healing and the art of war. Rampant disease took an enor-mous toll on people's lives. Pre-Islamic Arabs thought supernatural beings such as the jinn had power over death and sickness. The continual state of war was dev-astating. As one tribe commenced a truce with a neighboring kingdom, another tribe declared war somewhere in the Arabian Peninsula.

Love between humans and jinn was often linked to the belief jinn could dwell in some animals, as previously discussed. People maintained jinn dwell especially in deer. Pre-Islamic Arabs firmly believed deer were sacred animals. It was claimed goddess al-'Uzza was worshiped surrounded by deer as her sacred animals.[3]

The most notorious of pre-Islamic myths related to love and animals is undoubtedly that of the Arab Queen Balqis from Yemen. This myth recounts that

> Balqis's father, a king named al-Hadhad, went one day to hunt the deer. He encountered a flock of deer but didn't kill them. The king of the jinn appeared to him and thanked him for preserving the lives of his people, the jinn, who were thought to dwell in these "sacred" animals. The myth claims he expressed his gratitude to al-Hadhad and offered him the hand of his daughter, Ruwaha bint Sakan. The king of the jinn requested, however, that he never question her if her behavior appears sometimes odd to him. Ruwaha bint Sakan gave birth to two sons and a girl they named Balqis. At the birth of each child, a female dog would come and snatch away the newborn. The father didn't ask for any explanation at the request of the king of the jinn, except at the third time. Ruwaha then revealed to him this female dog was in fact a jinniyah that took the children to raise them in the jinn's realm. She then departed from the conjugal house and never returned because her husband broke the covenant of silence and asked about the secret of the jinn.[4]

After her father's death, Balqis became the queen. People accepted her author-ity. They abided by her rules, and attributed to her immense powers because of her mythical origins.

ISLAMIC THEOLOGY AND THE LOVE BETWEEN HUMANS AND JINN

The idea jinn embody a human form when they fall in love with a human, of either sex, persisted in Islam. Anecdotes on love affairs and marriages between both intelligent beings became very popular. In the bibliographical work of ibn al-Nadim (d. 1047), there is a whole section entitled "Names of humans who loved the jinn, and vice-versa."[5]

Despite an authorized prohibition against marriages between jinn and humans, as mentioned in the writings of Muslim jurists, it was believed these claimed unions continued to take place in Islam. Stories of people possessed by jinn proliferated, and the names of renowned persons who fell in love with jinn were commonplace. Ibn al-Nadim, however, cautions us that many of these stories were purely fabricated by some compilers to satisfy the demands of people under the Abbaside Caliphate, and especially under the Caliph al-Muqtadir (d. 932).

Because of these beliefs, Muslim theologians were bound to lay down a set of conventions and a code of moral principles to prohibit marriages between the two intelligent species. The various religious schools concurred these marriages were unlawful. They agreed to strictly forbid them on the grounds humans and jinn belong to different species.[6] Al-Suyuti (d. 1505) alleged the Prophet mentioned the illegality of these marriages on several occasions. He attributed to him the following Hadith: "The end of time will not come until the children of jinn multiply among you."[7] Many commentators on this prophetic saying maintained the Prophet was referring to the "illegitimate" progeny of jinn and humans. But despite this official ban, the majority of Muslims continued telling stories about marriages between the two species. Serious difficulties came up, especially when dealing with what was believed to be the offspring of these unions.

Religious experts had to provide a juridical and theological status to this progeny. They basically raised the question of identity: is a jinni or jinniyah a person? What does it mean to claim a human "contracted marriage" with a jinni or a jinniyah? Al-Shibli (d. 1368) recounted various anecdotes about humans and jinn intermarriages to make obvious marriages between humans and jinn occurred both before as well as during his time. He cited one of his friends, a jurist, who had been married to a jinniyah for three days when he was traveling with his father. Al-Shibli went to see him and heard the story from him directly, and substantiated it really did occur.[8] Al-Shibli also reported some stories in which Muslim authorities specifically had forbidden unions with jinn, such as the following: "A man came to al-Hasan al-Basri [b. 642] and said to him: 'A jinni wants to be engaged to one of our girls.' Al-Hasan said to him: 'Do not marry her to him and do not honor him!' Then the man went to another sheikh, surnamed Qatadah, and asked him the same. The latter repeated an identical injunction: 'Do not marry her to him, and, if he comes to you, say to him: We beg you—if you are a Muslim jinni—to leave us alone and not hurt us!'"[9]

The Qur'an alludes to this interrelation: "In these gardens [of Paradise] will be maidens restraining their glances, untouched before them by humans or jinn" (Qur'an 55:56 and 74*). Muslim theologians have concluded from these two verses the Qur'an implies humans had contracted unions with jinn. But a much more important question was posed: Is the Qur'an implying therefore these marriages are tolerable, irrespective of their apparent illegality?

In Qur'an 30:20 we read: "And of His signs is that He created for you, *of your-selves,* spouses, that you might find repose in them, and He has set between you love and mercy." Commentators of the Qur'an concurred that "of yourselves" in this context means "from your own kind," and these verses, therefore, imply God excludes beings other than humans as partners in marriage. They argued if God wanted humans to contract unions with jinn, he would have explicitly stated so. Al-Shibli, in interpreting this verse, mentioned the aversion and fear that have always existed between humans and jinn, and concluded humans cannot find peace and tenderness in unions with supernatural beings. He also quoted other verses, such as Qur'an 72:6 and 33:50, where the Qur'an speaks of marriage in general, and of the wives of the Prophet in particular, without mentioning humans are permitted to marry jinn. Imam Malik ibn Anas (d. 796) expressed his moral apprehension and ethical concern for the Muslim society: "It is not against the religion, but I hate to see a woman pregnant from marrying a jinni, and people would ask, 'Who is the husband?' and then corruption would spread among Muslims."[10]

In general, people were anxious about the mixing of species and the hybrid progeny of jinn and humans. It is reported from the Prophet's wife 'A'ishah that a group of people came to visit the Prophet, who said to them: "There are strangers among you." They asked him, "Who are the strangers?" He answered, "Some who are half jinn."[11] Based on this idea of otherness and foreignness, Islam forbade these unions.[12]

Many stories proliferated about these intermarriages. Thus, it is alleged the fourth Caliph 'Ali has met those "unfamiliar" children. Once he noticed a child in his council who was acting oddly, and he asked, "Who knows this child?" Someone replied, "I know him. His name is 'Aws, and there is his mother." 'Ali asked the mother, "Who is the father?" She said, "I don't know. One day I was pasturing the sheep for my parents—this was before Islam—when something in the form of a cloud mated with me. I became pregnant, and gave birth to this child."[13]

The "cloud" figure mentioned by the woman in this story is significant. Jinn are thought to be "subtle" beings, invisible, composed of air and fire, capable of changing forms ad infinitum. As for the clouds, they are evanescent and fine forms. They are also shape-shifters; it is enough to look for a few seconds at passing clouds in the sky to see them changing appearances. The symbol of the cloud across traditions refers to confusion, vagueness, and imprecision; clouds are threshold figures between the visible and the invisible. In religious texts, they refer to epiphanies and the spirit. Interesting enough, fairies have been often described as "subtle" and "aerial" too. Peter Rojcewicz, contemporary specialist of folklore, maintains, "fairies have something of the nature of a mist or condensed cloud, having been called 'astral,' 'crazed,' or 'sidereal.'"[14]

In the same context, Rojcewicz maintains a scientist, Ogilvie Crombie, claimed he contacted fairies and elemental entities at the Findhorn Community in Scotland. According to Crombie, "Their [fairies] primary state is what may be termed a 'light body.' Not easy to describe in words, it is nebulous like a fine mist, being a whirl or a vortex of energy in constant motion."[15]

The woman at the Caliph 'Ali's council seems to be hinting at a subtle being, to a source or "vortex" of energy she claimed hit her. It may well be one of these spirits of the imaginal realm that manifested itself to her in the shape of a cloud.

As in pre-Islam, stories of men marrying (female) jinn that suddenly depart like Balqis's mother continued to spread in Islam. Occasionally, the "alien" wife leaves just after giving birth to a child without any explanation. The husband will look for her in vain, for the absence of the supernatural bride is always ultimate. And if the husband delves into an over-curious questioning about her nature, this supernatural woman could harm him: "A jinniyah in the shape of a woman came once to al-Madinah and said to a man, 'We have come to live in your neighborhood, please marry me.' So he married her. One day she said to him, 'I must leave now, so divorce me.' While he was accompanying her for the last time, browsing together in the streets of al-Madinah, he saw her picking up grains from the ground and eating them. He spoke up, and said, 'Do you like these grains?' She stared at him angrily, and raised her finger towards his eyes, which instantly melted."[16]

Joseph Campbell (d. 1987), authority on myths across traditions, speaks of "the Wild Women of the woods" who are well known by the Russian peasants. These "alien" creatures "enjoy human lovers, have frequently married country youths, and are known to make excellent wives. But like all supernatural brides, the minute the husband offends in the least their whimsical notions of marital propriety, they disappear without a trace."[17] Eliade (d. 1986) in turn mentions, "The Maori people speak of a hero called Tawhaki, whom his wife, a fairy, came down to earth from heaven, and abandoned him after giving birth to a child."[18]

The purpose of these short marriages between humans and supernatural beings is mysterious because we are dealing with a dubious motive from the "alien" figure who desires to mate with a human only to bring forth a "hybrid" child she then leaves behind. One wonders why in all these stories across the world the supernatural wife never takes her children with her. Her love for her children seems to be different from that of a human mother. One could conjecture the supernatural mother is on a mission, which is only to bring these "hybrid" children to the world for reasons that remain unknown. Generally speaking, ambiguity, elusiveness, impulsivity, and swiftness seem to characterize these spiritual entities from a different realm. Indeed, intermediary beings strike rapidly. They trick their victim, and promptly leave the scene. Between one blink of an eye and the next, they appear and vanish, leaving behind them stunned humans who have difficulty coping with the event they just experienced.

LOVE BETWEEN HUMANS AND JINN IN POPULAR ISLAM:
THE ARABIAN NIGHTS

The Nights, this monumental literary material, undoubtedly overflows with the most outlandish and stunning stories on the theme of love between jinn and humans. It is the most prolific and the most ingenious popular source. *The Nights'* narratives are totally different from the anecdotes we have included above from orthodox Islam. Despite their prolific use of the Holy Book and Islamic tradition, the storyteller, and later the scribe, are not anxious about the prohibitions and injunctions we find in orthodox Islam. Located farther from the source of Islamic law, this body of texts indulges in portraying love stories between the two species. The narrative as an open realm grants freedom to the heroes in their quest for a non-human love. Here, one experiences an extraordinary mingling of fantastic, religious, and mystical dimensions. The connection with these beings of the imaginal is always imbued with reminiscences from Persian, Chinese, and Indian literatures. The daily life of humans in love with supernatural beings constantly combines the unfamiliar with the historical and the social. It is a realm where pure logic is of no avail for here and there, past and present, human and alien persistently fuse to create a perplexing reality.

In what follows, I will interpret three aspects in three different tales related to this theme in *The Nights*.

Jinn's Love and the Game of Shape Shifting

The love between humans and jinn appears in *The Nights* as characterized by the game of shape shifting. The invisible jinni or jinniyah manifests himself/herself to the beloved in a human shape to hide his/her true identity to the human beloved. In the tale of "The Merchant and the Jinni," for example, the jinniyah appeared to a man in the form of a woman dressed in tatters. She begged him to marry her and promised to reward him for his compassion and charity, adding these mysterious words, "Don't be misled by my poverty and my present condition."[19] So, he married her, and took her with him on a ship with his two brothers who were setting up his death. One day, the two brothers threw him and his wife in the sea while they were asleep. It is only at that moment that he discovers the true nature of his wife: "When we awoke, my wife turned into a [jinniyah] and carried me out of the sea to an island. When it was morning, she said, 'Husband, I have rewarded you by saving you from drowning, for I am one of the jinn who believe in God. When I saw you by the seashore, I felt love for you and came to you in the guise in which you saw me, and when I expressed my love for you, you accepted me.' Afterward, she took me and flew away with me until she brought me home and put me down on the roof of my house."[20]

Obviously, the human is bewildered, and his mind has little time to process his wife's swift metamorphosis. Everything happens in a glance, beyond the laws of nature, beyond time and place. It is not chaos that quakes the narrative, but rather a new set of laws, the laws of the fantastic that originate in the invisible realm and suddenly manifest themselves in our physical world.[21]

The idea of supernatural beings falling in love with humans is widespread in myths and religious traditions across the world. These supernatural beings, sometimes gods, put on human appearances to hide their true nature, for they have at hand many lines of attack to lure humans. The god Zeus himself fell in love with Europa, daughter of the king of Sidon. He saw her one morning while she was playing with her friends, and instantly desired her. So he transformed himself into a bull and appeared to her. The legend goes that she rode on his back, but he leapt into the sea and swam with her to Crete, then to his own domain, Olympus. There he married her, and she soon gave birth to the god Minos.

It was also acknowledged in Greek mythology the Greek heroes were the sons of nymphs. These ocean beings who visited Prometheus on the crag in the Caucasus spoke only the most ordinary common sense when they said to him: "May you never, oh never behold me, sharing the couch of a god. May none of the dwellers in heaven draw near to me ever. Such love, as the high gods know, from whose eyes none can hide, may that never be mine!"[22]

The Bible also tells about physical love between supernatural beings, the Beni Elohim, and the daughters of humans. In Genesis 6:2, we read: "It was at that time that the Elohim, these beings from the spirit world, looked upon the beautiful earth women and took any they desired to be their wives." In Celtic and Irish lore we stumble on comparable stories of fairies falling in love with humans. Briggs (d. 1980) claims, "The fairies are apparently near enough in kind to mate with humans—closer in fact than a horse is to an ass, for many human families claim a fairy ancestress."[23]

Jinn Carry Off the Woman They Love the Night of Her Wedding

The Prologue of *The Nights* already opens with a story of a jinni who comes up from the sea in front of the two brothers, Shahzaman and Shahrayar. He appears with a chest in his hands: "He took out four keys and, opening the locks of the chest, pulled out a full-grown woman. She had a beautiful figure, and a face like the full moon, and a lovely smile. He took her out, laid her under the tree, and looked at her, saying, 'Mistress of all noble women, you whom I carried away on your wedding night, I would like to sleep a little.'"[24]

And in the story of "The Porter and the Three Ladies," the second Kalandar (a particular type of Sufi) also tells his own story, in which we learn he lived for a short time with a woman who was carried off by a jinni the night of her wedding.[25]

This pattern unveils a jinn's desire to desecrate the human lovers' bond at the wedding, to transgress a cherished ritual by irrupting into the joyful gathering, and seizing away the bride.[26]

Although the first story of the jinniyah who saved her human husband from drowning sheds light on the jinn's affection and good will toward humans, the abduction of human brides by jinn in the second set of stories unveils the intentions of evil jinn, and their wish to subdue human females. At the same time, it underscores humans' fears of the invisible realm and its inhabitants. Finally, it reminds us of the official injunctions of Islamic theology not to embark on close and intimate relations with the jinn. In any case, whether the jinn abuse humans or express their affection toward them, the latter would always articulate their qualms and suspicions of these subtle entities. The opposite is also true, inasmuch as the jinn are said to be doubtful and apprehensive of human intentions concerning them.[27]

Three Tales of Initiation

The third aspect of love relationships between jinn and humans is the initiation the human hero undertakes to earn his beloved jinniyah. It is exemplified in three stories of *The Nights*: "The Tale of Janshah," "The Tale of Hasan al-Basri," and "The Tale of the Prince Sayf al-Muluk and the Princess Badi'at al-Jamal."

The Tale of Janshah

The tale of the prince Janshah begins, as in many fairy tales and folk tales across traditions, with a hunt. Hunting is an act loaded with symbols. On a first manifest level, hunting seems simply a game, or a sport, mostly royal, as in this story. But on a deeper level, it is a search of the unknown symbolized by the animal hidden somewhere in the forest or in the fields. The hunter is not pursuing the animal inasmuch as he is following the road this particular animal is taking. The hero's journey, or rather his destiny, is nothing other than this specific path unfolding in front of him.

The prince Janshah, accompanied by his slaves and friends, chase a beautiful deer that vanishes from their sight each time they come closer to it. We immediately recognize the game of hide and seek intermediary beings undertake to draw the human to their net. The more the group moves forward looking for the animal, the more the animal recedes deep in the forest. As we have seen, animals have always been representations of something higher than their physical forms. In this context, the deer are interesting because they are often imbued with magic in fairy tales. They are "the supernatural animals of the fairy world and are fairy cattle and divine messengers."[28] By hunting the deer, prince Janshah is unconsciously hunting for a supernatural message. Little by little, the prince loses his companions and slaves, one after the other, until he becomes the only survivor of the group. He finds himself in a wild, isolated environment. It is as if the experience of the supernatural, the search for meaning entails solitude, the sole company of beasts and virgin nature, and the freedom from all human bonds. Janshah doesn't find the deer, but follows her traces without capturing her, and keeps advancing forward. For the first time in his life, Janshah is confronted with his own self in total solitude. This is the first degree of a long initiation unraveling to the hero, who is only fifteen years old. This means he is neither a child nor an adult; he is at that junction in his life where puberty manifests itself.

Janshah's journey is long; it takes him to unfamiliar places. He faces all kinds of perils, and encounters various weird creatures, and finally, he perceives a faraway castle. He walks day and night until he reaches it. He enters it and meets sheikh Nasr, a very old jinni who rules over birds from the time of the prophet Solomon.[29] The second stage of the prince's initiation will begin at the hands of his "mentor" and spiritual guide. Sheikh Nasr grants him refuge and allows him to browse throughout the entire castle with the exception of one room. As in all fairy tales, Janshah, naturally, transgresses the orders of Sheikh Nasr, as his destiny needs to be fulfilled, and in this forbidden place, he finds his beloved, a jinniyah of ravishing beauty. But no sooner does he set eyes on her than she becomes a bird and flies away. Janshah is enraptured and a feverish passion burns in his heart at the scene of this being. In his grief, he wastes away to skin and bones. One day, he tells his secret to Sheikh Nasr who informs him his beloved is a jinniyah called Shamsah.

His third stage of initiation consists of his long wait for the beloved jinniyah because he must linger for a whole year, when all the birds come again to the castle. During this time, Janshah pines and laments for his beloved bird/ jinniyah. He experiences the torments and afflictions of the separation from the beloved. The following year, Shamsah and her friends return. Janshah, as his mentor sheikh Nasr advised him, steals her feathered dress; he promises to return it if she marries him, which she does. She stays with him for some time, but one day she unearths her dress Janshah had hidden from her, and flies away. The tale continues:

> For the lady Shamsah had said to her parents, "Janshah loveth me with passionate love and for sure he will follow me; for when flying from his father's roof I cried to him, 'If thou love me, seek me at Takni, the Castle of Jewels!'"[30]

Janshah must embark on a second journey to recover his beloved. This signals his fourth and last stage of initiation. The hero once again comes across a series of strenuous ordeals that he overcomes to be reunited with his beloved jinniyah.

The Tale of Hasan al-Basri

This gripping tale's title carries the name of a Sufi of early Islam called al-Hasan al-Basri, which signals a special mystical tone embedded in the narrative. It is a story of a youth named Hasan who embarks on a trip with a Magian in search of gold. He discovers that the Magian is an evil sorcerer who leaves him on top of a mountain after collecting the jewels. Like Janshah, Hasan is lost in the wilderness. He navigates through exotic and alien places, and encounters all kinds of treacherous beings before finding a castle. Here again, the inhabitants of the castle are jinniyat living at the margins of the human world and, as in the story of Janshah, Hasan is forbidden to enter a certain room. He defies the directives and encounters a beautiful jinniyat with whom he falls frantically in love. She too, like the jinniyat Shamsah, transforms herself into a bird and flies away. He yearns and languishes for a whole year. At moments, the reader has the feeling he/she is reading again the story of Janshah with some discrepancies.[31]

Like Janshah, Hasan takes his beloved jinniyah to Baghdad, his native city, and marries her. She bears him two sons, al-Nasir and al-Mansur. As in the previous story, one day she too flies away, and Hasan undertakes a second "initiatory journey" before being reunited with his beloved.

These two tales exhibit the same central pattern, which is known in folklore studies as the swan-maiden tale found across the world. Stith Thompson, one of the world's leading authorities on folklore (d. 1976), summarizes the pattern as follows,

> The hero in his travels comes to a body of water and sees girls bathing. On the shore he finds their swan covering, which shows him that the girls are really transformed swans. He seizes one of the swan coats and will not return it to the maiden unless she agrees to marry him. She does so, and, as a swan, takes him to her father's house where she again becomes human. From this point on the story may go in either one of two directions. The hero may be set difficult tasks by the girl's father and may solve them with her help. In other tales of the swan-maiden the hero is careful to hide her swan coat, so as to keep her in her human form. Once when he is absent, she accidentally finds the wings and feathers, puts them on, and disappears. The main part of tales containing this motif is concerned with the disappearance and painful recovery of the wife.[32]

The swan-maiden is here akin to the nymph, which is considered across traditions an emanation of the feminine, and a guardian spirit. We also know from folktales across the world nymphs have contracted marriages with humans. Many heroes and gods in Greek mythology, for example, are believed to be the outcome of a relationship between a man and a nymph. Water is treacherous. The feminine in water is ensnaring and enticing. In *The Nights'* stories, the dive in the water carries cosmological symbolism. It is that of the undifferentiated, the pre-formed, and the un-manifested. Water is transmuted into a magical liquid when the god or the supernatural being or spirits like the jinn dive in it. Water seems to invite the two partners, the human and the alien, to fulfill their passion.[33]

In Welsh stories, the supernatural brides are always fairies, very often lake maidens as well.[34] An example of love between fairies and humans can be found in a Celtic tale entitled "Connla and the Fairy Maiden." It is the story of a fairy who falls in love with the son of a king, and who then comes to the court to declare her love to Connla of the Fiery Hair, son of Conn of the Hundred Fights. The fairy gives Connla an apple and vanishes. "For a whole month from that day, Connla would take nothing, whither to eat or to drink, save only from that apple. But as he ate it, it grew again and always kept whole. And all the while there grew within him a mighty yearning and longing after the maiden he had seen."[35] Finally he decides to join his fairy maiden and the folktale ends: "So Connla and the Fairy maiden went forth on the sea, and were no more seen, nor did any know whither they came."[36]

In Indian mythology, it is also believed the spirits of water, known as *Nagi* (female) and *Nagini* (male), often seek the love of humans. One of the legends tells the story of a love affair between one Nagi and the famous king Arjuna, the interlocutor of Krishna in the *Bhagavad-Gita*. The story goes as follows:

> One day, Arjuna descended to the shore of the Ganges and entered into the water to perform his ritual ablutions. When he finished it, he was preparing himself to go out of the river in order to celebrate the prayer of the morning, when he was seized, he the hero with strong arms, and he was carried along to the deep water by Ulupi, the daughter of the king of Naga [plural of Nagi], who was tormented by love of him.
>
> And Arjuna the hero entered into a marvelous palace, the palace of Kauravya, the king of the genies Naga. Arjuna asked Ulupi: "Gentle lady, what an execrable act you have committed here! To whom belongs this splendid place, and of whom are you the daughter?"
>
> "Prince," she replied, "I am the daughter of the famous Kauravya, king of the genies Naga, and my name is Ulupi. O you Tiger among men, when you entered into the waters to perform your ablutions, the god of love enraptured my spirit! O you irreproachable person, know that I am not married; how can I survive, I who am tormented by desire for you! Grant me the grace to marry me, today!"
>
> Arjuna replied: "On order of the king Yudhisthira, I made a vow of chastity for twelve years! I am unable, O beautiful one, to act as it pleases me. However, I promise to satisfy you, and I have never lied in my life! Hence, O Nagini, tell me how to please you without being guilty of lying and without breaking my vow."
>
> The Nagini replied: "If you do not act as required, know, O hero Arjuna, that I will commit suicide! Win a great merit, O hero with strong arms, and save my life. I take refuge beside you, O the best of all men! You who always had protected and will always protect the afflicted, those without defense; you owe me protection! See my tears and my pain!" When he heard the words of the Nagi, Arjuna satisfied all her desires, through virtue. That night he spent in the palace of the Naga, and he left only when the sun rose, in the early morning. (*Mahabharata* 1.216)[37]

There is more than water and attraction in these tales, which I found replete with symbols. The symbol of the swan combines the two elements of air and water. As for the jinniyat, they connect with opposite elements such as water and fire. They fly and swim in two different mediums: air and water. Jinn hate immobility and constancy. And those who love them in these stories imitate their incessant roving. The element fire of which the jinn are composed stirs ardent passions in humans that only the encounter with the jinni or jiniyyah quenches. In their metamorphosis into birds or swans, jinn become overcharged with spirituality. After all, birds are a symbol for the soul across traditions, from the *Ancient Egyptian Book of the Dead* to Hinduism where the Supreme Swan refers to the Self or Reality.

There is another set of symbols worth decoding. It is related to the two journeys both Janshah and Hasan undertake. In the two tales, love is revealed in a flash; it is like a vision the hero perceives, or maybe an illusion he tries to decipher. It is a swift contact with beings from the hidden realm, as one of the swan-maidens explains to Janshah when he enquires about their nature: "'Who are ye, o illustrious Princesses, and whence come ye?' Replied the youngest damsel, 'We are from the invisible world of Almighty Allah and we come hither to divert ourselves.'"[38]

The hero witnesses the irruption of the swan/jinniyah from behind the veil, hidden in his corner. Filled with passion, he literally dies to the world to live only in the vision he witnessed until the second apparition of the jinniyah, when he resurrects to capture her. He must demonstrate to himself that although the jinniyah is from the hidden realm, she is not an illusion but a spirit from the unseen manifesting herself in our physical world.

The Tale of Sayf al-Muluk and the Jinniyah Badiʿat al-Jamal

The third tale, "Prince Sayf al-Muluk and the Princess Badiʿat al-Jamal," is also a love story between a human and a jinniyah. Sayf al-Muluk discovers a picture of this jinniyah at home, wrapped in a bundle of cloth his father, the king, gave him on the day of his coronation. Immediately, he is infatuated with her: "He spread it out and saw on the lining of the back the portraiture wroughten in gold of a girl and marvelous was her loveliness; and no sooner had he set eyes on the figure than his reason fled his head and he became jinn-mad for love thereof, so that he fell down in a swoon and presently recovering, began to weep and lament, beating his face and breast and kissing her."[39]

Sayf al-Muluk decides to search for the jinniyah of the picture, whose name is Badi'at al-Jamal. Like Janshah and Hasan, he endures many trials until he reaches India and China. When he finally encounters her, she refuses to marry him, on the grounds all humans are unfaithful. He ultimately succeeds in convincing her of the falsehood of this assertion, and they get married. It is noteworthy that the refusal of the jinnyyah could be seen as Sheherazade's revenge because most men in *The Nights* believe women are wily and unworthy of their trust. One can see in the three stories a return to the myth of the goddess, with the three jinniyat representing patterns of feminine ascendancy humans almost worship.

All three tales display an inevitable and mesmeric attraction exerted by spiritual entities on humans. They also reveal the same motives of initiation: the youth who leaves for the first time his protective home; the adventure that occurs at a crucial age in his life when he needs to be initiated into the other, the feminine, the *ying,* the hidden part of his own self; the motif of the castle where the beloved is found in the first place, lost for a time, and then recaptured. The castle in the three tales is not to be found on the map. It is, rather, timeless and placeless, where the hero enters to be trained in the secrets of the invisible by a sheikh. The castle itself is the intersecting point of two levels of reality: the human one and the jinn one, the seen and the unseen. Finally, it is captivating that beings from the two realms of the visible and the invisible worlds travel freely form one realm to the other. The hero undertakes a trip to the jinn world to recapture his beloved jinniyah. The latter leaves behind her home and family and accompanies her human husband to his world. The movement from one dimension to the other is constantly open both ways. From the perspective of these Muslim folktales, it is quite natural for humans and jinn to constantly circulate between the two realms as the scriptures and the tradition certify, while many folktales and fairy tales in the West display rather preserved domains for each species. In medieval French literature, for example, two particular kinds of tales exist about the Fairy Morgan and the Fairy Melusine. The tales woven around Fairy Melusine are characterized by the fact the fairy agrees to leave her fairyland in the forest and comes to live with her human lover among humans, while in the tales woven around Fairy Morgan the human agrees to leave his life among humans and follows the fairy to her domain. But there is no possibility for travel from one realm to the other. It is once again the paradigm of either/or.[40]

Generally speaking, the notion of excessive love, called ʿishq, was perceived as pernicious in classical Islam. Popular books were written to elucidate its dangers. Lovers were warned of the consequences of extreme passions, which could lead to all kinds of mental disorders, particularly epileptic fits, to madness, and even to death. One of the interesting books on ʿishq was written by Jaʾfar al-Sarraj (d. 1106), and entitled "*masariʿ al-ʿushaq,*" which literally means "The lovers' [path to] death." Al-Sarraj compiled various anecdotes related to excessive love. There is also a whole chapter entitled "Lovers from the jinn" in which the author narrates alleged love affairs between jinn and humans.[41]

In the same vein, one can classify the verse of the poet Qays ibn al-Mulawwah (d. 668), surnamed Majnun Laila.[42] His love story became famous in Islam like the romance of Romeo and Juliet in the West, especially after many Sufis took their inspiration from it to express their ecstatic states. They found in the poet's woes something analogous to their pain of being separated from the Divine.

The story of Majnun Laila is that of a man estranged from his beloved, who was forced to marry another man. When Majnun knew about this marriage, he ran away from his tribe and Laila's neighborhood. He roamed deserts and wilderness in search for something that could quell his thirst for Laila. In his wanderings, Majnun reaches the edge where reality and imagination interpenetrate. Relentlessly and hopelessly, the poet endeavors to capture the image of the absent beloved. Laila appears in his verse akin to those women/jinniyat mentioned in the stories above, whose presence is elusive, prevailing, and inexorable.

Distance and excruciating pain compel Qays to rapidly drift toward the non-human and the unseen realms. He wanders naked among animals and snakes, and lives in caves. As French writer Jean-Claude Vadet maintains, Majnun himself becomes similar to one of the jinn.[43] It is not true the jinn inspire him, as Asʿad Khairallah, contemporary Lebanese critic, maintained.[44] Although it was known jinn inspire poets and, often, the daemonic and the poetic thrive side by side, the case of Majnun is different. Majnun has forsaken the world of humans, and integrated himself with the irrational forces of nature.

The legend tells that people were even afraid of him, and often wondered if he were a jinni.

Away from his beloved, Majnun hallucinates, often identifying Laila with the deer. Whenever he sees one, he sings his love for her. He talks to the deer and asks her if she is not Laila or at least Laila's sister.[45] As we have seen, people claimed jinn dwell in deer. When a hunter wanted to kill a deer he captured, Majnun would offer him all he had to free the poor animal.

The help of his family and friends were of no avail, for Majnun continued to live in delusion seeking his missing love.[46] Having left behind the world of humans, Majnun, in one verse, desperately calls upon a physician from the jinn to cure him: "O doctor of the jinn, woe unto you, find me a cure, for the doctor of humans is helpless against my ill."[47]

The internal violence of passion is mingled with the harshness of the wilderness where the poet wanders. The dark cave where Majnun chose to live instigates chthonic forces. Majnun, at the end of the book, is found dead, far from his family and friends, in the land of the non-human.

Sufis in turn brought into play the legend of Majnun, especially in the book of the Sufi Ganjavi Nizami (d. 1209) precisely entitled *Majnun Laila*. In this romantic epic, Majnun, the lover, is the Sufi himself, and his object of love is none other than God. Majnun in this Sufi version is even closer to the animal kingdom and the elements. Like Majnun, the lover often stumbles into the kind of absence we call fainting. Between sleep and awareness, he grasps, as if in a glance, the borderline that separates the invisible realm from the manifest one and illusion from reality. The correlations with the jinn shapes are numerous in Nizami's verse. Majnun seems to have borrowed from the jinn their secrecy, invisibility, and elusiveness. The emaciated body of the lover, his nakedness, his sojourn among the beasts, and his distance from humans almost correlate with that of a jinni that lives in the ruins, and that has forsaken human company. In one verse, Nizami describes how Majnun roamed deserts and mountains after he heard of Laila's death, crying aloud her name:

> Climbs to the mountain's brow, over hill and plain
> Urged quicker onwards by his burning brain,
> Across the desert's arid boundary hies;
> Zayd, like his shadow, following where he flies;

And when the tomb of Laili [Laila] meets his view;
Prostrate he falls, the ground his tears bedew;
Rolling distraught, he spreads his arms to clasp
The sacred temple, writhing like an asp,
Despair and horror swell in his ceaseless moan,
And still he clasps the monumental stone.[48]

The allusions to the asp evoke the jinn who are thought to embody the shapes of snakes. Like them, the possessed lover creeps between the stones, wriggles, and writhes like any slinking lizard.

CONCLUSION

These alleged love stories between jinn and humans, whether in *The Nights* or in other classical Muslim sources, have almost no sexuality. I argue this is because of the subtle and shape-shifting nature of the jinni or the jinniyah whose love for a human remains elusive and intangible despite the jinn's embodiment in physical forms. This claimed passion between a human and a spiritual entity resembles some kind of evanescence, almost a loss of conscience that engulfs the human in its mysterious darkness. It is a kind of withdrawal from the world. Sexuality is of a totally different order, more substantial and more concrete. It cannot thrive in an indefinable relationship such as this.

This love is depicted as stronger than the love between two humans; it may be because of the strangeness of the spiritual partner and the curiosity otherness triggers in the human.

It is an uneven relation between a mortal and a spiritual entity in which the latter has always more operational power than the human who seems in most of our stories subjugated and infatuated at the same time.

8
Jinn Inspiring Poets

He was bizarre, a man made out of brass . . .
He said to me, "Recite some poetry!" Then he recited poetry to me.
I said: "Who are you?" He said, "I am your double from the jinn!"
That is how I started reciting poetry.
 — Umayayd love poet, Kuthayyir 'Azzah (d. 723)[1]

*J*inn meddle in the lives of humans as lovers, warriors, teachers, helpers, or healers. They also manifest themselves in mystifying modes in the lives and verses of Arab and Muslim poets. Jinn's incursion reveals itself sometimes as a whispering, sometimes as a powerful voice from another world which calls upon poets, drowns them into its inebriated power, and commands them to write its words. These stubborn spirits seem to display a staunch and mysterious power poets rarely can resist. Their insidious storming of the poets' intimacy is enthralling and subjugating. Many in classical Islam described this "contact" with jinn as the source of their writing. Many mused in their verses on the origin and nature of these spirits: are they coming from deep inside the human well or rather dashing from outside the forests of nature?

POETICAL INSPIRATION BEFORE ISLAM

It is known that seminal mythological texts in the world were written and chanted in rhymed prose. In Sumerian mythology—which goes back four thousand years before the Christian era—the tragedy of the goddess Inanna and her descent in the underworld, as well as the Sumerian epic of the hero Gilgamesh, are both brought to us through rhyme. Similarly, most of the old epics of humanity were conveyed in verse-like language, from the *Odyssey* to the Nordic *Edda*. The magnificence of the poetical text and the melody of its rhyme, whether in epics, myths, or religious texts, imbued poets with a particular aura. Poetry was considered sacred, "the language of the gods," and the first language of humanity that carried within it an unfathomable and hypnotic power.[2] Some poets, such as Orpheus and Empedocles, were even considered divine, possessing supernatural talents. Their poetry was mysterious and tinged with the shadows of the invisible.

In the Greek tradition, for example, the poet is described as being the mouthpiece of the Muses who were nine in number, the so-called daughters of Zeus and *Mnemosyme* (memory). Greek poets often began their poems by invoking the muse, as in the *Odyssey,* where Homer begs her to enthuse him: "Sing in me, Muse, and through me tell the story of that man skilled in all ways of contending."[3] In this tradition, the god of poetry is Apollo, the sun deity who drives his fiery chariot across the skies. But it is primarily in Plato's *ion* one discovers a thorough discussion of poetic inspiration. Plato conveys the idea poets are channels for a superior power that invests them with its knowledge. In this sense, poetry is not the result of the poets' work; it is not similar to reasoning, and doesn't have its source in the determination of the will. Socrates mentions the case of *Tynnichos of Chalcis* who was a mediocre poet until the god chose him to sing divinely beautiful songs: "that we listeners may know that it is not they who utter these precious revelations while their mind is not within them, but that it is the god himself who speaks, and through them becomes articulate to us."[4]

People in the pre-Islamic Arabian Peninsula likewise believed poets received their inspiration from a hidden source, from the invisible world of the jinn.[5] The latter were thought to follow the poets and read out to them verses of majestic beauty. Arabs at that time honored their poets because their words resembled those of seers.

The likeness between soothsayers and poets comes also from the fact they both used rhymed speech. It is interesting to note prophets too recourse to a similar language. The words of all three are filled with alliterations, parallelisms, elliptic formulas, forewarnings, and imprecations.[6]

The belief in a spirit guiding the poet's pen was not limited to old traditions. In fact, it was revived and embraced during the Romantic period. In a letter to historical painter and writer Benjamin R. Haydon (d. 1846), Keats (d. 1821) wrote: "I remember you saying that you had notions of a good Genius presiding over you—I have of late had the same thought."[7]

Analogous to the inspiration brought by the Muse, or the Genius to the Greek poet, and later to the Romantic poets is the stimulation brought by the Duende to the Spanish poet. The Duende is also similar to the Muse or the jinni in that the poet, in both cases, has no control over its manifestations. The Spanish poet too feels helpless and baffled in front of this divine and devastating power. He senses the force of inspiration climbs into him from the feet to the throat. He fights with it in vain, and finally surrenders to its invasion. Federico Garcia Lorca (d. 1936) is one of the most eloquent exponents of the Duende: "Before reading his poems in front of the audience, the first thing one must do is to invoke the Duende."[8]

The source from which the poetical inspiration flows can even be the Holy Spirit. It was believed Christian English poet John Milton (d. 1674) was carried through *Paradise Lost* by the descent of the Holy Spirit.[9]

Throughout the Christian Middle Ages, and even afterwards, poets sought the help of the Greek god Apollo in the composition of their verses. This god was identified with the monotheistic Spirit itself. Dante (d. 1321) promised to crown himself with a wreath from the Apollonian tree, the laurel.[10]

Even as modern a poet as American Jack Spicer (d. 1965) talked about "dictation" as the source of his poetry, and struggled with it in terms of its origin, whether from psychic movements within him or from outside him altogether.[11]

THE QUR'ANIC CONCEPTION OF POETRY

The word in Arabic for poet is *sha'ir,* which means literally "the one who feels, who perceives." Poetry in the Arab/Muslim world has always been considered a bona fide form of knowledge inexplicably received from the invisible. This notion persisted in Islam as well as the tradition of the poet accompanied by a jinni. Arab and Muslim accounts speak of a flowing and unremitting dialogue between poets and their inspirers. Early Islam poet Hassan ibn Thabit (d. 674) spoke of his own jinni who always followed him and helped him write the verse, as shall be seen later in this chapter.

However, some changes were introduced to this relationship between poets and jinn. To better understand the modifications that occurred, I will elucidate first the concept of poetry as it appears in the Qur'an. In many verses, the Qur'an maintains Arabs in the beginning rejected the prophethood of Muhammad because they perceived him as a poet rather than a prophet. In Qur'an 21:5, we read: "Nay, but they say: [A muddled jumble of dreams!] Nay, he has forged it; nay, he is a poet! Now therefore let him bring us a sign, even as the ancient ones were sent as messengers."

The Qur'an replies to the Prophet's opponents, and differentiates between poetical inspiration thought to come from the jinn and revelation bestowed upon Muhammad through the intermediacy of the angel Gabriel: "We have not taught him poetry; It is not seemly for him. It is only a Remembrance and a clear Qur'an" (Qur'an 36:69).[12] Moreover, the Qur'an disparages the poets of pre-Islam who concoct things unrelated to reality, and pay heed only to their egos: "And the poets—the perverse follow them; Hast thou not seen how they wander in every valley and how they say things they do not do? Save those that believe, and do righteous deeds, and remember God [repeatedly], and help themselves after being wronged" (Qur'an 26:225–26).

The Qur'an does not, however, condemn poetry as such. It is reported Muhammad alluded at several occasions to his own fascination with rhetoric. He once said to Hassan ibn Thabit, after listening to one of his poems: "The Holy Spirit is with you!"[13] By that, Muhammad meant the poet receives the spiritual influence and sings it back to the world. It should be mentioned, however, the poetry of Hassan became completely devoted to Islam after his conversion to the new religion to the point he was called "the Prophet's poet." Whether Muhammad was praising poetry in general, or just the poetry devoted to the faith, remains unresolved.

Be that as it may, the verse of Hassan ibn Thabit, as well as that of other poets, contributed to the creation of a new and different poetry after the advent of Islam. It is noteworthy most of this new verse was not dedicated to the praise of the new religion. In fact, erotic and wine poetry was more prevalent than religious poetry. This prompted literary critic Ihsan 'Abbas (b. 1920) to maintain, "Islam did not prohibit the idea of jinn as inspirer to poets. It rather acknowledged that poets have their independent imaginary world, and this is the meaning of [Qur'anic verse] 'they roam in every valley.'"[14]

Islamic civilization soon developed a sophisticated culture of both Arabian music and dance. Cities such as Madinah, Mecca, and Ta'if played a major role in helping poetry and singing to burgeon. Poems were sung by great singers, such as ibn Surayj (d. 726). And people flocked to Mecca to listen to the love poetry of 'Umar ibn abi Rabi'ah (d. 711) and others. Luxury, refinement, sophistication, and art proliferated in cities like Damascus, Mecca, and al-Hirah.

POETS INTERACT WITH THE JINN IN ISLAM

An Imaginal Parallel World

Andalusian poet Abu 'Amir ibn Shuhayd (d. 1035) tackles most of the issues related to jinn and poets in Islam in his book entitled *The Treatise of Familiar Spirits and Demons.*[15] This work remains one of the most original texts written in Arabic on this subject. In his introduction to the *Treatise,* ibn Shuhayd unveils the motives behind writing his book. After the death of his beloved, he desired to write an elegy to her memory, but he was beleaguered by grief. Suddenly, his inspiring jinni, by the name of Zuhayr ibn Numayr, appeared before him and assisted him in composing the poem. The jinni mentions to the poet he belongs to the banu Ashja', which is the poet's tribe. As I mentioned in the second chapter of this book, it is alleged the jinn's society is modeled after the human's one. It is a kind of parallel world, so if there is a human tribe by the name of banu Ashja', then there should be a jinn tribe by the same name.

From that time onward, the jinni of ibn Shuhayd would appear to him whenever he needed assistance. Soon, he becomes to him a helper and a kind of spiritual master who carries him to the country of the jinn to visit the inspirers of famous poets of both pre-Islam and Islam. In the "land of the jinn," ibn Shuhayd meets the jinn of many poets who lived before him, such as the jinni of pre-Islamic poet Imru' al-Qays (d. 540) who appeared as "a knight riding a glowing mare."[16] The jinni of al-Buhturi (d. 897) looks like "a gracious adolescent carrying a lance in his hand, and who came toward us on a white-spotted horse."[17] As for the jinni of Tarafah (d. 569), the author of the longest of the Seven Odes in the celebrated collection of pre-Islamic poetry, the *mu'allaqat,* he described him as "a beautiful knight bearing a sword."[18]

These jinn inspirers look more like human poets than spiritual beings coming from another world. The similarity with medieval Arab society is overwhelming. Like their poets, the jinn inspirers are knights, are armed, and have horses. Ibn Shuhayd, obviously, is intent on producing a copy of the humans' society. I argue this is because of his strong belief in the parallelism of the two worlds of jinn and humans, as depicted in the religious sources where both intelligent species are thought to correspond in many ways. Many poets in the pre-Islamic time, as well as in classical Islam, immortalized their bonds to their jinn inspirers in their poetry. The affinity between both comes up as even more strange than if these poets had created a fantastic world.[19]

The notion of a world parallel to ours inhabited by spiritual beings that act like us is indeed more "alien" to us than the "fantastic" we meet in our readings and visual arts. In a way, this kind of fantastic has been continually repeated to the point it became almost ordinary.

Two Different Jinn Inspirers for One Poet

Many Arab poets told of their encounters with two jinn inspirers instead of one. It is related, for example, al-Qays had two different inspirers. There is no agreement between critics on the exact names of his jinn inspirers.[20]

Compiler Abu Zaid al-Qurashi (d. 786), for example, explains as follows the reason for the existence of two jinn inspirers instead of one: "A man came to the poet al-Farazdaq [d. 728] and recited a verse to him and asked him his opinion. The poet answered by saying that, 'Poetry has two jinn. One of them is called Hawbar and the other is called Hawjal. If Hawbar is your inspirer, then your poetry is good, but if your inspirer is Hawjal, then your poetry is bad. Both were your inspirers in this verse. Hawbar inspired the first part of it, and Hawjal inspired the second part of it, and he damaged it!'"[21]

These two inspirers are almost homonyms, which could convey either a resemblance or an opposition. Briefly, they look like pairs.

The Command to Recite

In *al-Aghani,* this compendium of literature of classical Islam, one finds many stories about jinn following Muslim poets. For example, Umayayd love poet Kuthayyir 'Azzah (d. 723) was once asked, "When did you start reciting poetry?" He replied, "I did not start reciting poetry until it was recited to me." Then he was asked, "And how was that?" He replied, "One day, I was in a place called Ghamim, near Madinah. It was noon. A man on horseback came toward me until he was next to me. I looked at him. He was bizarre, a man made out of brass; he seemed to be dragging himself along. He said to me, 'Recite some poetry!' Then he recited poetry to me. I said: 'Who are you?' He said, 'I am your double from the jinn!' That is how I started reciting poetry."[22]

This story is interesting on many levels. The poet seems to play the role of a *rawi* rather than that of a poet. The *rawi* (the reciter) was the person who would follow the poet, and whose function was to memorize his poetry for it not to be lost. In this story, Kuthayyer seems to be the one to memorize the verse while the jinni is the real poet.

Although he didn't compose the verse, Kuthayyir developed into a poet when he recited what was "dictated" to him. In other terms, he identified with the jinni's voice. From where did this "double" come: from the murky waters of the self, or from the imaginal realm where the jinn are supposed to lurk, or more likely from both?

The Gender of the Inspirer

As in pre-Islam, the gender of the spiritual entity inspiring the poet remained noticeably masculine. Hassan ibn Thabit told of his encounter with his inspirer he addressed as "my brother the jinni."[23]

When the poet designates the jinni as "brother," he is insinuating intimacy and familiarity with the spiritual entity. The poet might also be looking at the jinni as his alter ego, a double or a shadow with whom he converses, and from whom he draws his words. This dialogue between the visible poet and the "invisible source of inspiration" takes place in an introspective environment where the poet is absorbed in his feelings, and engrossed in his thoughts and vision.

Talking about one's inspirer or even one's double as of a close presence is common to many traditions. Yeats (d. 1939), in a poem written in 1915 entitled "Ego Dominus Tuus," described also his haunting "other" as one who "shall look most like me, being indeed my double."[24]

One wonders, however, when reading the poets of classical Islam, why spirits that inspired the poets are often masculine. Is this simply because of the centrality of the male in the Arab/Muslim medieval society in his many roles of warrior, chief of the tribe or the clan, and poet? And why are the Muses in the West mostly feminine? English writer Robert Graves (b. 1895), specialist in classical literature, depicts this feminine aspect of inspiration as follows: "The reason why the hairs stand on end, the eyes water, the throat is constricted, the skin crawls, and a shiver runs down the spine when one writes or reads a true poem, is that a true poem is necessarily an invocation of the White Goddess, or Muse, the Mother of All Living, the ancient power of fright and lust—the female spider or the queen-bee whose embrace is death."[25]

Although one could reject the insistence on the "masculine" inspirer in Islam, one couldn't accept the image Graves gives of the feminine Muse. Not only is it not very flattering, but also pejorative, because this feminine entity is an epitome of fear, death, and lust. Both Hassan ibn Thabit and Graves lack the vision of the mysterious and highly spiritual feminine.

Rejecting the Jinn's Inspiration

The idea of a jinni inspiring the poet weakened in some significant way at the beginning of the fourth century of Islam, especially in Baghdad where the Mu'tazilite School of philosophy gave priority to reason over inspiration, and affected all fields of Islamic thought. Two poets especially rejected openly and categorically the notion of inspiration by the jinn. The first one was Abu Nuwas (d. 810), whose odes immortalized the wine taverns of Baghdad. He made a jinni kneel down in submission in one of his poems. The second poet was Bashshar ibn Burd (d. 783), a blind and licentious poet who celebrated Eros magnificently. He declined the inspiration of Shiniqanaq (one of the most famous chiefs of the jinn) in a well-known verse: "Shiniqanaq called me to ride behind him. I said, 'Leave me alone—I prefer solitude.'"[26]

At the same time, some poets went so far as to ridicule other poets who blindly accepted their jinni's inspiration. The debate between the two camps is epitomized in the following dialogue: "One poet said to another, 'I compose a poem every hour, and you compose a poem every month! How come?' The latter replied: 'Because I don't accept from my jinni what you accept from yours!'"[27]

It must be noted this dismissal of the jinn's inspiration existed already in pre-Islam. It was not, however, very widely known. 'Amru ibn Kulthum (d. 584) nicknamed the poets who accepted the jinn's inspiration "dogs of the jinn."[28]

One can clearly see two conceptions of poetry in these squabbles. Poets of reason insinuated it is only the craft that brings about a good verse, while poets of inspiration asserted over and over poetry springs solely from an invisible spiritual source. These disagreements between the two visions of poetry exist across traditions. Czeslaw Milosz, Lithuanian–Polish poet who won the 1980 Nobel Prize in Literature, criticized this belief in spiritual entities as inspirers as follows: "What reasonable man would like to be a city of demons, who behave as if they were at home, speak many tongues, and who, not satisfied with stealing his lips or hand, work at changing his destiny for their convenience?"[29]

Each poet has a particular attention to the source of inspiration, whose location is sometimes determined as inside of the self and sometimes outside of it. Some poets are more turned to the realm within, while others are more alert to the world outside of them. But isn't it the same power, voice, and entity that is captured differently?

The Risks of Having Jinn as Inspirers

Whether in pre-Islam or in Islam, a poet often acknowledges he might risk his life if he accepts the assistance of the jinn. Jinn could abduct him, or he could become mad.[30] A poet born in pre-Islam and converted to Islam by the name of ibn al-Sharqi was one night passing near the encampments of the jinn tribe of Banu 'Amir when the jinn carried him away to their land "in a span of time shorter than the flight of a bird."[31] He remained with them for three years. Some poets became totally insane after their "sojourn" in the land of the jinn. Early Islam poet Jarir (d. 728) referred to this state of affairs when he said, "It is possible to cure people from physical disease, but not from the insanity incurred after staying with jinn! Only jinn can cure those whom they enthralled."[32]

In Irish folklore too, the Muses were believed to persecute poets and bring lunacy upon them as Yeats maintains: "The Leanhaum Shee [fairy mistress] seeks the love of mortals. She is the Gaelic Muse for she gives inspiration to those she persecutes. The Gaelic poets die young for she is restless, and will not let them remain long on earth—this malignant phantom."[33]

THE ALLEGED JINN'S POETRY

As we have seen earlier in this chapter, a jinni commanded Hassan ibn Thabit to recite his jinni poetry. Jinn boasted not only that they put the words in the mouths of poets, but also that their poetry is by far better than that of humans, when and if the latter ever write it.

As for those poems attributed to the jinn and scattered in medieval Arab sources, we have no knowledge whatsoever of their real authors. One finds, however, a thorough discussion of the poetical jinn's superiority in *Risalat al-Ghufran*, the *Epistle For Forgiveness,* a monumental book of divine comedy written by al-Ma'arri (d. 1057). The narrator encounters in his travel to the jinn's paradise, Abu Hadrash, one of the jinn's great ancestors. He asks him about the poetry of the jinn and about their [lost] collection of poems entitled *ash'ar al-jinn* (odes of the jinn). Hadrash arrogantly replies: "What humans know about poetry except what cows know about cosmology and geodesy? Humans have fifteen kinds of meters poets rarely go beyond, while we have thousands of meters humans have never heard of."[34] Furthermore, the jinni adds that he himself composed poems eons before God created Adam.[35] The narrator then seems tempted to write down some of the jinni's poetry. However, he remembers he memorized and put down the poetry of others in his earthly life. So he refrains from doing it this time in paradise.[36]

Once again, it seems we have no access to the poetical treasure of the jinn or to their authors. All we know is humans claim the jinn wrote poetry that is better than theirs. It is alleged, for example, jinn portray themselves as protectors of animals, and particularly of serpents. We have previously discussed that jinn are thought to embody serpents. They appear to humans and recite poetry to them whenever the latter abuse an animal in general, or kill a serpent in particular. In their poetry, the jinn talk about their own lives and habits, their relations to animals as in this verse: "I rode on all mounts but found none/Nicer and more desirable than the mount of wolves."[37]

It is also maintained the jinn's verse is not limited to discussing poetical matters, animals, or their relationships with humans. The latter seem to have heavily involved them in all their political and religious discussions, in pre-Islam and in Islam as well. The jinn's poetry was used or rather invented, particularly in early Islam, to defend the new religion and to criticize its enemies. One finds, for example, verses of praise to the Prophet and his companions were assigned to the jinn. It is also alleged the jinn recited poetry of lamentations at the death of the Prophet's grandson, al-Hussein in the holy place of Karbala', where al-Hussein was assassinated, and where his tomb remains one of the greatest Muslim shrines.[38] It is also alleged the jinn lamented the death of the second Caliph of Islam, 'Umar ibn al-Khattab. We are even told 'A'ishah, the wife of the Prophet, heard jinn mourning his death before it actually occurred. In the same vein, people claimed the jinn bewailed the Prophet's mother.[39]

WHO IS THE AUTHOR?

If one accepts that poetry is inspired by a spiritual entity outside of the poet and that it puts the words in the mouths of poets, then one wonders: Who is the author? Is it the jinni that inspires and dictates, or is it the poet who receives and memorizes? Captivatingly enough, sometimes a poet acknowledges he shares his poetical terrain with his inspirer, as in this verse of Hassan ibn Thabit (d. 674): "My follower [jinni] is from *banu Shaysaban.* Sometimes, it is he who recites poetry. Sometimes it is I."[40]

Sharing the "poetical terrain" means the poet is constantly shifting from absence when it is the "other" (the jinni) who recites poetry, to awareness, when it is the poet himself who declaims the verse. The poet here mentions a different entity than himself is partaking of the verse. Poetry thus becomes the place par excellence where diverse psychological states manifest themselves with all transparency. It is the home where the self becomes aware of itself for a moment, then recedes, leaving a blank space to be swiftly filled by another power, be it jinni, Muse, or Duende.

Many stories were told in pre-Islam and in Islam of this participation between poet and jinni/inspirer. The following intriguing story is narrated about the poet al-'A'shah (d. 625), whose jinni was called Mish'al. It is told al-'A'shah was once on a journey to Hadramout, in Yemen, when all of a sudden he lost his way. He came upon a tent, and went inside. The host welcomed him, and asked him about his identity. The poet responded, "I am al-'A'shah." At this, his host started declaiming poetry to him. The poet was bewildered, for his host was reciting his own poetry back to him, in which he describes a girl named Sumayyah. Utterly baffled, the poet asked him, "Do you know who is Sumayyah?" The host called for Sumayyah, who came out before them. Al-'A'shah began to shiver and shudder. Finally, his host told him he was Mish'al, his jinni inspirer.[41]

Many points merit discussion here. First, al-'A'shah doesn't recognize his jinni. The familiarity between poet and jinni varies from one poet to another. Although Hassan seems to live with his follower jinni, al-'A'shah doesn't even recognize his when he meets him in the tent, although he too mentions him in his verse. Al-ʿAʾshah's case looks more like a vision in the desert that lasts for a short while. The poet lost his way and found himself in a tent. Moreover, the beloved he describes in his poetry is standing in front of him, alive and true, or so it seems. The world he imagined in his poetry is now made existent outside of him. His tremor comes from grasping in a second the imaginary realm of the poem that was within is now actual and exterior to the self. More shocking for him is he is no longer the inventor of this imaginary realm; someone else seems to own it. The poet is shattered because he is confronted with his own identity, so to speak.

More complex and gripping is the fact that sometimes the poet's jinni doesn't acknowledge his task is to inspire. He completely negates the authorship of the poet whom he assisted, as we read in *al-Aghani,* as in this following story:

> A traveler asked a jinni, "Who is the best poet among the Arabs?" The jinni replied, "Lafiz ibn Lahiz, Hiyab, Habid, and Hadhir ibn Mahir." The traveler said, "These names are new to me!" The jinni answered, "Oh well! Lafiz is the jinni of the poet Imruʾ al-Qays (d. 540), Habid is the jinni of the poet ʿAbid ibn al-Abras [d. before 540], and Hathir is the jinni of the poet [al-Nabighah], Ziyad al-Dhubyani [d. 604]."[42]

Here, there is sameness between poets and jinn, to the point it becomes superfluous to distinguish between giver and taker. This identicalness is clearly evoked in the *Treatise of Familiar Spirits and Demons* of ibn Shuhayd. Thus, the jinni of the Abasside poet Abu Nuwas (d. 812) is always drunk, and surrounded by wine jars just like the poet he inspires. The jinni of the poet al-Mutanabbi (d. 965), on the other hand, is always boasting, like the poet himself, well known for his bloated pride. Significantly, ibn Shuhayd gives the floor to the jinn rather than to the poets. By doing this, he is implying inspiration is the foundation of poetry, while craft is only secondary.

CONCLUSION

I have tried to elucidate the view that depicts the poet as being visited by some kind of spiritual entity, such as the Muses, the jinn, or—harking back to Lorca's definition—the Duende. However, a second view, considerably more down to earth, depicts a poet as an intensive laborer, achieving his or her abilities and perfecting his or her skills by dint of constant practice. The first view sees a poet as a person who is gifted, graced in an almost supernatural way with that which is defined as poetry. In the second view, a poet becomes so from the ground up, as it were, by means of a purely rational route.

The concept of inspiration as coming from the jinn should not imply total passivity on the part of the poet who simply submits to the jinn's reciting the verses that he then composes as his own. It was a well-known fact in Arabic poetry some poets would work endlessly their poems, continuously polishing them to the point they were called the slaves of poetry, and their poems were called *al-hawliyyat* (the chronicles), meaning a poet would spend a great length of time producing the poem. It was also known a poet would act as the *rawi* of an elder poet, which means he would receive training under him by assiduously studying the elder's work to be able to recite it properly. In this regard, the poet al-Hutay'ah (d. 674) was the reciter of the poet Zuhayr ibn abi Sulma (d. 609), and the poet Kuthayr 'Azzah (d. 723) was the reciter of the poet Jamil Buthainah (d. 701).[43]

In the context of the present study, it is important to point out not all traditions across the world have stressed a similar concept of inspiration as coming from the Muses, jinn, or Duende. The Far Eastern tradition, for instance, seems to be devoid of such a concept. There is not in Chinese poetics, for example, a possession by a spiritual entity, or the idea of a poet receiving his or her poem from a Muse. In these traditions, greatly inspired by Buddhism and particularly by Zen, poetry springs from silence and contemplation, which are the two meditative conditions that encourage inspiration.[44] As James J. Y. Liu (d. 1986) writes in *The Art of Chinese Poetry*, "The poet, like the follower of Zen, should seek to attain to a calm contemplative state of mind. When one has achieved this, one can then hope to capture the spirit (*shen*) of life, of Nature, in one's poetry."[45]

This last assertion simply means what we call jinn, Duende, Daemons, or Muse could come from inside the poet, if he/she listens in silence to the self. As I have tried to demonstrate throughout this book, and in this chapter in particular, the jinn could be hidden powers within the poet's self and outside of him as well. The poet's mind and imagination could create these spirits outside the self, making possible all kinds of interaction with them; he/she also could get them from where they lie dormant in the psyche, and slowly bring them to light.

Conclusion

The Sentience of Inside Out/Outside In

$\mathcal{T}$he exploration of the jinn's concept underscores that we and the universe are made from the same fabric. Each resembles the other. Most significantly, both are incessantly in contact. Like the human, the universe has a soul and is a living body. This is what our ancestors called "Anima Mundi," or "the Soul of the world." Both are endowed with intelligence. Plato (d. 347 BCE) evoked in the *Timaeus* the universe as a living being, a vital force that embraces all other living entities, which by their nature are all linked.

Quantum physics and traditional societies teach us the world of mental meaning and that of physical reality are not separate. They flow into each other. This is what Hinduism refers to as the Vedanta, which is a state of non-duality, of awareness, achievement, and cosmic consciousness. In such a condition of alertness, the human knows and lives the absence of borders between the external powers of the universe and the internal powers of the psyche. He/she understands there is only one sentience common to both the Self (Atman) and the Source of All Things (Brahman). As Huston Smith puts it, "Consciousness proper—pure consciousness, consciousness with no images imposed upon it—is the common property of us all."[1]

The jinn, being part of the Creation, partake in this general sentience inherent in all beings. The jinn are also subtle and elusive spirits. They are psychic powers that could appear as if they were real. They eternally travel between the seen and the unseen realms, between inside out/outside in, like waves that advance into the ocean of existence, then recede into the *ghayb*, the invisible. In a blink of the eye, they retreat into our collective darkness, to emerge again out there when we least expect them. They enlighten us that physical reality is not the only reality.

It is impossible to locate them on our physical map. We have to seek them out on the atlas of the imaginal where they invent their transformations before emerging into our material plane, dressed in their impermanent bodies to ensnare us. Each time they reveal to us they are "differently" real. Their multifarious manifestations provide evidence not only of the energy of the imaginal, but also of the infinite power of the universe to renew itself, or rather to be renewed by the Creator, the Highest Sentience of all.

Appendix

Notes

Glossary of Arabic Words and Names

References

Index

Appendix

The Different Classes of the Jinn

The Qur'an mentions only three terms related to the species of jinn: the generic "jinn," *marid,* and *'ifrit.* However, Arabic and Islamic literature provides preposterous descriptions of many others it claims belong to the jinn's species. Allegedly, the jinn's realm is filled with numerous eerie and alarming beings.

THE GHOUL

Its remarkable shape shifting characterizes this second category of jinn. In fact, the Arabic word ghoul is defined as "every supernatural creature that is capable of taking on infinite forms."[1] It is used in poetic language as "a general synonym for anything perpetually changing."[2]

The pagan Arabs of pre-Islamic period thought the act of shape shifting is an indication that ghouls want to kill. It is mostly in the darkness of the night and in the desert, far from civilization, in the bottomless human fear, that ghouls manifest themselves, luring and seducing their victims by constant metamorphosis until they bring madness or death upon them. This has given rise to the idea of the ghoul being associated with inevitable destruction.[3] The term ghoul comes in fact from an Arabic root (gh-w-l) that means "to annihilate" or "to assault." The phrase, "A ghoul carried him off" is sometimes used in Arabic metaphorically to refer to death.

Arab poets before Islam gave free reign to their imaginations in their descriptions of ghouls. The pre-Islamic poet of the sixth century 'Ubayd ibn Ayyub, for example, wrote of his various encounters with ghouls.[4] He narrated a story about a *ghoulah* (a female ghoul) who was drawn to the fire he had kindled, and assaulted him one night in the desert. He managed, however, to behead her. Similar stories can be found in odes of pre-Islamic poets such as Ka'b ibn Zuhayr and Imru' al-Qays (d. 540), who penned images such as "arrows sharp as the canine teeth of a ghoul." The poet 'Antarah ibn Shaddad al-'Absi (d. 615), portrayed the suddenly appearing and disappearing nature of the ghoul in the following verse: "Like the flickering flame of a torch, the ghoul / sometimes appears and sometimes disappears in my hands."[5]

The best known poems about ghouls, however, are undoubtedly those of Thabit ibn 'Amir al-Fahmi, known as Ta'abbata Sharran (d. 540), which literally means "he carried evil under his arm." This refers to a *ghoulah* he contended to have encountered in the night and killed, carrying her body with him under his arm to show his people the following morning.[6] Ta'abbata Sharran wrote that he met the *ghoulah* one night while he was traveling in the desert, hunted her down, and finally killed her without even getting a good look at her. Then he recited the following lines:

I spent the night bearing down on top of her,
Waiting for morning to see what I had caught.
Then I found two eyes in an ugly head,
Similar to the head of a cat, but with a forked tongue.[7]

Poets were not the only ones who would seem to have encountered ghouls. Well-known pre-Islamic figures also appear to have found themselves face to face with ghouls. Some of the companions of the Prophet maintain 'Umar [the second caliph of Islam] encountered before Islam a ghoul one day on his way to Damascus, and killed it with his sword.[8]

Many extravagant legends circulated in Medieval Islam about this kind of jinn, especially regarding its long life span and its supernatural resistance to death. It was believed the ghoul dies with one blow, but can come back to life if it is struck a second time. After that it remains alive forever, even if it is wielded a deathblow a thousand times over.[9]

The most intriguing stories are those that speak of ghouls' conversion to Islam. As with other classes of jinn, ghouls were invited to convert to Islam, seem to have obeyed the call, and joined the new religion. The story of "The King's Son and the Ogress" from *The Nights* tells about a young prince who encountered a *ghoulah* in the forest, and how she attempted to seduce him. The young prince prayed to God for help. At first, the *ghoulah* mocked him for worshiping God and sarcastically asked him: "Aid thyself against him with thy father's monies and treasures. He whom I fear will not be satisfied with wealth. Ye hold that ye have in Heaven a God who seeth and is not seen, and is Omnipotent and Omniscient." "Yes, we have none but Him." "Then pray thou to Him; happily He will deliver thee from me, thine enemy!" So the king's son raised his eyes to heaven and began to pray with his whole heart, saying, "O my God, I implore Thy succour against that which troubleth me." Then he pointed to her with his hand, and she fell to the ground, burnt black as charcoal.[10]

A popular belief states ghouls can become good if they hear someone reciting the Throne Verse of the Qur'an (Qur'an 2:255), known for its effectiveness in dispelling the power of evil, and convincing ghouls to follow the straight path of Islam.[11] Islamic medieval literature speaks of cooperation between human Muslims and jinn Muslims after the latter's conversion. All of a sudden, these eerie creatures become close to humans, forsake their wilderness, and even join human Muslims in the effort of spreading the Word of God. The story of "'Ajib and Gharib" from *The Nights* illustrates the consequences of this conversion's act. A ghoul named Sa'dan and his children convert after a long discussion with the human hero, Gharib: "[Said] Gharib, 'It is my will that you enter my faith, the faith al-Islam, and acknowledge the Unity of the All-knowing King whose All-might created Light and Night and every thing—there is no God but He, the Requiting King!—And confess the mission and prophethood of Abraham the friend [of God] (on whom be peace!).' So the Ghoul and his sons made the required profession after the goodliest fashion, and Gharib bade loose their bonds."[12]

The ghoul Sa'dan and his children, afterward, aided Muslims in their ambitious objectives.[13] An interesting point must be made here: It is usually human Muslims who cross the borders separating them from ghouls. It is the hero, Gharib, who, empowered by his religion, enters the land of the ghoul to convince him to join Islam. It is as if submission to God breaks all barriers, reuniting species, and healing old antinomies. One could also read it as a reciprocal awareness. Through submission to God, the human Muslim tames the ghoul's monstrosity on one hand, but also becomes sensitive to the existence of domesticated wilderness.

Similar stories of conversion can be found in Hinduism and Buddhism as well. In Hinduism, the Hindu sages tried to convert the Rakshasas, the evil spirits of forests to Hinduism. It is told in *The Ramayana,* the old Indian epic, that the prince Rama waged a ferocious battle against them, chased them in the deep of their dominion, and defeated them, thus establishing peace and order to the woods. As in the case of Sa'dan above, it is again the human who crosses the boundaries that separate the two species and comes to tame these spiritual entities hidden in the heart of the wilderness.

It is rather difficult to find Western folktale stories of conversion to Christianity similar to the ones mentioned in *The Nights* and in the texts of Hinduism and Buddhism. One story comes to mind; "Le Petit Poucet" in the French fairy tales collected by Charles Perrault (d. 1703). In this story, the ghoul intends to eat the seven boys, but the youngest of them tricks him and steals his boots and all his wealth. At no moment of the story is there mention of the possible redemption of the ghoul by his conversion to Christianity, and hence, of his eventual metamorphosis into a pacifist being.

THE *HINN*

The *hinn* are an offspring of a tribe of weak jinn and seem to be close to animals. In this context, they often appear in the shape of dogs, as mentioned in the prophetic tradition:

"Dogs belong to the category of hinn, and hinn are weak jinn. If they approach you, throw some food at them and chase them away, for they have evil souls."[14]

Some pre-Islamic poets immortalized the *hinn* in their verses. They chanted their playful evil as follows: "Jinn and hinn frolic around me!"[15] Another poet describes his predicament among them: "I continued falling among ringing devils, jinn and hinn, with wildly different faces."[16]

THE *'IFRIT*

The term *'ifrit* is mentioned only once in the Qur'an, when the prophet king Solomon asked for the throne of the Queen of Sheba to be brought to him. One *'ifrit* from among the jinn consented to fulfill his request: "An *'ifrit* of the jinn said, 'I will bring it to thee, before thou risest from thy place; I have strength for it and I am trusty" (Qur'an 27:39).

The term *'ifrit* often presents a problem for the scholars trying to classify the jinn. Many commentators on the verse cited above maintain the word *'ifrit* is an adjective referring to a specific powerful jinni rather than a separate and distinct type among the jinn. Later the word came to describe any powerful and cunning man; in which case, it could refer to dark powers within the human psyche.[17]

THE *MARID*

In the Qur'an, the *marid* is an unruly force always striving to predict the future by means of astrological hearsay. The term *marid* is mentioned only once in the Qur'an in the following verse "We have adorned the lower heaven with the adornment of the stars and to preserve against every [rebel satan (*shaytan marid*)]; they listen not to the High Council, for they are pelted from every side" (Qur'an 37:7–8). This kind of jinn is mostly found in popular medieval literature, in particular in the stories of *The Nights* dealing with Solomon. Finally, as with the term *'ifrit,* the term *marid* could also be applied to humans. Used as an adjective, it denotes a rebellious man.[18]

THE *NASNAS*

Like the *shiqq* and the ghoul, the *nasnas* moves in locales far away from urban centers. Some maintained he is "in China and other distant kingdoms."[19] Others asserted he lives beyond the dam of Ma'rib (in Yemen), beyond what the eye can see, in the realm of the unknown and the unpredictable.[20] In all cases, he seems to dwell further away from the

Arab/Muslim center, in other people's habitats, which makes him less of a threat, and less subject to be tamed and incorporated into the system of beliefs.

These uncanny beings appear to have, like humans, a physical environment, on and through which they act. The supernatural places carry a special power and energy. The Arabs approached them with awe and even paid reverence to the supernatural beings dwelling in them. It is there, across sand storms, mirages, and solitude, supernatural beings manifest themselves.

The *nasnas* seems a sad copy of the *shiqq*, a lower form of jinn, a hybrid between animal and man, a kind of weak, archaic, and abnormal creature. Muslim historians and geographers describe men hunting him rather than the reverse. Humans seem to terrify him; when he sees them, he tries to escape by leaping as swiftly as a mare.[21]

The etymology of *nasnas* means "twice people," since *nas* in Arabic means "people." This designation, instead of making him closer to humans, transformed him, on the contrary, into an enigmatic entity, an oddity.[22]

Some sources add "nasnases belong to the very ancient Arab tribe of 'Ad, that rebelled against their prophet, so God transformed them into nasnases. They hop like birds and graze like beasts."[23]

One description of this lower form of jinn seems, however, to offer a more empowering image of the *nasnas* and at the same time a more fictitious one. He appears a kind of alien capable of frightening humans and carrying them off. Najm al-din al-Razi (d. 1256) writes "nasnas: a mythical being combining both human and demonic features. It is an animal found in the deserts of Turkestan. It is tall, with an upright stature and broad fingernails. It is extremely fond of humans, and whenever it sees a human, it throws sand in his path and enthralls him with its gaze. If it meets a solitary traveler, it is said it will carry him off and take seed from him."[24]

In Najm al-din al-Razi's description, the *nasnas* seems the opposite of what other sources described him. Instead of being frightened of humans, he appears here as fond of them. This inconsistency in the Muslim sources makes this kind of jinn even more mysterious and might illustrate at the same time that it is a product of people's fantasy.[25]

THE *SHIQQ*

The term *shiqq* means in Arabic "half of." The uncanny being called *shiqq* manifests itself in the shape of half a man with one foot, one eye, one hand, etc. In a way, it could be surnamed "the incomplete being," because only half of it is created, and thus lacks the usual symmetry that exists in all beings. Like other eerie beings, it appears to humans far from the traffic of civilization, in the wilderness where there is no other witness to its oddity, and where imagination can wander. It traps the traveler alone, when in a journey, and invites him to a fight.[26]

The belligerent relationship between humans and *shiqq* is prominent in the many narratives depicting their encounters. Al-Jahiz (d. 868) recounts a story in which a certain Arab by the name of 'Alqamah ibn Safwan met with a *shiqq* at a place called Hazman's grove. They fought, and then they recited poetry to each other before they fell to beating one another to death.[27] This act of reciting poetry to a foe or someone from a different species comes up often in the narratives of medieval Islam, reminding us that poetry played the vital role of catalyst in the lives of people during that time.

Shiqq is also the proper name of a historical figure, a soothsayer in pre-Islam who was transformed into a supernatural being with the advent of the new religion.[28] Because this change took place in Islam, it is possible to argue it was part of a waged war against seers, diviners, and soothsayers. The figure of the *shiqq* was then demonized, or at least disfigured, to incite Muslims to reject the diviners of the past, and seek help from the Qur'an alone.

The figure of this intriguing being seems to be found across cultures as well, illustrating the constant migration of stories from one culture to another, and epitomizing at the same time the archetypes that inhabit each of us. The half man could indeed refer to the split self. If the fight is positive and the victim alive, the two parts of the self will be reconciled and integration will occur. However, if the victim dies in the narrative, then there is a suggestion the crack between the two parts will remain opened. Joseph Campbell relates the following: "A dangerous one-legged, one-armed, one sided figure, the half-man invisible if viewed from the off-side, is encountered in many parts of the earth. In Central Africa, it is declared such a half-man says to the person who has encountered him: 'Since you have met with me, let us fight together.' If thrown, he will plead: 'Do not kill me. I will show you lots of medicines;' and then the lucky person becomes a proficient doctor. But if the half-man (called Chiruwi, 'a mysterious thing') wins, his victim dies."[29]

Needless to say, this fantastic Central African being is similar to the Arab *shiqq*. Strangely enough, it behaves in the same manner and utters the same words.

THE *SI'LAT*

The *si'lat* resembles the ghoul in many aspects. She, too, is a temptress, a first-class trickster. She likes dancing relentlessly with men and playing with them as a cat plays with a mouse.[30] People in medieval Islam told stories the *si'lat* would attract a man to her by imitating a woman's voice and screaming a wolf is eating her![31]

The pre-Islamic Arabs maintained one of their forefathers, 'Amr ibn Yarbu', fell in love with a *si'lat*. He married her, and she gave birth to human children. There was even a belief an entire Arabian tribe sprang from this marriage. Whether this fictional ancestry was originally regarded as an honor or a dishonor, however, is not recorded. The tribe was called Banu Siʿlat (children of *siʿlat*). It is alleged this eerie *siʿlat* "one day saw lightning in the sky and interpreted it as a sign that her clan was calling her back. So she left children and husband, and returned to her clan."[32]

The difference between a *siʿlat* and a ghoul remains indistinct. Some texts mention that *siʿlat* acts in the broad daylight, while the ghoul manifests itself only in the night.[33] Others relate "the fire that a ghoul kindles in the night is different from a fire kindled by a siʿlat."[34] But we don't know how. As for the relationships between a *siʿlat* and a ghoul, some sources further refine the differences between these classes of jinn by claiming the ghoul's wife is a *siʿlat!*[35]

CONCLUSION

Islamic theology has tried to establish a hierarchical ranking for the classes of jinn mentioned above based on their abilities to perform marvels, their different spiritual powers, their specific interaction with humans, their closeness or distance from angels and animals, the extent to which they can shape-shift themselves, and the time and place they choose to manifest themselves.[36]

Some medievalist Muslim scholars gave full reign to their imagination, like al-Masʿudi (d. 956) for example, who found the classes of jinn mentioned above could not exhaust the list of these spiritual entities. He claimed there are thirty-one types of jinn. They are all children of *al-jann,* the father of all jinn, and his unnamed wife.[37]

Even with the best efforts of Muslim lexicographers, geographers, and historians, the distinctions between the diverse classes of jinn remain unclear. For example, some Muslim medieval sources maintain that the ghoul is exclusively female, while others claim it is exclusively male. The popular belief during the pre-Islamic period was that there existed a masculine ghoul along with its female counterpart or mate, a *ghoulah.*[38]

Androgyny and Womanhood

This indecision with regard to the gender of both *siʿlat* and ghoul might suggest the possibility of androgyny. Some supernatural beings, such as the phoenix and the dragon, are considered androgynous across cultures. It is this characteristic that partly gave them mythical attributes. Indeed, androgynous beings are looked at as perfect beings that existed before time, before the partition of life into masculine and feminine.

One could also find that sometimes *siʿlat* and ghoul are associated with womanhood rather than androgyny. Alone in the desert, a *siʿlat* keeps changing shape until she manages to draw a man to her. Iraqi historian Mahmud Shukri al-Alusi (d. 1924) recounts the Arabs call any attractive, witty, slim, and powerful woman a *si'lat*.[39] These kinds of associations indicate a negative approach to women perceived as inconstant, unfaithful, and bringers of death. It is possible to compare it to the Hindu Maya as the destructive and seductive powers of the senses and the realm of illusion.

The Blurring of Species

Although some of these diverse classes of jinn could be androgynous, others are depicted as hybrid. For example, *si'lat* and ghouls are fashioned out of two or even more species. Thus, a ghoul is sometime depicted as half man and half donkey, or has the features of one animal that can be mixed with the features of another.[40] It is recounted a ghoul has the head of a cat and the tongue of a dog, and it could change everything in its appearance except its feet, which remain donkey's hooves, no matter what shape it takes.[41] One wonders if this peculiarity is not meant to recognize the ghoul despite all the luring and disguise it recourses to. It is worthy of note this oddity is in the lower part of the body as if to encapsulate the bestiality of this being.

In general, all kinds of jinn have a body peculiarity that distinguishes them from each other. Thus, a *shiqq* has only half a body, a *shaytan* has one eye, a *nasnas* is half demonic half human and hops like a bird, a ghoul has a donkey's hooves, etc.

The Arab/Muslim lore is not alone in picturing ghouls as having a foot oddity. Such beings seem to have existed since early times, as R. Campbell Thompson (d. 1941), specialist in ancient Near-Eastern incantations and author of many works on the Assyrian, Babylonian, and Hittite literatures seems to allude: "Herodotus describes some people who were supposed to live beyond the region inhabited by the Scythians as having goats' feet."[42]

A Fleeting Concept

When dealing with the various classes of the jinn, it seems impossible to catalogue them the way a modern zoologist would do with his thousands of real, measurable, and identifiable animals. All of them show a remarkable resistance to systemization. In the domain of the jinn, forms shift ceaselessly because jinn are essentially tricksters. Even their habitat is constantly being displaced, and apparently wanders around just as they do. The following saying of the Prophet Muhammad is often quoted to epitomize the transitory and elusive nature of these spiritual entities, "The jinn are of three kinds: one has wings and flies, serpents and dogs are another, and the third keeps roaming."[43]

As we have seen, the Qur'an mentions jinn only, and refers to *'ifrit* and *marid* in rare instances. The Qur'an addresses its message to humans and jinn, both considered intelligent and responsible. How then one should understand the inclusion of all these supernatural beings in the inventory of jinn? It is obvious Muslim geographers, historians, and lexicographers were under the sway of a widely spread popular and oral literature that dealt with the most unheard of among creatures.

In fact, there are two ways of reading this list of the jinn's classes. The first reading would suppose the inclusion of these supernatural beings degraded the "pure" and intelligent concept of jinn as unfolded in the Qur'an into supernatural and uncanny beings. It assumes there was a constant conflict between an orthodox Islam and a popular Islam. The second reading, however, stresses there is no conflict, and claims jinn are essentially shape shifters who could appear in animal shapes. Within this second reading, one is reminded that throughout human history, spirits, gods, and animals have often lived together and often completed each other. It even happened that one of them took on the appearance and the life force of the other.

Notes

INTRODUCTION

1. See for example the book of Ahmad Saqr, *al-Jinn* (Lombard, IL: Foundation for Islamic Knowledge, 1994). This book is simply quotation upon quotation of Qur'anic verses and prophetic tradition, Hadith, that mention jinn and demons without any interpretation or analysis whatsoever. It stands as an example of contemporary naïve and unsophisticated Islamic views on this topic.

2. Samuel M. Zwemer, *The Influence of Animism on Islam* (New York: Macmillan, 1920).

3. William James, *The Varieties of Religious Experience* (New York: Modern Library, 1991), 61.

4. Ibid., 64.

5. Ake Hulkrantz, *Soul and Native Americans* (Quebec: Spring Publications, 1997), 65.

6. Fritthjof Schuon, *The Feathered Sun: Plains Indians in Art and Philosophy* (Bloomington, IN: World Wisdom Books, 1990), 18–19.

7. Thomas Kasulis, *Shinto: The Way Home* (Honolulu: Univ. of Hawaii Press, 2004), xiii.

8. Ibid., from book cover.

9. For more details about these entities in Hinduism and Buddhism, see especially T. O. Ling, *Buddhism and the Mythology of Evil: A Study in Theravada Buddhism* (Oxford: Oneworld Publications, 1997), 15.

10. On the interaction of the Yaksas with humans in Hinduism and Buddhism, see especially Ananda K. Coomaraswamy, *Yaksas: Essays in the Water Cosmology* (New Delhi: Indira Ghandi National Center for the Arts; New York: Oxford Univ. Press, 1993.) See also Gail Hinich Sutherland, *The Disguises of the Demon: The Development of the Yaksa in Hinduism and Buddhism* (Albany: State Univ. of New York Press, 1991.)

11. Katharine M. Briggs, *The Fairies in English Tradition and Literature* (Chicago: Univ. of Chicago Press, 1967), 95.

12. Françoise Durand and Christiane Zivie-Coche, *Gods and Men in Egypt. 3000 BCE to 395* (Ithaca, NY: Cornell Univ. Press, 2004), 168.

13. Plato, *Great Dialogues of Plato,* trans. W. H. D. House (New York: New American Library, 1984), 445.

14. Paul Friedlander, *An Introduction* (London: Routledge and Kegan, 1958), 1:41

15. Jalal al-din al-Suyuti, *Laqt al-murjan fi 'ahkam al-jann* (Beirut: Dar al-kutub al-'ilmiyyah, 1986), 52.

16. Patrick Harpur, *The Philosophers' Secret Fire: A History of the Imagination* (London: Penguin Books, 2002), 38.

17. Joseph Campbell, *Inner Reaches of Outer Space: Metaphor as Myth and as Religion* (California: New World Library, 2002), 59. Campbell here quotes Japanese philosopher, Daisetz T. Suzuki.

18. Amit Goswami, *The Self-Aware Universe* (New York: Penguin, 1995), 17. Goswami mentions on the same page "when Descartes divided the world into matter and mind, he intended a tacit agreement not to attack religion, which would reign supreme in matter of mind, in exchange for science's supremacy over matter."

19. Arthur Zajonc, ed. *The New Physics and Cosmology. Dialogues with the Dalai Lama* (Oxford: Oxford Univ. Press, 2004), 150.

1. THE POETICS OF THE INVISIBLE: MUSLIM IMAGINATION AND THE JINN

1. *Al-zahir* (the Outward) and *al-batin* (the Inward) are two of God's ninety-nine Most Beautiful Names: *'asma' allah al-husna*. These two names summarize in themselves many aspects of my discussion of the two realms. See especially 'Abdul Karim al-Qushayri, *al-Tahbir fi al-tadhkir: sharh 'asma' allah al-husna* (Beirut: Dar al-kutub al-'ilmiyyah, 2006). See William Chittick, *The Self-Disclosure of God: Principles of ibn al-Arabi's Cosmology* (Albany: State Univ. of New York Press, 1998), 62. Ibn 'Arabi underscored the relation between these two Divine names and jinn and humans as follows: "God takes into account from the cosmos only the human species and the jinn. He appointed manifestation for the human beings, from His name the Manifest, and He appointed nonmanifestation for the jinn, from his Name the Nonmanifest."

2. Seyyed Hossein Nasr, *Knowledge and the Sacred* (New York: Crossroads, 1989), 134.

3. By *al-'alamin*, the Qur'an is referring to all kinds of existence, whether physical or nonphysical.

4. "Behold, Thy Lord said to the angels, 'I will create a deputy on earth'" (Qur'an 2:30*).

5. Muhyi al-din ibn 'Arabi, *Kernel of the Kernel,* trans. Ismail Hakki Bursevi (Sherborne, UK: Beshara Publications, 1981), 9. Ibn 'Arabi mentions the following Hadith of the Prophet, "God has 18,000 universes and this your world is just one universe among them." See also Rauf Bulent, "Universality and ibn Arabi." *Journal of Muhyi al-din ibn 'Arabi Society* (1985) 4:1.

6. "Do you not see that God has subjugated to your [use] all things in the heavens and on earth?" (Qur'an 31:20*). Also in the Qur'an 55:33*, we read: "O people of jinn and men, if you are able to pass through the confines of heaven and earth, pass through them! You shall not pass through except with an authority." Thus, humans and jinn could explore all things in the heavens and on Earth with an authority from God.

7. J. C. Cooper, *An Illustrated Encyclopedia of Traditional Symbols* (New York: Thames and Hudson, 1978), 117.

8. Ibid.

9. Jamal al-din Muhammad ibn Manzur, *Lisan al-'arab* (Beirut: Dar sader, n.d.), 8:147. He mentions "seven, seventy, and seven hundreds are mentioned several times in the Qur'an and the Hadith. Arabs in general use these terms to indicate a large amount of things or beings."

10. As mentioned in Qur'an 65:12, "It is God who created seven heavens, and of earth their like."

11. 'Ali Ahmad 'Abd al-'Al al-Tahtawi, *Fath rab al-falaq: Sharh kitab bid' al-khalq* (Beirut: Dar al-kutub al-'ilmiyyah, 2004), 414.

12. Sadr al-din Muhammad ibn Ibrahim Shirazi, *Mafatih al-ghayb* (Beirut: Mu'assasat al-tarikh al-'arabi, 1999), 1:415.

13. Henry Corbin, *Spiritual Body and Celestial Earth: From Mazdean Iran to Shi'ite Iran,* trans. Nancy Pearson (Princeton, NJ: Princeton Univ. Press, 1976), 131–39.

14. Al-Shirazi, 1:130.

15. Henry Corbin, *Spiritual Body and Celestial Earth,* 137.

16. Ibid., 137.

17. Ibid., 137.

18. Ibid., 139.

19. Ibid., 138.

20. Ibid., 139.

21. Ibid., 140.

22. Ibid., 141.

23. See ibn 'Abdullah al-Hamawi Yaqut, *Mu'jam al-buldan* (Beirut: Dar ihya' al-turath al-'arabi, n.d.), 7:12. Yaqut depicts the mountain of Qaf as follows, "it surrounds the earth, and it is very close to the sky. Some claimed that behind it are multiple worlds and beings known only by Almighty."

24. Henry Corbin, *Spiritual Body and Celestial Earth,* 131. See also Kathleen Raine, "The Underlying Unity: Nature and the Imagination," in *The Spirit of Science: From Experiment to Experience,* ed. David Lorimer (New York: Continuum, 1999), 216–20. Raine (d. 2003) spoke, in turn, of our world as filled with all possible kinds of living beings, "There may be other beings, attuned not to the spectrum of our human senses, but to other, larger, ampler magnitudes; and in every hedgerow."

25. Muhyi al-din ibn 'Arabi, *al-Futuhat al-makkiyyah* (Beirut: Dar sader, n.d.) 3:506–7.

26. Nur al-din 'Abd al-Rahman Jami, *Lawa'ih: A Treatise on Sufism,* trans. E. H. Winfield and Muhammad Kazvini (London: Theosophical Publishing House, 1978), 33.

27. Ibn 'Arabi, *Kernel of the Kernel,* 9.

28. Mircea Eliade, *Images and Symbols: Studies in Religious Symbolism,* trans. Philipe Mairet (Princeton, NJ: Princeton Univ. Press, 1991), 61.

29. Dick J. Steven, "Plurality of Worlds," in *Cosmology: Historical, Literary, Philosophical, Religious, and Scientific Perspectives,* ed. Norriss S Hetherington (New York: Garland Publishers, 1993), 515–32.

30. George Gale. 1993. "Multiple Universes," in *Cosmology: Historical, Literary, Philosophical, Religious, and Scientific Perspectives,* ed. Norriss S Hetherington (New York: Garland Publishers, 1993), 533–45.

31. To those who criticize the hierarchical perspective of the world as 'oppressive,' Huston Smith, contemporary American historian and philosopher of religion replies in these terms: "The notion that hierarchies as such—all hierarchies—are oppressive is simplistic, misguided, and flatly untrue. We live in a hierarchical universe, in which gradations of size, power, and complexity confront us at every turn. In addition, the social world, animal as well as human, couldn't last a week without chains of command that are honored." Phil Cousineau, ed. *The Way Things Are: Conversations with Huston Smith on the Spiritual Life* (Berkeley: Univ. of California Press, 2003), 155.

32. Ibid., 208. Emphasis added.

33. Henry Corbin, *Swedenborg and Esoteric Islam,* trans. Leonard Fox (West Chester, PA: Swedenborg Foundation, 1995), 1.

34. Ibid., 9.

35. Ibid., 10.

36. Ibid., 18.

37. The science of dreams developed very much in medieval Islam in large part because of this intense thinking on the imaginal realm and its relation to dreams. Many works were written on how to interpret dreams. See especially Muhammad ibn Sirin, *Dictionary of Dreams According to Islamic Inner Traditions,* trans. Muhammad M. al-'Akili (Philadelphia: Pearl Publishing House, 1992). See also John C. Lamoreaux, *The Early Tradition of Dream Interpretation* (Albany: State Univ. of New York Press, 2002).

38. Corbin, *Swedenborg and Esoteric Islam,* 6. It is interesting to mention in this context that the expression of al-Suhrawardi, "inside out," inspired the title of a book on Corbin: Tom Cheetham, *The World Turned Inside Out: Henry Corbin and Islamic Mysticism* (Woodstock, CT: Spring Journal Books, 2003).

39. Corbin, *Swedenborg and Esoteric Islam,* 3.

40. Ibid., 12.

41. The same meaning comes again in Qur'an 25:53 where it is mentioned that the two seas meet without transgressing each other. Ibn 'Arabi, *al-Futuhat al-makkiyyah,* 1:304.

42. Ibid., 304.

43. Ibid., 304.

44. Regarding this issue, see especially Mahmud Qasim, *al-Khayal fi madhab Muhyi al-din ibn 'Arabi* (Cairo: Univ. of Cairo Press, 1969), 79–85.

45. I will develop this particular issue of seeing the jinn toward the end of the following chapter.

46. Ibn 'Arabi, *al-Futuhat al-makkiyyah,* 2:313.

47. In this context see especially William Chittick, *Imaginal Worlds: Ibn al-Arabi and the Problem of Religious Diversity* (Albany: State Univ. of New York Press, 1994), 70–82.

48. Ibn 'Arabi, *al-Futuhat al-makkiyyah.* 2:390. See also William Chittick, *Ibn al-Arabi Metaphysics of Imagination: The Sufi Path of Knowledge* (New York: State Univ. of New York Press, 1989), 29.

49. See especially Su'ad al-Hakim, *al-Mu'jam al-sufi* (Beirut: Dar dandarah, 1981), 280.

50. René Guénon, *The Great Triad*, trans. Peter Kingsley (Cambridge: Quinta Essentia, 1991), 75.

51. Fred Alan Wolf, *The Dreaming Universe: A Mind-Expanding Journey into the Realm Where Psyche and Physics Meet* (New York: Simon and Schuster, 1994), 285.

52. Henry Corbin, *The Man of Light in Iranian Sufism*, trans. Nancy Pearson (New York: Omega Publications, 1994), 60.

53. James Hillman, *Revisioning Psychology* (New York: Harper Perennial, 1992), 27.

54. Nasr, *Knowledge and the Sacred*, 131. Nasr indicates "Ibn 'Arabi refers to this coincidence between knowledge and being when he speaks about the hierarchical orders of reality and calls them '*hadrah*' or 'Divine presence' because, metaphysically speaking, being or reality is none other than presence *hadrah* or consciousness *shuhud*. These presences include the divine Ipseity itself *hahut*, the Divine Names and Qualities *lahut*, the archangelic world *jabarut*, the subtle and psychic world *malakut*, and the physical world *mulk*," (161).

55. Corbin, *Swedenborg and Esoteric Islam*, 7.

2. CORRESPONDENCES BETWEEN JINN AND HUMANS

1. Ibn Manzur, 6:118. However, not all Muslim thinkers agree on the rationality of the jinn. See Yves Marquet, *La philosophie des alchimistes et l'alchimie des philosophes: Jabir ibn Hayyan et les frères de la Pureté* (Paris: Editions Maisonneuve et Larose, 1988), 73. Marquet maintains "Jabir ibn Hayyan, as well as Ikhwan al-Safa' proclaim that the angels are endowed with reason, but not the jinn." Some folkloric texts depict the jinn as being stupid. See especially Husain Haddawy,trans. *The Arabian Nights* (New York: W. W. Norton, 1990), 30. In the story of "The Fisherman and the Jinni," a cunning fisherman manipulates a jinni and compels him to return to the jar. The story underscores the human intelligence and the jinn's dumbness. See also Sou'ad al-Hakim, "Knowledge of God in ibn Arabi," in *Ibn Arabi: A Commemorative Volume*, ed. Stephen Hirtenstein and Michael Tiernan (Rockport, MA: Element, 1993), 264–90. Al-Hakim mentions "for ibn 'Arabi, only jinn and humans are endowed with mental faculties, which allows them to acquire knowledge." Jinn and humans are referred to in the Qur'an and in the Hadith as *al-thaqalan*, which could be translated as "the two weighty communities." Islamic scholars gave many interpretations of this term. Ibn Manzur, 1:88, states: "God Almighty called jinn and humans *thaqalan* in order to prefer them to all other beings on earth." See also geographer Kamal al-din al-Damiri, *Hayat al-hayawan al-kubra* (Beirut: al-Maktabah al-islamiyyah, n.d.), 1:180. He gives the additional meaning of "honor" to the term: "They have been called thaqalan because they carry weight on earth, and because they are extremely honorable. Every honorable person is said to be 'weighty.' They are also called thaqalan because they are sin-laden beings." Another term applied to both humans and jinn is the term *nas*, which literally means "people." See Qur'anic commentator, 'Abdul Karim al-Qushayri, *Lata'if al-'isharat: Tafsir sufi kamil li al-qur'an al-karim* (Cairo: al-Hay'ah al-misriyyah al-'ammah li al-kitab, 1981), 3:356. Al-Qushayri states "nas is a word which refers to both jinn and humans."

2. The *shahadah*, is the Muslim declaration of belief in the oneness of God and in Muhammad as his messenger. Recitation of the *shahadah* is one of the Five Pillars of Islam.

3. Muhyiddin abu Zakariyya Yahya ibn Sharaf al-Nawawi, *Riyad al-salihin* (London: Curzon Press, 1975), 191. The call to prayer includes the *shahadah:* "I bear witness that there is no divinity but God. I bear witness that Muhammad is God's Messenger."

4. Al-Damiri, 1:212.

5. Fakhr al-din al-Razi, *al-Tafsir al-kabir li al-qur'an: Mafatih al-ghayb* (Cairo: al-Matba'ah al-bahiyyah al-masriyyah, 1934), 30:153.

6. Ibn Manzur, 4:566. Some say 'Asr is not a tribe, but rather a place where the jinn dwell.

7. Murtada al-Zabidi, *Taj al-'arus min jawahir al-qamus* (Kuwait: Matba'at hukumat al Kuwait, 1965), 4:310. See Abu al-'Ala' Ahmad al-Ma'arri *Risalat al-ghufran* (Cairo: Dar al-ma'arif, 1950), 287. See also Badr al-din Muhammad ibn 'Abdullah al-Shibli, *Akam al-murjan fi ahkam al-jan* (Beirut: al-Maktabah al 'asriyah, 1988), 157. Al-Shibli mentions another tribe of jinn called *'Ukaysh*. See also Muhammad ibn Jarir al-Tabari, *Tarikh al-rusul wa al-muluk* (Cairo: Dar al-ma'arif, n.d.), 2:349.

8. Al-Husayn ibn 'Ali al-Mas'udi, *Akhbar al-zaman* (Beirut: Dar al-andalus, 1980), 34.

9. Ibn 'Arabi, *al-Futuhat al-makkiyyah*. 1:132.

10. Jawad 'Ali, *al-Mufassal fi tarikh al-'arab qabla al-islam* (Beirut: Dar al-'ilm li al-malayin, 1970), 6:711. See also Fakhr al-din al-Razi, 30:152. When discussing the Qur'anic chapter entitled "al-jinn," Fakhr al-din al-Razi suggests the jinn who listened to Muhammad were from the Shaysaban's tribe. See Wallis Budge, *Amulets and Talismans* (New York: Carol Publishing Group, 1992), 43. Budge claims that he found an amulet in Egypt. He writes, "the fifth line of this amulet contains the names of the kings of the jinn; Mudhahhab, Marra, Ahmar, Abyad, Ma'mun, Buskan, Shamhurash."

11. Richard Burton, trans. *The Book of the Thousand Nights and a Night* (London: Burton Club, 1885), 8:39. "And her father had dominion over men and jinn and wizards and Cohens and tribal chiefs and guards and countries and cities and islands galore and hath immense wealth in store."

12. Ibid., 7:331.

13. Katharine M. Briggs, *The Personnel of Fairyland* (Oxford: Alden Press, 1953), 67. In the story, there is a fascinating description of one of the fairies' revels led by their king and queen: "Then out came the little knights in green and gold, and their bevies of fairy ladies, singing more beautifully than nightingales, and then the tiny beautiful king and queen. They all moved to the top of the Gump, and settled themselves in thousands at the banquet that appeared there. It was a sight, which no man that saw it could forget, though he lived to be a hundred. Every *firze* bush around the hill glittered with fairy lights; the whole ground was starred with tiny flowers, and the air sweet with the scent of them. Each little figure of the thousands, which sat at the feast, was perfect in form and feature." Ibid.

14. The word used in Arabic for "differing" is *qidad,* meaning "fragmented," referring to the slight differences between the jinn's sects.

15. *Al-Shibli,* 70.

16. Muhammad 'Abd al-Rahim, ed., *Tafsir al-hasan al-basri* (Cairo: Dar al-hadith, 1992), 368. For more details on these different religious movements, see Muhammad ibn 'abd al-Karim al-Shahristani, *al-Milal wa al-nihal* (Beirut: Matba 'at al-naser, 1975).

17. See Fayd al-Kashani, *Tafsir al-safi* (Beirut, al-Mu'assasah al-'amiyah li al-matbu'at, 1982), 5:18.

18. There are many other verses in the Qur'an that carry the same meaning as Qur'an 22:18: "Hast thou not seen how to God bow all who are in the heavens and all who are in the earth, the sun and the moon, the stars and the mountains, the trees and the beasts, and many of mankind?" In Qur'an 16:50, the same meaning is reiterated: "To God bows everything in the heavens, and every creature crawling on the earth, and the angels."

19. Fakhr al-din al-Razi, 29:1130.

20. Fayd al-Kashani, 5:111.

21. Isma'il ibn Kathir, *The Signs Before the Day of Judgment* (London: Dar al-taqwa, 1992), 21–22.

22. See also Qur'an 46:18–19; Qur'an 7:38; Qur'an 55:39; and Qur'an 7:179.

23. Al-Damiri, 204.

24. See Husayn ibn Muhammad Diyarbakri, *Tarikh al-khamis fi ahwal anfas nafis* (Beirut: Mu'assasat sha'ban, 1970), 1:32. Diyarbakri prefers to leave the question unanswered: "Only God knows if the believers among jinn will be in Paradise or in Hell!"

25. Ibn Qayyim Muhammad ibn abi Bakr al-Jawziyyah, *al-Tafsir al-qayyim* (Beirut: Dar al-kutub al-'ilmiyyah, 1978), 461.

26. Al-Ma'arri, 282.

27. Ibid., 285.

28. 'Ali Burhan al-din al-Halabi, *'Aqd al-murjan fima yata 'allaqu bi-al-jann* (Cairo: Maktabat ibn Sina, n.d.). The author even questioned if angels see God and determined the answer was negative as well. In general, Muslim theologians agreed angels simply obey God from behind the veil, *hijab*.

29. Al-Ma'arri, 282.

30. It is important to mention in this context that Muslims believe Jesus will come at the end of time.

31. Ibn Kathir, 52. It is crucial, though, to mention that many other books on the Apocalypse do not mention the Antichrist might be a jinni. See also 'Abd al-Rahman al-Sakhawi, *Ashrat al-sa'ah* (Jordan: Dar al-bayareq, 1997).

32. Ibid., 70.

33. Muhammad ibn 'Ali al-Tahanawi, *Mawsu'at istilahat al-'ulum al-islamiyya* (Beirut: Dar khayyat, 1966), 2:264.

34. Abu 'Ubaydah Mashhur ibn Hasan, al-Sulayman, *Fath al mannan fi jam' kalam shaykh al-Islam ibn Taymeyah 'an al-jinnan* (Bahrein: al-Manamah maktabat al-tawhid, 1999), 1:54.

35. Some theologians consider the Mu'tazilah a school of rational theology, but most of those who wrote about the history of Muslim philosophy (Ibrahim Madkur, Majid Fakhri, and M'an Mohammad Sharif) have indicated it was in fact a school of philosophy or a theological-philosophical movement. See Albert Nasri Nadir, *Le système philosophique des Mu'tazilah* (Beirut: Editions les Belles Lettres, 1956).

36. Al-Tahanawi, 2:264.

37. Jalal al-din al-Suyuti, *Laqt al-murjan fi 'ahkam al-jann*, 29.

38. Ibn 'Arabi, *al-Futuhat al-makkiyyah*, 3:541.

39. Shihab al-din al-Suhrawardi, *Treatises of Shihabuddin Yahya al-Suhrawardi*, trans. W. M. Thackston, Jr. (London: Octagon Press, 1982), 79.

40. Haddawy, 33.

41. Ibid., 35.

42. Ibid., 97.

43. Ibid., 17 and 43.

44. Ibn 'Arabi, *al-Futuhat al-makkiyyah*, 3:48.

45. Ibid. Although it may be true the jinn are generally closer to the hidden realm than are humans, it is also mentioned in the Qur'an they don't always have access to it. The jinn who worked hard for the prophet Solomon, according to Qur'an 27:17, for example, were unable to predict his death. He died leaning on a staff. The jinn serving him did not even know he was dead until ants gnawed through the staff and the corpse fell down. See Qur'an 34:14.

46. See especially Sulayman 'Attar, *al-Khayal 'inda ibn 'Arabi: al-nazariyyah wa al-majalat* (Cairo: Dar al-thaqafah li-al-nashr wa al-tawzi', 1991).

47. Ibn 'Arabi, *Al-Futuhat al-makkiyyah* 2:333. "Not all those who witness imaginal bodies distinguish between these bodies and bodies that are material in their view. That is why the companions of the prophet didn't identify the angel Gabriel when he came disguised in the appearance of a Bedouin."

48. Ibid., 1:133. See also Duncan Black MacDonald, *The Religious Attitude and Life in Islam* (Beirut: Khayats, 1965), 272. MacDonald compares the spirits of Irish folklore to the jinn as described by ibn 'Arabi.

49. See especially 'Ali ibn Muhammad al-Jurjani, *al-Ta'rifat* (Cairo: Maktabat mustafa al-babi al-halabi, 1938), 235. See also Seyyed Haydar Amoli, *Inner Secrets of the Path*, trans. Assadullah al-Dhakir Yate (Shaftesbury, Dorset: Elements Books, 1989), 75–76.

50. Ibn 'Arabi, *al-Futuhat al-makkiyyah*, 1:160–61.

51. Al-Damiri, 213.

52. Najm al-din al-Razi, *The Path of God's Bondsmen from Origin to Return* (North Haledon, NJ: Islamic Publications International, 1980), 109.

53. Ibn 'Arabi, *al-Futuhat al-makkiyyah*. 1:133.

54. Ibn Manzur, 4:167.

55. Edwyn Robert Bevan, *Sibyls and Seers: A Survey of Some Ancient Theories of Revelation and Inspiration* (London: George Allen and Unwin Limited, 1928), 86.

56. Briggs, *The Fairies*, 97.

57. Jalal al-din al-Suyuti, *Laqt al-murjan fi 'ahkam al-jann*, 221.

58. Sulayman 'Attar, *al-Khayal 'inda ibn 'Arabi*, 1:211.

59. Jalal al-din al-Suyuti, *Laqt al-murjan fi 'ahkam al-jann*, 103.

60. Ibid., 104.

61. Ibid., 244. Sibawayh (d. around 793) was one of the earliest and greatest grammarians of the Arabic language. Moreover, the jinn seem to like intellectual discussions, as illustrated by the jurisprudent al-imam al-Bayhaqi (d. 1100), whose work imagines a debate between a group of scholars from the jinn and a group of human scholars on issues involving freedom of choice and submission to one's fate.

62. Ibn 'Arabi, *al-Futuhat al-makkiyyah,* 3:3. This is not a clear indication, contrary to what some theologians have written, that the Prophet Muhammad personally entered into discussions with the jinn, and was aware of their presence other than in the revelation of the Qur'an, as we shall see further in the fourth chapter of this book.

63. The jinni who transports Badr al-din Hasan tells him, for example, "know that I have brought thee hither, meaning to do thee a good turn for the love of Allah." Burton, 1:214.

64. Ibid., 5:174.

65. Ibid., 3:231.

66. Ibid., 1:214. This help from spiritual entities such as the jinn is not restricted to Islam, but rather is present in most folkloric traditions across the world. However, although Muslim jinn in *The Nights* always acknowledge they are mere performers of Divine orders, spiritual beings in other folkloric traditions are not necessarily centered on religion, and they do not see themselves as instruments in the hands of God. In some world folklore stories, one finds a pattern of reward and punishment created by the spiritual beings. The latter would punish the humans who don't respond to their calls and would reward those who run to their rescue. See Idries Shah, *World Tales: The Extraordinary Coincidence of Stories Told in all Times, in all Places* (New York: Harcourt Brace Jovanovich, 1979), 164. In the story of "The Water of Life," for example, a dwarf rewards a young prince who has helped him. The prince's two elder brothers humiliate him, heaping contempt upon him, and refuse to assist him. So the dwarf punishes them by transforming them into statues. In this context, see also Charles Perrault, *Contes* (Paris: Collection de l'imprimerie nationale, 1987), 225–29. Perrault (d. 1703), a famous French fabulist, tells the stories of two sisters, one ugly and the other beautiful. Their mother used to prefer the ugly one because she resembled her, and hate the beautiful one simply because she was beautiful. One day, the mother sent the beautiful one to the forest with the intention of getting rid of her. Once in the forest, however, the girl saw a fairy who asked her to bring her some water. The girl gave her the water as she requested. To reward her, the fairy told her "each time you speak, jewels will fall from your mouth." She returned home to her mother, and when she started to speak, jewels fell from her mouth as the fairy had promised. The greedy mother, to increase her fortune even more, now sent the ugly daughter into the forest. However, when the ugly daughter met the fairy, she refused to obey her request. So, to punish her, the fairy made a wish that each time she spoke, frogs would come out of her mouth. When she returned to her mother, she started speaking and frogs spewed out, so her mother chased her away from the house and kept the beautiful daughter instead. See also W. B. Yeats. *Irish Fairy and Folk Tales* (New York: Boni and Liveright, 1979), 90. In a story entitled "Master and Man," Yeats tells how a dwarfish spirit punished a human and made him his slave because the spirit helped him, but the human did not acknowledge it, and even refused to help him in return. The dwarf forces the human to work for him: "'Billy Mac Daniel,' said the little

man, getting very angry, 'you shall be my servant for seven years and a day, and that is the way I will be paid; so make ready to follow me.' When Bill heard this, he began to be very sorry for having used such bold words toward the little man; and he felt himself, yet could not tell how, obliged to follow the little man the live-long night about the country, up and down, and over hedge and ditch, and through bog and brake, without any rest." See finally W. Y. Evans Wentz, *The Fairy-Faith in Celtic Countries* (New Jersey: New Page Books, 2004), 116, where a woman refuses the hospitality of a fairy who offers her food. Consequently, the fairy imprisoned her and made her work for her in the hillock.

3. BEINGS OF LIGHT AND OF FIRE

1. Ibn Manzur, 13:92 and 2:366.

2. For a more modern interpretation of this mixing of air and fire in the jinn, see also 'Abdul-Razzaq Nawfal, *'Alam al-jinn wa-al-mala'ikah* (Cairo: Mu'assasat dar al-sha'b, 1968), 16.

3. For more details regarding the analysis of the two elements in the jinn, see ibn 'Arabi, *al-Futuhat al-makkiyyah* 1:131. See also al-Hakim, 280.

4. Nasri Nadir Albir, ed., *Min rasa'il Ikhwan al-Safa' wa khillan al-wafa'* (Beirut: al-Matba'ah al-katholikiyah, 1964), 188.

5. Ibn 'Arabi, *al-Futuhat al-makkiyyah,* 1:130–34.

6. Arthur Edward Waite, ed. *Hermetic and Alchemical Writings of Paracelsus the Great* (Edmonds, WA: Alchemical Press, 1992), 211. Paracelsus explained in detail the nature and force of the inhabitants of the four elements: the sylphs in the air, the salamanders in the fire, the undines and nymphs in the water, and the gnomes and all kinds of dwarfs in the earth.

7. On this issue, see in particular Gaston Bachelard, *Psychoanalysis of Fire,* trans. Alan C. M. Ross (Boston: Beacon Press, 1964).

8. Ibn Manzur, 13:197.

9. Toufic Fahd, "Anges, démons et djinns en Islam," in *Génies, anges et démons,* ed. Denise Bernot (Paris: Editions du Seuil, 1971), 153–215.

10. Joseph Chelhod, *Les structures du sacré chez les Arabes* (Paris: G.P. maisonneuve et Larose, 1964), 78. On the Aramaic source of the word *malak,* see also Philip Hitti, *History of the Arabs* (London: Macmillan, 1943), 106.

11. Jawad 'Ali, 6:738.

12. Ibid., 1:187.

13. On this issue, see also Toufic Fahd, *La divination arabe: Etudes religieuses, sociologiques et folkloriques sur le milieu natif de l'Islam* (Leiden: E. J. Brill, 1966), 70.

14. Muhammad ibn Jarir al-Tabari, *Tarikh al-rusul wa al-muluk,* 1:314–15. Al-Tabari relates the story of the custody of the Ka'bah. He also mentions that Ismael, to coexist with his powerful new neighbors, eventually had to marry a woman of the Jurhum, Sayyidah bint Mudad, who bore him twelve sons.

15. Hisham ibn al-Kalbi, *The Book of Idols [al-asnam]* trans. Nabih Faris (Princeton, NJ: Princeton Univ. Press, 1952), 24.

16. On the relationship of the goddesses to their temples, see especially Montgomery Watt, *Muhammad at Mecca* (Oxford: Clarendon Press, 1960), 103. Watt states "we hear of Medinian nobles having wooden representations of Manat in their houses, but on the whole the Arabs of that period probably hardly ever thought of the worship of any deity apart from the ceremonies that took place at particular shrines."

17. Mahmud Shukri al-Alusi, *Bulugh al-'arab fi ma'rifat ahwal al-'Arab* (Cairo: al-Maktabah al-ahliyah, 1924), 2:205.

18. On this issue of the religion of South Arabia, see in particular Hubert Petersman, "Le culte du soleil chez les Arabes, suivant les témoignages gréco-romains," in *L'Arabie préhistorique et son environment historique et culturel: Actes du colloque de Strasbourg, 24–27 Juin 1987*, ed. Toufic Fahd (Strasbourg: Université des sciences humaines de Strasbourg, 1989), 215–31.

19. On this issue, see also Mahmud Shukri al-Alusi.

20. See especially Qur'an 43:16 and Qur'an 52:39.

21. Theodore E. Mullen, Jr., *The Divine Council in Canaanite and Early Hebrew Literature* (Cambridge, MA: Harvard Semitic Monographs 24, Scholars Press, 1980), 184–85.

22. Ibid.

23. See also Qur'an 16:57–59.

24. On this issue see particularly 'Abd al-Salam Harun, ed. *Jamharat ansab al-'arab li ibn Hazm, 'Ali ibn Ahmad* (Cairo: Dar al-ma'arif, 1962), 451 where the names of the poet 'Abdul-jinn al-Tanukhi is mentioned, as well as the name of 'Amru ibn 'abd al-jinn.

25. On this issue, see Philip Hitti, *History of the Arabs* (London: Macmillan, 1943), 76. He draws attention to the fact that the Arabs who settled at Palmyra spoke "a dialect of Western Aramaic not unlike the Nabataean and Egyptian Aramaic." See also J. G. Février, *La religion des Palmyriens* (Paris: Librairie Philosophique J. Vrin, 1931), 209. See H. J. W. Drijvers, *The Religion of Palmyra* (Leiden: E. J. Brill, 1976), 6.

26. On this issue, see especially W. F. Albright, "Islam and the religions of the Ancient Orient," *The Journal of the American Oriental Society*, no. 60 (1940): 283–86.

27. Albright writes: "On Aramaic incantation bowls of about the sixth or seventh century from Babylonia, we find the '*gene*' appearing in the sense of 'evil spirit.' In Syriac, the derived '*genyata*' (emphatic feminine plural) means 'pagan shrines,' and sometimes 'female divinities' (the passage from an Aramaic '*ganya*' or '*genya*,' feminine '*geenita*,' 'demon,' to Arabic jinni, jinniyah offers no difficulty when one remembers that Aramaic '*gena*' and Arabic '*janna*' are synonymous." Ibid. 283. See also Javier Teixidor, *The Pagan God: Popular Religion in the Greco-Roman Near-East* (Princeton, NJ: Princeton Univ. Press, 1977), 77. Teixidor speaks of Arab gods worshiped in Palmyra as "tutelary deities." See Jean Starcky and Salah al-din al-Munajjid, *Palmyra, Bride of the Desert* (Damascus: The General Directorate of Antiquities, 1948), 248–57. The authors state "the term '*ginaya*,' found in inscriptions around Palmyra, was derived from Arabic."

28. Jean Starcky, *Palmyre* (Paris: Editions Adrien Maisonneuve, 1952), 85.

29. Cyril Glassé, ed., *The Concise Encyclopedia of Islam* (New York: Harper and Row, 1989), 210.

30. Teixidor, 79. On the Latin concept of "genie," see also Penelope Murray, *Genius: The History of an Idea* (New York: B. Blackwell Inc., 1989), 67. See Jane Chaucer Nitzche, *The Genius Figure in Antiquity and the Middle Ages* (New York: Columbia Univ. Press, 1975), 24.

31. Wentz, 291.

32. See al-Mas'udi, *Akhbar al-zaman,* 33. See also al-Shibli, 237, where he adds that the jinn even killed one of their kings named Yussef, Joseph.

33. Al-Harith is one of the names given to Satan in Muslim theology. In this context, he is still an angel sent to fight disobedient jinn/angels on Earth.

34. Diyarbakri, 1:33. See also Muhammad ibn Ahmad al-Ibshihi, *al-Mustatraf min kul fann mustazraf* (Cairo: Maktabat al-babi al-halabi, 1952), 2:149.

35. The confusion between spiritual entities in pre-Islam is in a way similar to the mythology of ancient Greece, where the concepts of angel, daemon, and god were not clearly defined as well. In Homer, for example, one finds the terms *angelos, theos* and *daimon* all refer to god.

36. For more details on the battles between spiritual entities, see Muhammad ibn 'Ali al-Kisa'i, *The Tales of the Prophets,* trans. W. M. Thackston, Jr. (Boston: Twayne Publishers, 1978), 21. See also al-Mas'udi, *Akhbar al-zaman,* 33. See Isma'il ibn Kathir, *Tafsir al-qur'an al-'azim* (Beirut: Dar al-qalam, 1983), 1:55.

37. Albir Nasri Nadir, ed., *Min rasa'il Ikhwan al-Safa',* 2:228–29. Brackets added to citation to separate the words of Ikhwan al-Safa' from the Qur'anic verse.

38. Al-Shibli, 20.

39. On this issue of jinn/angels, see especially Muhammad Mokri, "L'ange dans l'Islam et en Iran," in *Anges, démons et êtres intermédiares,* ed. Muhammad Mokri (Paris: Labergerie, 1969), 66–80. Mokri says "Le peuplement de la terre par les djinns a été traité par la plupart des exégètes qui sont restés dans le vague au sujet de la nature de ces entités."

40. Muhyi-al-din ibn 'Arabi, *Shajrat al-kawn,* trans. A. Jeffrey (Lahore: Aziz Publishers, 1980), 64.

41. Salim al-Hut, *Fi tariq al-Mitholojiya 'inda al-'Arab* (Beirut: Dar al-nahar, 1979), 265.

42. See Ahmad ibn Muhammad al-Maydani, *Majma' al-amthal* (Beirut: Dar al-kutub al-'ilmiyyah, 1988), 1:191. Al-Maydani mentions that "the saying: 'We let the country speak for itself' means wild deserts where no one lives except the jinn."

43. Al-Ibshihi, 2:149.

44. Muhammad ibn 'Abd Allah al-Azraqi, *Akhbar makkah wa ma ja'a fiha min al-'athar* (Makkah: Dar al-thaqafah, 1965), 37.

45. Isma'il ibn Kathir, *Qisas al-anbiya'* (Cairo: Dar al-kutub al-hadithah, 1968), 70.

46. As mentioned by 'Abdul-Hamid Kishk, *The World of Angels* (London: Dar al-taqwa, 1999), 44.

47. On the function of the angel as a carrier of knowledge to the prophets and an interpreter of divine messages, see also Jeffrey Burton Russell, *The Devil: Perceptions of the Evil from Antiquity to Primitive Christianity* (Ithaca, NY: Cornell Univ. Press, 1977), 198.

48. Ibn 'Arabi, *al-Futuhat al-makkiyyah,* 2:253. On the Sufi perspective of Revelation and prophethood, see William Chittick, *The Sufi Path of Love: The Spiritual Teachings of Rumi* (Albany:

State Univ. of New York, 1983), 120. Chittick maintains "Rumi often employs the term 'revelation' in referring to the special knowledge of the saint."

49. Ikhwan al-Safa', *The Case of the Animals Versus Man before the King of the Jinn: A Tenth Century Ecological Fable of the Pure Brethren of Basra,* trans. Lenn Evan Goodman (Boston: Twayne Publishers, 1978), 202.

50. See also Henry Corbin, *The Voyage and the Messenger: Iran and Philosophy* (Berkeley: North Atlantic Books, 1998).

51. 'Abd al-Qader al-Gilani, *Futuh al-ghayb* (Cairo: Maktabat al-thaqafah al-diniyyah, 2005), 16. It is worthy of note that some medieval Western scholars maintained that attaining the angelic state is not possible in this life, but only in the next one. "The just in heaven shall become like to the angels: similes angelis effecti." See Emil Schneweis, *Angels and Demons According to Lactantius* (Washington, DC: Catholic Univ. of America Press, 1944), 4.

52. Ibn 'Arabi, *Tafsir al-qur'an al-karim* (Beirut: Dar al-yaqazah, 1968), 1:40.

53. Ibid.

54. Al-Damiri, 1:210.

55. Ibid.

56. See Fahmi Jad'an, "Les anges dans la théologie musulmane" [Angels in Islamic Theology]. *Studia Islamica,* no. 41 (1975): 26. He presents the opinions of the *Mu'tazilah* regarding the nature of Iblis through their interpretation of Qur'an 18:50 "They bowed themselves, except Iblis; he was one of the jinn." Jad'an quotes al-Jahiz who provided the following gloss on the angelic origin of Iblis: "The one who is excepted, who is Iblis in the verse, belongs to the same kind of creation as the angels, hence the necessary angelic origin of Iblis."

57. Najam al-Din al-Razi, 22.

58. As in Qur'an 2:204; 3:155; 4:16–121; 16:63; and 35:6.

59. Ibn 'Arabi, *Shajrat al-kawn,* 64–65.

60. 'Abdullah ibn 'Umar al-Baydawi, *Anwar al-tanzil wa asrar al-ta'wil* (Cairo: Matba'at mustafa al-babi al-halabi, n.d.), 1:17–18.

61. Ibn 'Arabi, *al-Futuhat al-makkiyyah,* 3:367.

62. Ibid., 1:132.

63. See Kishk, 46.

64. Al-Suyuti, Jalal al-din 'Abd al-Rahman, *al-Haba'ik fi akhbar al-mala'ik* (Egypt: Maktabat al-Qur'an, 1990), 96.

65. See Seyyed Hossein Nasr, *An Introduction to Islamic Cosmological Doctrines* (Albany: State Univ. of New York, 1993), 270. Nasr describes the ascension of the soul to the heavens in Avicenna's philosophy as follows: "The soul, moreover, has contact with beings made of pure fire called *genis* [jinn] or *parsis* which exist in a realm below the terrestrial angels."

66. Henry Corbin, *Avicenna and the Visionary Recital,* trans. Willard R. Tresk (Texas: Spring Publications, 1980), 357.

67. Kishk, 76.

68. On this issue, see especially al-Tahanawi, 3:450.

69. Ibn ʿArabi, *al-Futuhat al-makkiyyah,* 1:133.

70. See al-KisaʾI, 19. He described the procreation of the jinn in these terms: "God created the first jann and called him marij (the mixed one). From him he also created a mate called marijah. Then marij lay with marijah, and she bore him a son called jann, from whom all the tribes of the jinn proceeded. Iblis, the accursed, also sprang from this race. Jann produced male jinn and female jinn. The males were mated to the females, and they grew to number seventy thousand tribes, ever increasing, until their number was like unto the sands of the desert."

71. Georg Luck, *Arcana Mundi: Magic and the Occult in the Greek and Roman Empire* (Baltimore: Johns Hopkins Univ. Press, 1985), 207.

72. One may see in these stories a kind of popular and naïve imagination that stresses the "conversion" of the jinn to the new religion.

73. Ibn ʿArabi, *al-Futuhat al-makkiyyah,* 1:133.

74. Georg Luck, 173.

75. Al-Shibli, 88.

76. Ibn ʿArabi, *al-Futuhat al-makkiyyah,* 1:132. On this issue, see also al-Shibli, 43–44. He mentions the following Hadith of the Prophet: "When the jinn of Nusaybin came to me (and they were good jinn) and asked me for food, I prayed to God that each time they pass by a bone, they might find nourishment in it."

77. Ibn ʿArabi, *al-Futuhat al-makkiyyah,* 1:132.

78. Ibid., 1:210. See appendix for more information on the different classes of the jinn.

79. Najm al-Din Razi, 70.

4. DIVINATION, REVELATION, AND THE JINN

1. For more information on the *baru,* see especially Morris Jastrow, *Aspects of Religious Belief and Practice in Babylonia and Assyria* (New York: B. Blom, 1971).

2. As defined by lexicographer ibn Manzur, 13:362. See also Toufic Fahd, "Kihana," *Encyclopedia of Islam* (Leiden: E. J. Brill, 1991), 4:421. Fahd attempted to find a solid definition for the term *kahin,* seer, and wrote: "To begin with, the etymological origin of the term kahin itself is obscure; possible roots are the Semitic root k.w.n 'to be,' 'to stand up,' and the Akkadian root k'n, which implies the idea of prostration."

3. Seers across traditions have been known to be poets, storytellers, and preservers of oral culture. On this issue, see particularly Mircea Eliade, *Myths, Dreams and Mysteries* (London: Harvill Press, 1960), 78. Eliade maintains "they [the soothsayers] are the principal custodians of the rich oral literature. The poetic vocabulary of a Yaqyt shaman comprises some 12,000 words, whilst his ordinary speech—all that is known to the rest of the community—consists of only 4,000. Among the Kasakh-Kirghizes the *baqça,* singer, poet, musician, seer, priest, and doctor, seems to be the guardian of the popular religious traditions, the custodians of legends several centuries old."

4. Ibn Manzur, 8:150.

5. See Toufic Fahd, *Encyclopedia of Islam* 4:421. In this article on the *kahin* (soothsayer), Fahd states "these functions are similar to the functions of the Hebrew *Kohen* before the institution of Monarchy, as described by the Bible." See also Ann Jeffers, *Magic and Divination in Ancient Palestine and Syria* (Leiden: E. J. Brill, 1996), 25–35. Jeffers gives the various classes of diviners in ancient Israel, such as *ro'eh, kohen, hakamin, gazerin, harasim,* etc.

6. For more details on the *sadanah* (guardians of the sanctuary), see especially al-Hut, 141. See also Abu al-Qasim Jarullah Mahmud ibn 'Umar al-Zamakhshari, *al-Kashshaf 'an haqa'iq al-tanzil* (Cairo: al-Maktabah al-tijariyah al-kubra, 1953), 207.

7. See especially ibn al-Kalbi, 49. The author mentions "the custody of the god Wudd was kept within the descendants of 'Amir al-Ajdar until the advent of Islam."

8. See 'Ali al-Mas'udi, *Muruj al-dhahab,* 2:150–52. Al-Mas'udi defines the jinn as "pure souls who predict of things to come."

9. Ibn al-Kalbi, 54.

10. Ibn Manzur, 5:84.

11. Mahmud Shukri al-Alusi, 3:269. For more details on how the jinn transmitted their knowledge to soothsayers in the pre-Islamic era, see especially al-Shibli, 154. See also al-Hut, 230.

12. Al-Mas'udi, *Akhbar al-zaman,* 122.

13. See Jurgi Zaydan, *al-A'mal al-kamilah* (Beirut: Dar al-jil, 1982), 13:285. Regarding the seer Satih, see in particular Abu Na'im Ahmad al-Isbahani, *Dala'il al-nubuwwah* (Beirut: 'Alam al-kutub, 1988), 75.

14. Shawqi Abdul-Hakim, *Madkhal ila dirasat al-folklore wa al-asatir al-'arabiyyah* (Beirut: Dar ibn khaldun, 1983), 125.

15. Al-Mas'udi, *Muruj al-dhahab,* 3:379.

16. Ibn Hisham, 'Abd al-Malik, *al-Sirah al nabawiyyah* (Cairo: Dar al-hadith, 1996), 1:131.

17. Mahmud Shukri al-Alusi, 3:296–98.

18. Jawad 'Ali, 6:762. 'Ali maintains "what is given to the seer does not belong to him but to his jinni. The latter cannot perform his job unless rewarded."

19. A. Bouché-Leclercq, *Histoire de la divination dans l'Antiquité* (Paris: Editions Leroux, 1882), 3:97.

20. Robert Flacelière, *Greek Oracles* (New York: W. W. Norton, 1965), 39.

21. Luck, 163.

22. See Michael A. Williams, "Higher Providence, Lower Providences and Fate," in *Neoplatonism and Gnosticism,* ed. Richard T. Wallis and Jay Bregman (Albany: State Univ. of New York Press, 1992) 6:493. See also the article of John P. Anton in the same book, where he speaks of "the priestly practices and the securing of the presence of daemons by means of certain rites and substances, and by employing the instructions the daemons afford, together with the interpreting of symbols, to inspect the good and attain communication with the gods." 6:19.

23. On this issue see especially E. R. Dodds, *The Greeks and the Irrational* (Berkeley: Univ. of California Press, 1951), 213.

24. Ibid., 172.

25. For further details on the Sibyls, see especially Luck, part 2: "Daemonology."

26. On this issue, see particularly H. W. Parke, *Sibyls and Sibylline Prophecy in Classical Antiquity* (New York: Routledge, 1988).

27. Al-Ibshihi, 2:91–95.

28. Ibn Manzur, 13:362.

29. Al-Shahristani, 101.

30. Ibn ʿArabi, *al-Futuhat al-makkiyyah* 2:253. In the Sufi perspective of revelation and prophethood, see Chittick, *The Sufi Path of Love*, 120.

31. See Chittick, *The Self-Disclosure of God*, 154. Did the Prophet receive revelation as a young child? Regarding Qurʾan 94:1: "Have we not expanded your chest?" it is sometimes considered as an indication that the child Muhammad was thrown to the ground by two individuals, who split him open and then washed his heart. See Muhammad Husayn Haykal, *The Life of Muhammad,* trans. Ismaʿil Raji al-Faruqi (Indianapolis, IN: American Trust Publications, 1976), 50. Haykal mentions the story of the opening of the chest, but seems not to give it any credit: "Orientalists and many Muslim scholars do not trust the story, and find the evidence therefore spurious. The biographers agree that the two men dressed in white were seen by children hardly beyond their second year of age—which constitutes no witness at all, and that Muhammad lived with the tribe of Banu Saʿd in the desert until he was five." It is worth mentioning, though, that both ibn Ishaq and ibn Hisham, the two most trusted biographers of the Prophet, did not deny this incident.

32. On the issue of how early Muslims conceived revelation as a continuation to divination, see also Toufic Fahd, *La divination arabe*, 68. Fahd asserts "certaines idées et certaines procédés divinatoires ont conservé une partie de leur prestige dans la jeune communauté islamique."

33. Many other verses in the Qurʾan deal with this view of the Meccans, that the Qurʾan is but poetry invented by the Prophet, such as Qurʾan 37:36, Qurʾan 3:30, Qurʾan 69:41, and Qurʾan 26:22.

34. The question of the differences between inspiration and revelation continues to be of great interest for Muslim scholars today. See Muhammad Sayyed Ahmad Musayyar, *al-Nubuwah al-muhammadiyah: Al wahy, al-muʿjizah, al-ʿalamiyah* (al-Jizah: Nahdat misr li al-tibaʿah wa al-nashr wa al tawziʿ, 2004). See also Muhammad Rashid Reda, *al-Wahy al-muhammadi* (Cairo: Maktabat al-manar, 1932).

35. Ibn Hisham, *Al Sirah al nabawiyyah* (Cairo: Dar al-hadith, 1995), 1:222.

36. Shawqi Dayf, *al-ʿAsr al-islami* (Cairo: Dar al-maʿarif, 1963), 30. On the impact of the Prophet on his audience, see ibn al-Hajjaj Muslim, *Sahih muslim* (Beirut: Dar al-kutub al-ʿilmiyyah, n.d.), 7:153. Meccans were not only alienated from the origin and nature of the revelation, but also perplexed and confounded regarding how to manage their lives after the advent of the new religion, as in the following address to Quraysh by al-Nadr ibn al-Harith, another notable Arab in Mecca: "Then you said he was a sorcerer, but he is not, for we have seen such people and their spitting and their knots; you said a diviner, but we have seen such people and their behavior, and we have heard their rhymes; and you said a poet, but he is not a poet, for we have heard all kinds of poetry; you said he was possessed, but he is not, for we have seen the possessed, and he shows no signs of their

gasping and whispering and delirium. Ye men of Quraysh, look to your affairs, for by God, a serious thing has befallen you" (Haykal, 136).

37. See Saleh ibn 'Abd al 'Aziz ibn Ibrahim, ed. *Mawsu'at al-hadith al sharif* (Ryad: Dar al-salam li al nashr wa al tawzi', 2000), 1. See also abu Na'im Ahmad al-Isbahani, 155, where "the voice" of revelation is "like someone throwing ironware on the rocky mountain of al-Safa."

38. On the subordination of the human receptacle to the power of revelation, see Frithjof Schuon, *The Transcendental Unity of Religions* (New York: Harper and Row, 1975), 21. Schuon wrote the following on this issue: "What man stands in absolute need of is not such and such a Revealer, but rather revelation itself, in terms that is, of its essential and unalterable content." Further, he adds: "This is to fail to realize that the ego which, in the revelations, speaks and gives law, can only be a manifestation of the divine subject and not this subject itself; one must distinguish in God—always from the point of view of revelation—firstly the one and essential Word, and then the manifestations of this Word in view of particular receptacles" (59).

39. Haykal, 75.

40. See Toufic Fahd, "Anges, génies et démons en Islam," 157.

41. The idea of converting both humans and spiritual entities to one's religion is not confined to Islam. We also encounter it in Buddhism, where we find the Buddha preaching his message to humans as well as to the *Nagas* and the *Yaqsas*. In Buddhist texts that narrate the spread of Buddhism into new territories, the conversion of spirits is a common element. See especially Sutherland, *The Disguises of the Demon,* 41. The author describes how the Buddha preached Buddhism to the spiritual entities called *Nagas*: "In the *Mahavamsa* and the *Dipavamsa,* the Buddha descends among Nagas spirits to establish the Buddhist belief: Hovering there in mid-air above the battlefield, the Master, who drives away [spiritual] darkness, called forth dread darkness over the Nagas. Then comforting those who were distressed by terror, he once again spread light abroad. When they saw the Blessed One, they joyfully did reverence to the Master's feet. Then preached the Vanquisher to them the doctrine that begets concord, and both [Naga] gladly gave up the throne to the Sage. When the Master, having alighted on the Earth, had taken his place on a seat there, and had been refreshed with celestial food and drink by the Naga-kings, he, the Lord, established in the three refuges and in the moral precepts eighty *kotis* of snake spirits, dwellers in the ocean and on the mainland."

42. Al-Shibli, 53.

43. Al-Kashani, 5:17.

44. See Mahmud Shukri al-Alusi, 13:188. Al-Alusi confirms the fact the Prophet had two significant encounters with the jinn. He cites several authorities on this issue, such as al-Tabarani, and says that some Islamic authors think that the jinn came to speak to the Prophet six times after that.

45. Muhammad Husein al-Tabatiba'i, *al-Makhluqat al-khafiyyah fi al-qur'an* (Beirut: Dar safwan, 1995), 39–40.

46. Al-Shibli, 64.

47. Cooper, 76

48. It is reported, for example, someone came to Muhammad and asked him, "O Prophet of God, I heard people quarreling and I didn't understand their language." He replied, "Muslim jinn and heretic

jinn brought a quarrel of theirs to me. They asked me to decide between dwellings for them. So I put the heretic jinn in the lowlands and the Muslim jinn in the villages between the mountains and the sea." Al-Damiri, 1:205. From this account, it is obvious popular literature highlighted the dualism between bad jinn and good jinn and added an appealing fantasy not present in the Qur'an. It emphasized acceptance of the Muslim good jinn and rejection of the heretic ones, those who refused to join the new religion. One could also find traces of this kind of popular literature in some of the prophetic tradition itself where we are told that an *'ifrit*, a kind of rebellious jinn, attempted to divert the Prophet from his prayer. God having given the Prophet power over him, he tied him to a pillar of the mosque, to show him to his Companions. Then he released him, remembering the prayer of Solomon: "Lord forgive me, and grant me a kingdom which will not be proper to any after me" (Qur'an 38:35). See Yaqut, 2:153.

49. Al-Azraqi, 2:200–201.

50. Al-Damiri, 1:208.

51. Ibid.

52. Abu Na'im Ahmad al-Isbahani, 262.

53. Ibid., 267 and 263. Al-Isbahani asserts "there were nine jinn who listened to the Prophet, one of whom was named Zawba'ah," and then he cites the names of some of the other jinn who were present, such as Hiss, Miss, Shashirah, al-Irb, Abin, and Adkham. Al-Isbahani even attempts to pinpoint the name of the first jinni who called the prayer the night the jinn came to listen to the Prophet. He says "'Abdullah ibn Mas'ud [one of the Prophet's companions] said his name was Samrah."

54. This opinion is expressed by al-Damiri, 1:204. See also Fouad 'Abd al-Baqi, *al-Lu'lu' wa-al murjan fi ma ittafaqa 'alayhi al shaykhan: Bukhari wa muslim* (Beirut: al-Maktabah al-islamiyyah, n.d.), 1:94.

55. Al-Ma'arri, 288.

56. Plutarch, *Essays*, trans. Robin Waterfield (London: Penguin Books, 1992), 294–358. Plutarch compares the voice that "visited" Socrates to what we usually experience in dreams. He finally adds this seminal remark, "The phenomenon in this case was, at a guess, not sound but a deity's voiceless message, which impinged on his intellective faculty as sheer meaning."

57. Luck, 219.

58. Fazlur Rahman, *Prophecy in Islam: Philosophy and Orthodoxy* Chicago: Univ. of Chicago Press, 1979), 74. On the issue of "internal" and "external" agents of the revelation, Rahman adds "in any case, the Muslim philosophical tradition of revelation does not envisage that total 'otherness' of the giver of revelation, which is characteristic of the Semitic tradition. The total 'otherness' was safeguarded by Philo, who regarded revelation as a suppression of the prophet's self by God, or by a divine agent."

59. Al-Zamakhshari, 3:279.

5. MAGIC, POSSESSION, DISEASES, AND THE JINN

1. Geraldine Pinch, *Magic in Ancient Egypt* (Austin: Univ.of Texas Press, 1994), 44.

2. On this issue, see especially Garth Fowden, *The Egyptian Hermes: A Historical Approach to the Late Pagan Mind* (Princeton, NJ: Princeton Univ. Press, 1993), 23.

3. Pinch, 133.

4. See especially Idries Shah, *Oriental Magic* (New York: Philosophical Library, 1957).

5. See on this issue John G. Gager, ed. *Curse Tablets and Binding Spells From the Ancient World* (Oxford: Oxford Univ. Press, 1992), 228.

6. Jeremy A. Black and Anthony Green, *Gods, Demons and Symbols of Ancient Mesopotamia: An Illustrated Dictionary* (Austin: Univ. of Texas Press, 1992), 75.

7. R. Campbell Thompson, *Semitic Magic* (London: Luzac, 1908, 97.

8. Homère, *L'Odyssée*, trans. Mario Meunier (Paris: Editions Albin Michel, 1961), 5:394–98.

9. On this issue see Pedro Entralgo, *The Therapy of the Word in Classical Antiquity* (Yale: Yale Univ. Press, 1970), 27.

10. Ibid., 10.

11. Ruth Padel, *Whom Gods Destroy: Elements of Greek and Tragic Madness* (Princeton, NJ: Princeton Univ. Press, 1995), 159.

12. Al-Zabidi, 1:478. See also al-Alusi, Mahmud Shukri, 2:323. This belief in the plague as "the spears of the jinn" can also be found in the poetry of pre-Islam; see in this context 'Amru ibn Bahr al-Jahiz, *Kitab al-hayawan* (Beirut: Manshurat al-majma' al-'arabi al-islami, 1969), 6:218.

13. Jawad 'Ali, 6:807.

14. See on this issue ibn Manzur, 11:689.

15. See on this issue Yaqut, 4:118. Yaqut speaks of a certain place near Kufa in Iraq, called *al-'azzaf* (the musician) because people claim they could hear the music played by the jinn.

16. Ibn Manzur, 9:244. To be possessed by the music of the jinn can be compared to the stories Briggs tells on the fairies in Ireland and England who bewitch humans by their music. When a human listens to this music, he becomes intoxicated and is drawn to their realm. Briggs, *The Fairies*, 21.

17. Ibn Manzur, 11:689.

18. On this issue, see Mahmud Shukri al-Alusi, 2:324. See also Dawud Dawud, *Adyan al-'arab qabla al-islam* (Beirut: al-Mu'assasah al-jami'iyyah, 1981), 375.

19. Al-Jahiz, 5:185–86.

20. Muhammad ibn Ishaq ibn al-Nadim, *al-Fihrist* (Tehran, 1971). See also Ahmad ibn Taymiyah, *Struggle Against Popular Religion and Kitab iqtida' al-sirat al-mustaqim wa-mukhalafat ashab al-jahim,* trans. 'Umar Muhammad Memon (Paris: Mouton-La Hague, 1976), 97. Ibn Taymiyah asserted "as to imitating the Persians and the Byzantines, so much of the theoretical and practical influence of Persia and Byzantium is felt in Islam that it is no secret to a Muslim learned in his faith and its fate."

21. G. Van der Leeuw, *Religion in Essence and Manifestation* (New York: Harper and Row, 1963), 609.

22. Al-Jahiz, 4:257. Al-Jahiz claims Arabs continued after the advent of Islam to believe the jinn can drink from any vessel, hence the call to cover them.

23. See Jawad 'Ali, 6:744. See also R. Campbell Thompson, 33.

24. Saleh ibn abd al-Aziz Ibn Ibrahim, ed., *Mawsu'at al-hadith al sharif* (Ryad: Dar al-salam, 2000), 264. See also ibn Khaldun, *Introduction,* trans. Franz Rosenthal (London: Routledge and Kegan, 1958), 2:156–64. Ibn Khaldun described "an act of sorcery" he witnessed in Morocco as follows: "Then he

tied a knot over the symbol in an object that he had prepared for the purpose, since he considered tying knots (and making things) stick together to be auspicious and effective in magical operations. He also entered into a pact with the jinn, asking them to participate in his spitting during the operation, intending to make the spell forceful. This (human) figure and the evil names have a harmful spirit. It issues from the sorcerer with his breath and attaches to the spittle he spits out. It produces (more) evil spirits. As a result, the things that the sorcerer intends (to happen to) the person who is cast under a spell actually befall him."

25. See Ahmad ibn Taymiyah, 1976.

26. Henry Cornelius Agrippa, *The Philosophy of Natural Magic* (Secaucus, NJ: Univ. Books, 1974), 219.

27. *Enuma Elish: The Seven Tablets of Creation,* trans. L. W. King (Escondido, CA: Book Tree Publishers, 1999), 1:73, lines 112–14.

28. Eliade, *Images and Symbols,* 92–124. Eliade devotes a whole chapter entitled "The God who Binds" to this major act of sorcery.

29. Ibn al-Nadim, 369.

30. Ibid.

31. For more information on the therapeutic value of certain verses, see especially Tewfik Canaan, "The Decipherment of Arabic Talismans," in *Magic and Divination in Early Islam,* ed. Emilie Savage-Smith (Burlington, VT: Ashgate/Variorum, 2004), 128.

32. See on this issue ibn Qayyim al-Jawziyyah, Muhammad ibn Abi Bakr, *Medicine of the Prophet,* trans. Penelope Johnstone (Cambridge: Islamic Texts Society, 1999), 128. The author mentions "Mujahid said, 'There is no harm in writing the Qur'an, washing it in water, and giving it to the sick person to drink.'" The same is reported from Abu Qilabah. It is mentioned on the authority of ibn 'Abbas: "For a woman who was having a difficult childbirth, he ordered two verses of the Qur'an to be written, soaked in water and given to her to drink."

33. Fowden, 60.

34. Ibid.

35. *The Holy Bible,* Contemporary English Version (New York: American Bible Society, 1995), 131.

36. Burton, 1:136. In the same story, one of the jinniyat converts to Islam in front of the Caliph (1:184). See also the story of "Badr Basim and Julnar of the Sea," where the wife of the king makes Badr return to his human form by reciting the Qur'an. See also al-Shibli, 123, where he tells a story of some jinn who were playing with human children, but when they heard the Qur'an's recitation, they left the children and ran away.

37. Jalal al-din 'Abd al-Rahman al-Suyuti, *al-Rahmah fi al-tibb wa al-hikmah* (Damascus: Maktabat al-hadarah, 1972), 147.

38. Ahmad ibn 'Ali al-Buni, *Shams al-ma'arif al kubra* (Beirut: Mu'assasat al-nur li al-matbu'at, 2000), 4:432. The same practices seem to have prevailed in Greece. See especially R. Campbell Thompson, 106. Thompson claims "in the *Greek Papyri* there are directions for driving out a demon by pronouncing the name, and applying sulphur and bitumen to the nostrils, whereat it will cry and go forth."

39. Jalal al-din al-Suyuti, *al-Rahmah fi al-tibb wa al-hikmah,* 174–77 and 177–83. The author mentions also that Muhammad himself cites all possible procedures to drive away the evil jinn from the body of the possessed, such as burning them with specific inhalants, striking them, and whipping them.

40. Al-Buni, 3:351.

41. Ibid., 3:350.

42. Ibn ʿArabi, *al-Futuhat al-makkiyyah,* 1:51.

43. Ibid., 1:68.

44. Al-Hakim, 320.

45. ʿAbdul-Hamid Hamdan, *ʿIlm al-huruf wa aqtabuh* (Cairo: Maktabat madbuli, 1990), 22–45 and 80. Hamdan distributes the Arabic letters following the four elements as well.

46. Al-Buni, 312.

47. See chapter 50 of the Qurʾan precisely entitled "Qaf," which starts as follows, "By Qaf and the Glorious Qurʾan."

48. See chapter 4 of this book.

49. Cooper, 36.

50. For the opponents' claims see: Qurʾan 15:6, 3:36, 44:14, and 68:51. For God's reply, see Qurʾan 52:19, 68:2, and 81:22.

51. Ibn Taymiyah, *Majmuʿ fatawa shaykh al-islam ibn taymiyah* (Riyad: Matbaʿat al-riyad, 1967), 19:58. See also R. Campbell Thompson, 101.

52. Ibn Qayyim al-Jawziyyah, 47.

53. Ibid., 48.

54. Huston Smith, *Forgotten Truth: The Primordial Tradition* (New York: Harper and Row, 1976), 44.

55. Ibn Taymiyah, *Majmuʿ fatawa shaykh al-islam ibn taymiyah,* 19:46.

56. Al-Jahiz, 6:66 and 6:215.

57. Cooper, 171.

58. Ibid., 70.

59. Yeats, *Irish Fairy and Folk Tales,* 34.

60. Jean Chevalier, and Alain Gheerbrant, *Dictionnaire des symbols* (Paris: Seghers, 1969), 3:220.

61. Ibn Qayyim al-Jawziyyah, 117.

62. In this context, see especially James George Frazer, *The Golden Bough: A Study in Magic and Religion* (London: Oxford Univ. Press, 1994) In 1890, Frazer wrote *The Golden Bough* in which he relegated magic to the lowest place in an evolutionary anthropological structure. Modern anthropologists such as Claude Lévi-Strauss rejected this classification.

6. JINN IN ANIMAL SHAPES

1. Ahmad Abu al-Hasan, *Al hayyah fi al-turath alʿarabi* (Beirut: al-Maktabah al ʿasriyah, 1997), 81.

2. Rupert Sheldrake, *The Sense of Being Stared At* (New York: Crown Publishers, 2003), 226.

3. Mircea Eliade, *Shamanism: Archaic Techniques of Ecstasy,* trans. Willard R. Trask (New York: Pantheon Books, 1964), 93–94.

4. Wallis Budge, *The Gods of the Egyptians: Studies in Egyptian Mythology* (New York: Dover Publications, 1969), 2:345. See also Henry Frankfort, *Kinship and the Gods: A Study in Ancient Near Eastern Religion as the Integration of Society and Nature* (Chicago: Univ. of Chicago Press, 1948), 162. Frankfort showed cattle were venerated in most areas of the ancient Near East, especially in Egypt. Frankfort spoke of "cattle images" and "cattle similes."

5. For a more detailed description of demons embodied in animal forms in Babylon, see especially Samuel Noah Kramer and Diane Wolkstein, *Inanna, Queen of Heaven and Earth: Her Stories and Hymns from Sumer* (New York: Harper and Row, 1983), 21. In this work, we find descriptions of "the wild haired *enkum* creatures who seized the boat of Heaven." See S. H. Hooke, *Middle Eastern Mythology* (New York: Penguin Books, 1963), 39. See also Stephanie Dalley, *Myths from Mesopotamia* (New York: Oxford Univ. Press, 1991).

6. On this issue, see especially Bernot, chapters 2, 3 and 4.

7. *Enuma Elish: The Seven Tablets of Creation,* 1:iix.

8. The term *deva* in Sanskrit means "shining one." Hinduism acknowledges three types of devas: mortals living on a superior domain to other mortals, enlightened people who have grasped the Divine, and a *Brahman* in the form of a personal God.

9. See Alain Daniélou, *The Gods of India: Hindu Polytheism* (New York: Inner Traditions International, 1985), 167–68.

10. Briggs, *The Fairies,* 11, 166. Briggs tells a story about a human child who was "exchanged" with a fairy child. When the parents discovered it, they threw the child into a fire, but, "As soon as the flame touched it, it turned into a black kitten and shot up the chimney." See also Peter M. Rojcewicz, "Between One Eye Blink and the Next: Fairies, UFOs, and Problems of Knowledge," in *The Good People: New Fairylore Essays,* ed. Peter Narváez (Lexington: Univ. Press of Kentucky, 1991), 483.

11. W. B. Yeats, *Writings on Irish Folklore, Legend, and Myth* (London: Penguin Books, 1993), 60. In the same work, Yeats tells the following intriguing story about an industrious Irish fisherman of great strength: "One night, he was coming home through the field, when he saw in front of him a small white cat. While he looked at it, the creature began to swell bigger and bigger, and as it grew in size he lost in strength, as though it sucked out his vitality. He stood for a time motionless with terror, but at last turned and fled, and as he got further away his strength came back."

12. In this context see especially Eliade, *Shamanism,* 89.

13. Jawad ʿAli, 6:817. See also al-Shibli, 121. The claim that jinn use animals for their mounts is astonishing inasmuch as jinn are thought to move with an extraordinary speed and do not need to ride on animals. One wonders, however, if this kind of assertion is not rooted in a popular belief the communication between animals and spirits could not take place without this act of riding.

14. Edward Langton, *Essentials of Demonology* (London: Epworth Press, 1981), 42.

15. Cooper, 123.

16. Al-Jahiz, 1:222.

17. Muslim ibn al-Hajjaj, 7:145.

18. Cooper, 53.

19. Abd al-Wahab ibn Ahmad al-Sha'rani, *Kashf al-hijab wal-ran 'an wajh 'as'ilat al-jann* (Beirut: Dar al kutub al-'ilmiyyah, 1999), 1.

20. Mashhur Hasan Mahmud al-Sulayman, *al-Ghoul bayna al-hadith al-nabawi wa al-mawruth al-sha'bi* (Dammam: Dar ibn al-qayyim, 1989), 20.

21. R. Campbell Thompson, 59.

22. Mahmud Shukri al-Alusi, 2:376. See also al-Shibli, 30. Al-Shibli adds other animals as mounts for the jinn, "like scorpions, cows, sheep, horses, mules, donkeys and birds."

23. Zakariya ibn Muhammad al-Qazwini, *'Aja'ib al-makhluqat* (Cairo: Dar al-tahrir, n.d), 260.

24. Al-Mas'udi, 2:294

25. Al-Ma'arri, 285–86.

26. Budge, *The Gods of the Egyptians*, 37.

27. W. R. Smith, *Lectures on the Religion of the Semites: The Fundamental Institutions* 3d ed. (New York: Macmillan, 1927), 168 and 588.

28. On this issue, see especially James Hastings, ed. *The Encyclopedia of Religion and Ethics* (New York: Scribner, 1928), 11:404.

29. The Holy Bible, 718.

30. S. H. Hooke, ed. *Myth and Ritual: Essays on the Myth and Ritual of the Hebrews in Relation to the Culture Pattern of the Ancient East* (Oxford: Oxford Univ. Press, 1933), 76.

31. Jean Varenne, "Anges, génies et démons dans l'Inde" in Bernot, 278.

32. Jawad 'Ali, 5:47.

33. Al-Damiri, 1:282.

34. Ibid., 283.

35. See the appendix, where *shaytan* is described as being a kind of jinn in pre-Islam.

36. Al-Maydani, 1:84. See also Hastings, 1:670 where the German orientalist Theodor Noldeke (d. 1930) states the use of the term *shaytan* to refer to a serpent is even older than the use of the term jinn.

37. Al-Azraqi, 2:16–17.

38. Ibn al-Athir, 34.

39. Ahmad ibn Muhammad al-Tha'labi, *Qisas al-anbiya'* (Cairo: Maktabat al-jumhuriyyah al-'arabiyyah, 1902), 25.

40. Ibid., 18.

41. See the section on ghouls in the appendix.

42. See the appendix, where the story of the ghoul Sa'dan is mentioned. For more information on the ghoul's conversion, see the whole tale in Burton, 4:137.

43. Timothy K. Beal, *Religion and Its Monsters* (New York: Routledge, 2002), 6.

44. See the appendix, the section on *nasnas*.

45. In contrast to this Islamic perspective, see Mircea Eliade, *The Sacred and the Profane*, trans. Willard R. Trask (New York: Harcourt Brace, 1959), 20. Eliade maintains "the former is the world

(more precisely, our world), the cosmos; every thing outside it is no longer a cosmos but a sort of 'other world,' a foreign, chaotic space, peopled by ghosts, demons, 'foreigners.' It is not difficult to see why the religious moment (i.e., the manifestation of the sacred) implies the cosmogonic moment."

46. Ikhwan, 1978.

47. Al-Damiri, 1:285. See also al-Qazwini, 170, who maintains "human beings are a kind of animals, the jinn are animals of fire, transparent, and capable of taking different forms." In this same context, see also Annemarie Schimmel, *Islam and the Wonders of Creation: The Animal Kingdom* (London: al-Furqan Islamic Heritage Foundation, 2003). Schimmel highlights the centrality of animals in Islamic literature. Equally seminal from the Islamic perspective is the fact all these forms of life, *al-hayawan,* are aware of the Divine and worship him, each in its own manner. It is in this context that ibn 'Arabi maintained there are some saints among these species, and he wishes one day to become as pious as they are, for their worship of God is exemplary. See al-Hakim, 368.

7. LOVE BETWEEN HUMANS AND JINN

1. Abdul-Sattar Ahmad Farraj, ed. *Diwan majnun Laila* (Cairo: Maktaba misr, 1963), 73.

2. Jawad 'Ali. 6:714. See al-Jahiz, 6:218. See also ibn Manzur, 8:29. See 'Abdul-Hakim, 37.

3. Ibid.

4. Ziad Muna, *Balqis: 'imr 'at al-'alghaz wa shytanat al-jins* (London: Riyad al-Rayyes, 1997), 65–66. The myth mentions also an interesting detail: Balqis's feet were similar to a donkey's hooves. This podal oddity is shared by many demons and spirits across traditions like, for example, the fauns, the satyrs, and some kind of Nereids who are pictured as having goats' feet. This characteristic indicates otherness and alerts the human to a deformity that might be dangerous. In any case, it creates distance and fear in the human, who is intrigued and cautious, even when in love with these supernatural beings.

5. Ibn al-Nadim, 367. The author claims two persons were known to invent these love stories between the two species. One was called Ahmad ibn Dallan, and the other ibn al-Attar.

6. Al-Damiri, 1:213.

7. Jalal al-din al-Suyuti, *Laqt al-murjan fi ahkam al-jann,* 66.

8. Al-Shibli, 89. The name of this jurist is Jalal al-din Ahmad ibn Husam al-Razi.

9. Ibid., 91.

10. Mahmud ibn Abdullah al-Alusi, *Ruh al-ma'ani fi tafsir al-qur'an al-'azim wa al-sab' al-mathani* (Cairo: Idarat al-tiba'ah al munirah, 1926), 14:118. The author mentions "as for claiming that jinn sleep with human women if their husbands do not mention the name of God during intercourse, there is no agreement among the scholars on this matter!"

11. Ibid., 56.

12. Jalal al-din al-Suyuti, *Laqt al-murjan fi ahkam al-jann,* 54.

13. Ibid., 57.

14. Rojcewicz, 482.

15. Ibid., 482.

16. Jalal al-din al-Suyuti, *Laqt al-murjan fi ahkam al-jann,* 64.

17. Joseph Campbell, *The Hero with a Thousand Faces,* 3d ed. (Princeton, NJ: Princeton Univ. Press, 1973), 40.

18. Mircea Eliade, *The Myth of the Eternal Return: or, Cosmos and History* (New Jersey: Princeton Univ. Press, 1991), 40.

19. Haddawy, 1:28.

20. Ibid.

21. In this context, see especially Tzvetan Todorov, *Introduction à la littérature fantastique* (Paris: editions du Seuil, 1970), 29.

22. Edith Hamilton, *Mythology: Timeless Tales of Gods and Heroes* (New York: Penquin Books, 1982), 114.

23. Briggs, *The Fairies,* 124–25.

24. Haddawy, 1:9.

25. Ibid., 96. She tells him her story, "I too shall tell you my tale. I am the daughter of Aftimarus, king of the Ebony Island. He married me to one of my cousins, but on my wedding night a jinni snatched me up, flew away with me, and a while later set me down in this place."

26. See Yeats, *Irish Fairy and Folk Tales,* 93. Allegedly, the same motif occurs with the fairies. It is believed maidens are taken into Fairyland unwillingly, on the eve of a human wedding. In the fairy story entitled "Master and Man," one of the "little people" goes to a place where a wedding is being celebrated to attempt an abduction of the bride: "And to that purpose," said the little man, "have I come all the way to Carrigogunniel; for in this house, this very night, is young Darby Riley going to be married to Bridget Rooney; and as she is a tall and comely girl, and has come of decent people, I think of marrying her myself, and taking her off with me." In the same work, Yeats mentions "On Midsummer Eve, when the bonfires are lighted on every hill on honor of St. John, the Fairies are at their gayest, and sometimes steal away beautiful mortals to be their brides" (2).

27. See also Ikhwan, 84. One of the sage jinn epitomizes the jinn's apprehension in these terms: "O company of jinn let us not become exposed to them (humans) and ruin our relations with them. Let us not incite their weakling hatred that would ignite that deeply rooted prejudice toward us which is so entrenched in their human nature."

28. Cooper, 50.

29. This is how the hero Janshah is described approaching the castle: "As he drew near the gates he saw an old man of comely aspect and face shining with light standing there with a staff of carnelian in his hand, and going up to him, saluted him." Burton, 5:343.

30. Ibid., 5:374.

31. Ibid., 8:45. "Wherefore he fell sick and abode on the palace-roof expecting her return and abstaining from eat and drink and sleep, and he ceased not to be so till the new moon showed, when behold, they again made their appearance according to custom and doffing their dresses went down into the basin."

32. Stith Thompson, *The Folktale* (New York: Dryden Press, 1946), 88.

33. See Lena Jayyusi, ed., *The Adventures of Sayf ben Dhi Yazn: An Arab Folk Epic* (Bloomington: Indiana Univ. Press, 1996), 172. A very similar story to the preceding two narratives exists as well in this popular Arab saga. The same pattern with similar details is carried out. Sayf finds the jinniyah of his heart in a castle. One look at her and he almost loses his mind: "Now as King Sayf gazed on her, he was seized with imaginings, becoming ever more possessed, transported from one state to another. As for Queen Munyat an Nufus, she went down into the fountain with the maidens and began to disport herself with them, and they with her, all making merry together, with none to keep watch over them. They began to embrace as a lover embraces his beloved, their perfumes wafting out from them, so that the garden was filled with musk and scent. At that King Sayf sensed fire and flame kindling in his loins, and was seized with torment; unable to endure, he was ready almost to lose his mind, afflicted by love's ailment over which no physician has power."

34. See Briggs, *The Fairies*, 17, 95.

35. Joseph Jacobs, ed., *Celtic Fairy Tales* (London: David Nutt Publisher, 1892), 2.

36. Ibid., 4.

37. Bernot, 276–77. It is said in this legend that the act of Arjuna is considered an act of virtue since by satisfying the *Nagini's* desires, he prevented her from committing suicide.

38. Burton, 5:346.

39. Ibid., 7:330. A very similar tale to Sayf al-Muluk's exists in Indian folklore. It is entitled "The Prince and the Painted Fairy." Like Sayf al-Muluk, the Indian prince Manohara falls instantly in love with the painting. Both princes pine and languish after these figures. In the case of the Indian tale, the fairy in the painting speaks to the prince and entrances him. Then she disappears: "The fairy vanished, and so did Manohara's reason. Bakula and the other friends were desperate when they saw his condition. But they had heard what the fairy had said, and, when the prince regained consciousness, they said: 'Enough! Don't despair, for Sukumarika is easily found.'" Van Johannes Adrianus Bernardus Buitenen, ed., *Tales of Ancient India* (Chicago: Univ. of Chicago Press, 1959), 171–72.

40. For more information on these two kinds of French fairy tales, see especially Laurence Harf-Lancner, *Les fées au Moyen Age: Morgane et Mélusine: La naissance des fées* (Genève: Editions Slatkine, 1984)

41. Ja'afar al-Sarraj, *Masari' al-'ushaq* (Amman: al-Maktabah al-wataniyyah, 2004), 484–87.

42. Meaning "mad about Laila."

43. Jean-Claude Vadet, *L'esprit courtois en orient dans les cinq premiers siècles de l'hégire* (Paris: G.P. Maisonneuve et Larose, 1968), 378. Vadet states "Le fou par excellence est aussi le poète par excellence, le poète surhumain celui qui vit comme les djinns, et qui a la clairvoyance des djinns parcequ'il a subi leur blessure mortelle mais libératrice."

44. Khairallah, 24.

45. Abdal-Sattar Ahmad Farraj, ed. *Diwan majnun Laila* (Cairo: Maktabtat misr, 1963), 215.

46. Ibid., 84.

47. Ibid., 73.

48. James Atkinson, *Laili and Majnun: A Poem From the original Persian of Nizami* (London: A. J. Valpy Publishers, 1836), 109–10.

8. JINN INSPIRING POETS

1. Abu al-Faraj al-Isbahani, *Kitab al-aghani* (Cairo: Dar al-sha'b, 1969), 9:3144.

2. On the relationship of poetry to sacredness and to primordial man, see in particular Martin Lings, *Symbol and Archetype: A Study in the Meaning of Existence* (Cambridge: Quinta Essentia, 1991), 58–67. See also Jacqueline de Romilly, *Magic and Rhetoric in Ancient Greece* (Cambridge, MA: Harvard Univ. Press, 1975), 4.

3. See Gerald Else, *Plato and Aristotle on Poetry* (Chapel Hill: Univ. Press of North Carolina, 1986), 63.

4. Edith Hamilton, ed. *The Collected Dialogues of Plato* (New York: Pantheon Books, 1961), 492.

5. Some orientalists hold the astonishing opinion the poetry of the pre-Islamic period is devoid of any originality or spirituality. See in particular. W. R. Smith, 49. The author claims "it is true that there is not much mythology in the poetry of heathen Arabic. But Arabian poetry has little to do with religion at all."

6. See Alfred Guillaume, *Prophétie et divination chez les sémites* (Paris: Payot, 1950), 243–98. Guillaume maintains "no prophet speaking in the name of Yahve would find an audience if he were not a poet."

7. Joseph Sendry, ed. *John Keats: A Thematic Reader* (Glenview, IL, Scott, Foresman, 1971), 196.

8. Federico Garcia Lorca, *In Search of Duende* (New York: New Directions, 1998), 49. It is interesting to note the Duende, unlike the Muse or the jinn, seems to affect not only the poet, but the audience as well.

9. On the issue of the Holy Spirit in the work of Milton, see also Merrit Hughes, ed. *John Milton: Complete Poetry and Major Prose* (New York: Odyssey Publishers, 1957), 64–72. See also Lings, 66.

10. See Lings, 6.

11. Lewis Ellingham and Kevin Killian, *Poet Be Like God: Jack Spicer and the San Francisco Renaissance* (New Hampshire: Univ. Press of New England, 1998), 183. "He became convinced that he was in touch with— and perhaps had been in touch for years—a great 'Outside' force, as powerful and omniscient as the spirits that visited Blake and attended the séances of William and George Yeats, or those who wrote the 'Sonnets to Orpheus' through Rilke. He was now a radio, picking up transmissions from 'ghosts.'"

12. Many other verses of the Qur'an refer to this issue. See especially Qur'an 53:30; 69:41 and 37:36.

13. See Ihsan 'Abbas, *Tarikh al-naqd al-adabi 'inda al-'arab: naqd al shi'r min al-qarn al thani hatta al-qarn al thamen al-hijri* (Amman: Dar al-shuruq, 1993), 26–27.

14. Ibid., 23.

15. Abu 'Amir ibn Shuhayd, *Risalat al-tawabi' wa al-zawabi'* (Beirut: Dar sader, 1967).

16. Ibid., 92.

17. Ibid., 102.

18. Ibid., 93.

19. An unknown poet of pre-Islam is believed to have composed the following verse in which he immortalizes his "friendship" with his jinni. He doesn't represent him as his double. However,

the bond between the two appears immensely strong. "I am a man whose follower is a jinni / I befriended him, and he befriended me for life / He drinks from my cup / And I drink from his cup / Thanks Be to God who gave him to me!" Ali, Jawad, 6:734.

20. Abu Zaid al-Qurashi, *Jamharat ash'ar al-'arab* (Beirut: Dar al-kutub al-'ilmiyyah, 1986), 40–55. The author gives the name of Imru' al-Qays's jinni as Lafiz ibn Hafiz.

21. Ibid., 7.

22. Abu al-Faraj al-Isbahani, 9:3144. See also 'Abdullah ibn Muslim ibn Qutaybah, *al-Shi'r wa al-shu'ara'* (Beirut: Dar al-thaqafah, 1969), 502.

23. 'Abd al-Rahman al-Barquqi, ed., *Diwan Hassan ibn Thabit* (Cairo: al-Maktabah al-tijariyah al-kubra, 1929), 174, 422.

24. Edward Hirsch, *The Demon and the Angel: Searching For the Source of Artistic Inspiration* (New York: Harcourt, 2002), 67.

25. Robert Graves, *The White Goddess: a Historical Grammar of Poetic Myth* (New York: Farrar, Straus and Giroux, 1966), 24.

26. Al-Jahiz, 6:228.

27. Ibid., 228.

28. Ibid., 1:141.

29. Hirsch, 74.

30. See Abu al-Faraj al-Isbahani, *Kitab al-aghani,* 7:3711.

31. Ibid., 13:4516.

32. Ibid., 8:2769.

33. Yeats, *Irish Fairy and Folk Tales,* 285–86.

34. Al-Ma'arri, 283. *Ash'ar al-jinn* (the jinn's poetry) is collected by literary compiler abu 'Ubaidillah al-marzubani (d. 994), and quoted by many literary sources. Nonetheless, it seems to have been lost, as is the case with many Arabic manuscripts. See also ibn al-Nadim, 147.

35. Al-Ma'arri, 283.

36. Ibid., 284. The jinni poet recites to the narrator a very long poem. It is a kind of synthesis of the jinn's behavior toward humans. See also Ibid., 286–88.

37. Al-Hut, 277.

38. Abu al-Faraj al-Isbahani, *al-Aghani,* 11:160–61.

39. Ibid., 2:339.

40. Ibn Manzur, 1:95. For more information on Hassan ibn thabit, see also Abu al-Faraj al-Isbahani, *al-Aghani,* 3:862–63.

41. Al-Jahiz, 6:225; al-Hut, 281; *Encyclopedia of Islam,* 1:689.

42. Abu al-Faraj al-Isbahani, *al-Aghani,* 2:595. See also al-Qurashi, 60–61.

43. See 'Abbas, 26–27.

44. For a view of Indian and Chinese poetics, see especially Ray Livingston, *The Traditional Theory of Literature* (Minneapolis: Univ. of Minnesota Press, 1962). See also Krishna Chaitanya, *Sanskrit Poetics: A Critical and Comparative Study* (New York: Asia Publishing House, 1965).

45. James J. Y. Liu, *The Art of Chinese Poetry* (London: Routledge and Kegan Paul, 1962), 81.

CONCLUSION: THE SENTIENCE OF INSIDE OUT/OUTSIDE IN

1. Huston Smith, *Why Religion Matters* (New York: Harper and Collins, 2001), 265

APPENDIX: THE DIFFERENT CLASSES OF THE JINN

1. Al-Jahiz, 6:48.

2. Al-Zabidi, 8:51.

3. Al-Jahiz, 6:220.

4. Ibid., 6:159.

5. Dawud, 365.

6. Abu al-Faraj al-Isbahani, 24:8323.

7. Dayf, *al-'Asr al-jahili* (Cairo: Dar al-ma'arif, 1977), 95.

8. Al-Mas'udi, *Muruj al-dhahab,* 2:135

9. Al-Jahiz, 6:158.

10. Burton, 6:142.

11. Ibn Kathir, *Tafsir al-qur'an al-'azim,* 6:289.

12. Burton, 7:274.

13. See also in this context the story "The Youth of Ispahan." In Shah, *World Tales,* 78.

14. Al-Mas'udi, *Muruj al-dhahab,* 2:208.

15. Al Jahiz, 2:131.

16. Ibn Manzur, 13:132. For more information on the nature of the *hinn,* see especially abu Bakr Muhammad ibn Durayd, *al-Ishtiqaq* (Beirut: al-Maktab al-tijari,1958), 548. See Yaqut, 2:313.

17. Ibn Manzur, 4:586.

18. Ibid., 3:400.

19. Al-Mas'udi, *Muruj al-dhahab* 2:208.

20. Al-Jahiz, 6:181. The same author also says, "The nasnas is a lower form of jinn" (7:178).

21. Abu hanifah Ahmad al-Dinawari, *al-Akhbar al-tiwa*l (Cairo: Wizarat al-thaqafah wa al-irshad al-qawmi, 1960), 12. See also al-Mas'udi, *Muruj al-dhahab,* 2:209.

22. Al-Mas'udi, *Muruj al-dhahab,* 2:208.

23. Ibn Manzur, 6:230–32.

24. Najm al-Din al-Razi, 82. See also al-Qazwini, 384. Al-Qazwini mentions "the nasnas was born from the union of a demon and a human being. He mainly lives in Yemen and speaks Arabic!"

25. There is still another definition of *nasnas* in some Indian sources. See Seyyed Hossein Nasr, *Science and Civilization in Islam* (Cambridge, MA: Harvard Univ. Press, 1968), 118. Nasr mentions a certain Indian author, Buzurg ibn Shabriyar, who considered the "apeman" similar to the *nasnas.*

26. Al-Mas'udi, *Muruj al-dhahab,* 2:140.

27. Al-Jahiz, 6:206.

28. Ibn Manzur, 10:605. For more details on the life of this intriguing pre-Islamic figure, see Mahmud Shukri al-Alusi, 3:278. See also al-Zabidi, 6:396; see al-Tabari, *Tarikh al-rusul wa al-muluk,* 1:911.

29. Joseph Campbell, *The Hero with a Thousand Faces,* 78.

30. Al-Jahiz, 7:375.

31. Ahmad ibn Faris, *Mu'jam maqayis al-lughah* (Cairo: Dar ihya' al-kutub al-'arabiyyah, 1946), 74.

32. Mahmud Shukri al-Alusi, 341.

33. Al-Damiri, 2:223.

34. Al-Jahiz, 4:481.

35. Al-Zabidi, 8:51.

36. Al-Jahiz, 6:190.

37. Al-Mas'udi, *Muruj al-dhahab,* 2:138. He describes the birth of all these weird jinn/beings as follows: "So the wife of the jann laid thirty-one eggs. From one of these eggs came qutrubah who is the mother of all the qutrubs. She has the shape of a cat. From another egg were born the iblises (demons), among whom is al-Harith abu Murrah. They live in the sea. The marids were born from another egg. They live on islands. Then the ghouls were born from yet another egg. They live in deserts and empty places. The si'lats came from a different egg. They live in heaps of dirt and in bathrooms. As for the *hawam,* they were born from another egg. They live in the air, and have the forms of flying snakes, etc."

38. Ibn Manzur, 11:336. See also al-Jahiz, 4:481–86, 4:158–59. See also *The Encyclopedia of Islam,* 2:1078.

39. Mahmud Shukri al-Alusi, 2:346.

40. Ibn Manzur, 11:507.

41. Mahmud Shukri al-Alusi, 2:342.

42. See R. Campbell Thompson, *Semitic Magic.*

43. Abu al-Hasan Ahmad, 81.

Glossary of Arabic Words and Names

'Abdal: a group of Muslim "saints," highly revered by Sufis.

'Abdul-Muttalib: the grandfather of Muhammad (d. 577).

'Abid ibn al-Abras: Pre-Islamic Arab poet and author of one of the ten *mu'allaqat* (the odes hanging on the walls of Ka'bah) (killed a few years before 540).

Abu, aba, abi: different grammar forms of "father of."

Abu Bakr al-Siddiq: the first caliph (d. 634).

Abu Hadrash: proper name of a jinni.

'Ad: 'Ad and Thamud were two of the perished Arabian tribes. They are mentioned in the Qur'an as rejecting their prophets and being destroyed by God as a result.

'Afarit (sing. 'ifrit): term used to describe the jinn. See appendix for further explanation.

'A'isha/'A'ishah: wife of the Prophet Muhammad.

'Ali ibn abi Taleb: the Prophet's son-in-law and the fourth caliph (d. 661).

'Amaliq: the Amalekite (lit.: giants).

'Amir al-Ajdar: one of the custodians of Wudd; a pre-Islamic idol.

'Amru ibn Luhayy: a seer of pre-Islamic period reputed to have lived in the third century CE.

'Amru ibn Yarbu': legendary forefather of an Arab tribe of Banu [children of] *si'lat*.

'Asatir (sing. 'usturah): myths.

Asha'ira: school of early Muslim philosophy and jurisprudence named after its founder, Abu al-Hasan al-Ash'ari (d. 945).

Asma' allah al-husna: God's Most Beautiful [99] Names.

al-Asnam [The idols]: title of a book on the pagan gods and goddesses in pre-Islamic Arabia authored by Hisham ibn al-Kalbi (d. 819).

'Asr: name of a tribe of the jinn.

Balqis: queen of Sheba.

Banu, bani: different grammar forms of "children of."

Banu 'Amru ibn 'Amir: tribe of jinn.

Banu Ashja': a tribe of jinn (lit.: children of snake).

Banu Dhi'b: an Arab tribe (lit.: children of wolf).

Banu Ghazwan: a tribe of jinn.

Banu Sa'd: an Arab tribe.

Banu Sahm: an Arab tribe.

Banu Shaysaban: a tribe of jinn.

Barzakh: isthmus.

al-Basrah: city in southern Iraq founded in 638 that played an important role in shaping the early Islamic culture. In *The Nights,* al-Basrah was the port from which the legendary Sindbad sailed.

al-Basri, al-Hasan: Muslim theologian and founder of the School of al-Basrah (b. 642). Among his many pupils was Wasil ibn 'Ata' (d. 761), the founder of the Mu'tazilah school of philosophy.

Beisan (Beth-Shan, House of Shan): a Canaanite god and a city in the Jordan Valley.

al-Bukhari, Muhammad ibn Isma'il: compiler of the first and most authentic collection of the Prophet Muhammad's sayings (d. 870).

Dahrash: a tribe of jinn.

al-Dajjal: anti-Christ (lit.: the Imposter).

Dhu al-Khimar: a false prophet who arose in Yemen in 632.

Dimiryat: king of the jinn.

Diwan: collection of poetry.

Dukhan: smoke; title of one of the Qur'an's chapters.

Dura: a place northwest of Palmyra, Syria.

Fatiha: the opening of the Book; the first *surah* (chapter) of the Qur'an.

Fatik: name of jinni, poetry inspirer.

Fatimah bint al-Nu'man: a woman-seer of the pre-Islamic period.

Fitrah: the human innate or natural disposition toward right and wrong. According to the prophetic tradition quoted by both al-Bukhari and Muslim: "Every newborn is born in this innate or natural disposition."

al-Ghasasinah (or the Ghassanides): an Arab Christian tribe. Long before the advent of Islam, they emigrated from Arabia and settled in south of Syria, where they founded their kingdom.

Ghayb: the unseen.

Ghoul/ghoulah: a category of jinn. See appendix.

Hadith: the prophetic tradition relating to the words and deeds of the Prophet Muhammad.

Hadith Qudsi: the sayings of the Prophet Muhammad, but unlike other Hadith, their authority is related to God.

Hajj: the pilgrimage to Mecca. It is a duty owed to God by all Muslims who are able to undertake it.

Hamah ibn Laqqis ibn Iblis: name of a jinni, grandson of Satan.

Hanafite, Hanafiyyah, Ahnaf: school of jurisprudence founded by the jurist Abu Hanifah, al-Nu'man in the eighth century.

Hawbar: name of a jinni, poetry inspirer.

Hawjal: name of a jinni, poetry inspirer.

Hayyah: snake.

Hijrah: the Prophet's migration to Madinah in 622 CE.

Hinn: a kind of jinn. See appendix.

Hira' (Cave of Hira'): located on a peak of Alnour (light) mountain near Mecca, it is where Muhammad received the first Revelation.

al-Hirah: an ancient Arab city in today's Iraq. In the fifth and sixth centuries, al-Hirah was the capital of the Lakhmide kingdom—the first Arab kingdom outside Arabia.

Hubal: a god worshiped in Mecca before Islam. Hubal's idol at the Ka'bah was the grandest of the idols.

Hudhayl: an Arab tribe.

Hulwan: a "sweet reward."

Iblis: Satan

Ibn 'Abbas, 'Abdullah: one of the Prophet's companions (d. 688).

Ibn al-'Awwam, Labid: the man who bewitched the Prophet Muhammad.

Ibn al-Mas'ud, al-Husayn 'Ali: one of the Prophet's companions (d. 652).

Ikhwan al-Safa(the Brethren of Purity): a group of philosophers who lived in Basra, Iraq, during the tenth century.

'Ifrit: a kind of jinn. See appendix.

Ilham: inspiration.

Israfil: According to popular Islam, Israfil is one of the archangels. He is responsible for signaling the Day of Judgment by blowing a horn (*sur*).

Jabal al-sha'r: a mountain northwest of Palmyra, Syria.

Jabalqa and Jabarsa: mythical cities.

al-Jahiz, 'Amru ibn Bahr: Mu'tazilite scholar and one of the most influential prose writers in classical Arabic literature (d. 868).

Jan: another name of the jinn and also the father of all jinn.

Jibril: Arabic for the angel Gabriel.

Jinni: one of the male jinn.

Jinniyah: one of the female jinn.

Jurhum: an Arab tribe.

Ka'bah: the holiest shrine in Islam for pagan Arabs before Islam. According to the Qur'an, the Ka'bah was built by Ibrahim (Abraham) and his son Isma'il (Ishmael).

Kahin: seer/soothsayer.

al-Kufah: An Iraqi city, founded and given its name by the Prophet's companion Sa'd ibn abi Waqqas in 637. Opposite to al-Basrah's liberal school of thought, al-Kufah was a center for conservative theology and scholarship.

al-Lat: pre-Islamic Arabian goddess worshiped in Mecca as one of God's daughters.

al-Lawh al-mahfuz: "The preserved record" of heaven upon which the Qur'an is inscribed since all eternity (Qur'an 85:22). Some commentators take this verse in its literal sense. For others, the verse has a metaphorical meaning.

al-Ma'arri, Abu al-'Ala' Ahmad: a cynical Arab poet and philosopher (d. 1057). Many literary historians, including Spanish scholar and Roman Catholic priest Miguel Asín Palacios (1871–1944) in his *La Escatología Musulmana en la Divina Comedia* (Islam and the Divine Comedy), hold that al-Ma'arri's divine comedy *Risalat al-Ghufran* (The epistle of forgiveness) clearly had an influence on, or even inspired, Dante's *Divine Comedy*.

Majnun Laila: "mad for Laila"; the seventh-century love poet Qays ibn al-Mullawwah (d. 668).

Mala'ikah (sing. **malaak** and **malak**): angels.

Manat: pre-Islamic Arabian goddess worshiped in Mecca as one of God's daughters.

Marid: giant jinni. See appendix.

al-Mu'allaqat: the best seven (or ten) odes by leading pre-Islamic poets. They were considered absolute masterpieces and were honored by being inscribed in gold and hung on the walls of Ka'bah.

Murji'ah: an early Islamic school of theology that emerged after the Khawarj rebellion against 'Ali ibn abi Taleb, the fourth caliph. It advocates the idea that only God has the right to judge who are the true faithful and who are not.

Muslim, Abu al-Qasim Muslim ibn al-Hajjaj al-Naysaburi: compiler of the second most authentic collection of Muhammad's sayings (d. 875).

Nas: Arabic for "people."

Nasnas: kind of jinn. See appendix.

Nasr: one of five gods mentioned in the Qur'an (71:22) worshiped by pre-Islamic Arabs.

Nusaybin: the city (now in Turkey) of the jinn delegation to the Prophet Muhammad.

Qadariyyah: a school of thought centered on the divine destiny of man and his acts.

Qaf: mythical mountain.

Qashqash: proper name of a *marid*, or giant jinni.

Qur'an: the holy book of Islam. Muslims regard it as a continuation of other divine messages including Judaism and Christianity. The Qur'an addresses both humans and jinn. One of its chapters (Qur'an 72) is entitled "al-Jinn."

Quraysh: the tribe of the Prophet.

Rabb al-'alamin: Lord of the Worlds. Muslims start their prayers with the *fatiha,* the opening chapter of the Qur'an, which begins with these words: "Praise belongs to God, the Lord of the worlds," *rabb al-'alamin.* Muslims repeat the expression *rabb al-'alamin* in the *fatiha* several times during their five daily prayers. By *al-'alamin',* the Qur'an is referring to all kinds of existence, whether physical or nonphysical.

al-Rahman (the merciful): one of the ninety-nine "Beautiful Names of God," and the title of one of the Qur'an's chapters.

Ra'i: visionary.

Rawi/Rawiyah: the person who follows the poet, and whose function is to memorize his poetry and recite it to others for it not to be lost (lit.: the narrator).

al-Ruh al-Amin: a designation of Jibril (Gabriel), the Angel of Revelation (lit.: the faithful or trustworthy spirit).

al-Ruh al-Qudus: another designation of Jibril (Gabriel). It is mentioned three times in the Qur'an in relation to Jesus, son of Mary (lit.: the Holy Spirit).

Sadin (pl. **sadanah**): custodian, guardian of the sanctuary.

al-Safa: al-Safa and al-Marwah are two relatively high places in the holy shrine of al-Ka'bah, Mecca, where Muslims perform part of their Hajj's rituals.

Satih: a legendary Arab seer in pre-Islam.

Shahadah: the Muslim declaration of belief in the Oneness of God and in Muhammad as his Messenger.

Sha'ir: poet.

Shaytan: devil.

Shiqq: the proper name of a historical figure, a soothsayer in pre-Islam.

Si'lat: a kind of jinn. See appendix.

Surah/Surat: chapter of the Qur'an.

Suwa': one of five gods mentioned in the Qur'an (71:22) worshiped by pre-Islamic Arabs.

Tafsir: a term used for the commentary on the Qur'an.

al-Ta'if: a city near Mecca.

al-Thaqalan: the humans and the jinn (Qur'anic term).

'Umar ibn al-Khattab: the second caliph.

'Ummar (sing. **'amer**): home-dwelling jinn in snake shape.

'Umrah: a pilgrimage to Mecca that can be undertaken at any time of year.

al-'Uzza: pre-Islamic Arabian goddess worshiped in Mecca as one of God's daughters.

al-Wahy: Islamic term for the Revelation of God to his prophets and messengers and certain privileged elites.

Wudd: one of five gods mentioned in the Qur'an (71:22) worshiped by pre-Islamic Arabs.

Zubayr: an Arab name and a name of poetry inspirer jinni.

References

IN ARABIC

'Abbas, Ihsan. *Tarikh al-naqd al-adabi 'inda al-'arab: naqd al-shi'r min al-qarn al-thani hatta al-qarn al-thamen al-hijri.* Amman: Dar al-shuruq, 1993.

'Abd al-Baqi. *See* 'Abdul-Baqi.

'Abd al-Hakim. *See* 'Abdul-Hakim.

'Abd-Allah. *See* 'Abdullah.

Abd al-Rahim, Muhammad, ed. *Tafsir al-hasan al-basri.* Cairo: Dar al-hadith, 1992.

'Abdul-Baqi, Fouad. *Alfaz al-qur'an al-karim.* Beirut: Dar al-fikr, 1983.

———. *al-Lu'lu' wa al-murjan fi ma ittafaqa 'alayhi al-shaykhan: Bukhari wa muslim.* Beirut: al-Maktabah al-islamiyyah, n.d.

'Abdul-Hakim, Shawqi. *Madkhal ila dirasat al-folklore wa al-asatir al-'arabiyyah.* Beirut: Dar ibn khaldun, 1983.

'Abdullah, Riyad. *al-Jinn wa-al-shayatin bayn al-'ilm wa-al-din.* Damascus: Dar al-hikmah, 1986.

Abu al-Hasan, Ahmad. *Al hayyah fi al-turath al-'arabi.* Beirut: al-Maktabah al-'asriyah, 1997.

al-A'lami, Husain, ed. *Tafsir al-safi li al-fayd al-kashani.* Beirut: al-Mu'ssasah al-a'lamiyah li al-matbu'at, 1982.

'Ali, Jawad. *al-Mufassal fi tarikh al-'arab qabla al-islam.* Beirut: Dar al-'ilm li al-malayin, 1970.

al-Alusi, Mahmud Shukri. *Bulugh al-'arab fi ma'rifat ahwal al-'arab.* Cairo: al-Maktabah al-ahliyyah, 1924.

al-Alusi, Mahmud ibn Abdullah. *Ruh al-ma'ani fi tafsir al-qur'an al-'azim wa al-sab' al-mathani.* Cairo: Idarat al-tiba'ah al-munirah, 1926.

'Attar, Sulayman. *al-Khayal 'inda ibn 'Arabi: al-nazariyah wa al-majalat.* Cairo: Dar al-thaqafah li-al-nashr wa al-tawzi', 1991.

———. *al-Khayal wa al-sh'ir fi al-tasawwuf al-andalusi: ibn'arabi, abu al-hasan al-shashtari, wa ibn khamis al-tilimsani.* Cairo: Dar al-ma'aref, 1981.

185

al-Azraqi, Muhammad ibn 'Abd Allah. *Akhbar makkah wa ma ja'a fiha min al-athar.* Makkah: Dar al-thaqafah, 1965.

al-Barquqi, 'Abd al-Rahman, ed. *Diwan Hassan ibn Thabit.* Cairo: al-Maktabah al-tijari-yah al-kubra, 1929.

al-Baydawi, 'Abdullah ibn 'Umar. *Anwar al-tanzil wa asrar al-ta'wil.* Cairo: Matba'at mus-tafa al-babi al-halabi, n.d.

al-Buni, Ahmad ibn 'Ali. *Shams al-ma'arif al kubra.* Beirut: Mu'assasat al-nur li al-matbu'at, 2000.

al-Damiri, Kamal al-din. *Hayat al-hayawan al-kubra.* Beirut: al-Maktabah al-islamiyyah, n.d.

Darwish, Muhammad Hassan. *Tarikh al-adab al-'arabi fi al-jahiliyyah.* Cairo: Maktabat al-kuliyyat al-azhariyyah, 1971.

Dawud, Dawud. *Adyan al-'arab qabla al-islam.* Beirut: al-Mu'ssasah al-jami'iyyah, 1981.

Dayf, Shawqi. *Al'asr al-islami.* Cairo: Dar al-ma'arif, 1963.

———. *Al'asr al-jahili.* Cairo: Dar al-ma'arif, 1977.

Diyarbakri, Husayn ibn Muhammad. *Tarikh al-khamis fi ahwal anfas nafis.* Beirut: Mu'assasat sha'ban, 1970.

Farraj, Abdul-Sattar Ahmad,ed. *Diwan majnun Laila.* Cairo: Maktabat misr, 1963.

al-Gilani, 'Abdul Qader. *Futuh al-ghayb.* Cairo: Maktabat al-thaqafah al-diniyyah, 2005.

al-Hakim, Su'ad. *al-Mu'jam al-sufi.* Beirut: Dar dandarah, 1981.

al-Halabi, 'Ali Burhan al-din. *'Aqd al-murjan fima yata'allaqu bi- al-jann.* Cairo: Makta-bat ibn Sina, n.d.

Hamdan, 'Abdul-Hamid. *'Ilm al-huruf wa aqtabuh.* Cairo: Maktabat madbuli, 1990.

Harun, 'Abd al-Salam, ed. *Jamharat ansab al-'arab li* ibn Hazm, 'Ali ibn Ahmad. Cairo: Dar al-ma'arif, 1962.

al-Hut, Salim. *Fi tariq al-mythologia 'inda al-'arab.* Beirut: Dar al-nahar, 1979.

ibn al-Athir, 'Izz al-din. *al-Kamil fi al-tarikh.* Beirut: Dar sader, 1965.

ibn al-Jawzi, abu al-Faraj 'Abdul-Rahman. *Talbis iblis.* Cairo: Almatba'ah al-muniriyyah, n.d.

ibn al-Nadim, Muhammad ibn Ishaq. *al-Fihrist.* Tehran, 1971.

ibn 'Arabi, Muhyi-al-din. *al-Futuhat al-makkiyyah.* 4 vols. Beirut: Dar sader, n.d.

———. *Tafsir al-qur'an al-karim.* Beirut: Dar al-yaqazah, 1968.

ibn Durayd, Abu Bakr Muhammad. *al-Ishtiqaq.* Beirut: al-Maktab al-tijari, 1958.

ibn Faris, Ahmad. *Mu'jam maqayis al-lughah.* Cairo: Dar ihya' al-kutub al-'arabiyyah, 1946.

ibn Hisham, 'Abd al-Malik. *Al Sirah al nabawiyyah.* Cairo: Dar al-hadith, 1996.

ibn Ibrahim, Saleh ibn Abd al Aziz, ed. *Mawsu'at al-hadith al sharif.* Ryad: Dar al-salam li al nashr wa al tawzi', 2000.

ibn Kathir, Isma'il. *al-Bidayah wa al-nihayah.* Cairo: Dar al-fikr al-'arabi, 1982.

———. *Qisas al-anbiya'.* Cairo: Dar al-kutub al-hadithah, 1968.

———. *Tafsir al-qur'an al-'azim.* Beirut: Dar al-qalam, 1983.

ibn Majah, Muhammad ibn Yazid. *Sunan ibn Majah.* Beirut: Dar ihya' al-kutub al-'arabiyyah, 1954.

ibn Manzur, Jamal al-din Muhammad. *Lisan al-'arab.* Beirut: Dar sader, n.d.

ibn Qayyim al-Jawziyyah, Muhammad ibn abi Bakr. *al-Tafsir al-qayyim.* Beirut: Dar al-kutub al-'ilmiyyah, 1978.

ibn Qutaybah, 'Abdullah ibn Muslim. *'al-Shi'r wa al-shu'ara'.* Beirut: Dar al-thaqafah, 1969.

ibn Shuhayd, Abu 'Amir. *Risalat al-tawabi' wa al-zawab'.* Beirut: Dar sader, 1967.

ibn Taymiyah, Ahmad. *Majmu' fatawa shaykh al-islam ibn taymiyah.* Riyad: Matba'at al-riyad, 1967.

ibn Wathimah. *See* al-Farisi, Umarah.

al-Ibshihi, Muhammad ibn Ahmad. *al-Mustatraf min kull fann mustazraf.* Cairo: Matba'at mustafa al-babi al-halabi, 1952.

al-Isbahani, Abu al-Faraj. *Kitab al-aghani.* Cairo: Dar al-sha'b, 1969.

al-Isbahani, Abu Na'im Ahmad. *Dala'il al-nubuwwah.* Beirut: 'Alam al-kutub, 1988.

al-Jahiz, 'Amru ibn Bahr. *Kitab al-hayawan.* Beirut: Manshurat al-majma' al-'arabi al-islami, 1969.

al-Jawziyyah. *See* ibn Qayyim al-Jawziyyah.

al-Jurjani, 'Ali ibn Muhammad. *al-Ta'rifat.* Cairo: Maktabat mustafa al-babi al-halabi, 1938.

al-Kashani, Fayd. *al-Tafsir al-safi.* Beirut: al-Mu'ssasah al-'amiyah li al-matbu'at, 1982.

al-Ma'arri, Abu al-'Ala'Ahmad. *Risalat al-ghufran.* Cairo: Dar al-ma'arif, 1950.

al-Mas'udi, al-Husayn ibn 'Ali. *Akhbar al-zaman.* Beirut: Dar al-andalus, 1980.

———. *Muruj al-dhahab.* Beirut: Dar al-andalus, 1965.

al-Maydani, Ahmad ibn Muhammad. *Majma' al-amthal.* Beirut: Dar al-kutub al-'ilmiyyah, 1988.

Muna, Ziad. *Balqis: 'Imr'at al-alghaz wa shytanat al-jins.* London: Ryad al-rayyes, 1997.

Musayyar, Muhammad Sayyed Ahmad. *al-Nubuwah al-muhammadiyah: al-wahy, al-mu'jizah, al-'alamiyah.* al-Jizah: Nahdat misr li al-tiba'ah wa al-nashr wa al-tawzi', 2004.

Muslim, ibn al-Hajjaj. *Sahih Muslim.* Beirut: Dar al-kutub al-'ilmiyyah, n.d.

Nadir, Albert Nasri, ed. *Min rasa'il Ikhwan al-Safa' wa khillan al-wafa'.* Beirut: al-Matba'ah al-katholikiyah, 1964.

Nawfal, 'Abd al-Razzaq. *'Alam al-jinn wa al-mala'ikah*. Cairo: Mu'assasat dar al-sha'b, 1968.

Qasim, Mahmud. *al-Khayal fi madhab Muhyi al-din ibn 'Arabi*. Cairo: Univ. of Cairo Press, 1969.

al-Qazwini, Zakariya ibn Muhammad. *'Aja'ib al-makhluqat*. Cairo: Dar al-tahrir, n.d.

———. *Athar al-bilad wa akhbar al-'ibad*. Beirut: Dar sader, 1960.

al-Qurashi, Abu Zaid. *Jamharat ash'ar al-'arab*. Beirut: Dar al-kutub al-'ilmiyyah, 1986.

al-Qushayri, 'Abd al-Karim. *Lata'if al-isharat: Tafsir sufi kamil li al-qur'an al-karim*. Cairo: al-Hay'ah al-misriyyah al-'ammah li al-kitab, 1981.

———. *al-Tahbir fi al-tadhkir: sharh 'asma'allah al-husna*. Beirut: Dar al-Kutub al-'ilmiyyah, 2006.

al-Razi, Fakhr al-din. *al-Tafsir al-kabir li al-qur'an: Mafatih al-ghayb*. Cairo: al-Matba'ah al-bahiyyah al-masriyyah, 1934.

Reda, Muhammad Rashid. *al-Wahy al-muhammadi*. Cairo: Maktabat al-manar, 1932.

al-Sakhawi, 'Abd al-Rahman. *Ashrat al-sa'ah*. Jordan: Dar al-bayareq, 1997.

al-Sarraj, Ja'afar. *Masari' al-'ushaq*. Amman: al-maktabah al-wataniyyah, 2004.

al-Sha'arani, Abd al-Wahab ibn Ahmad. *Kashf al-hijab wa al-ran 'an wajh as'ilat al-jann*. Beirut: Dar al kutub al-'ilmiyyah, 1999.

al-Shahristani, Muhammad ibn 'abd al-Karim. *al-Milal wa al-nihal*. Beirut: Matba'at nasir, 1975.

al-Shibli, Badr al-din. *Akam al-murjan fi ahkam al-jan*. Beirut: al-Maktabah al-'asriyyah, 1988.

al-Shirazi, Sadr al-din. *Mafatih al-ghayb*. Beirut: mu'assasat al-tarikh al-'arabi, 1999.

al-Sulayman, abu 'Ubaydah Mashhur ibn Hasan. *Fath al mannan fi jam' kalam shaykh al-Islam ibn taymeyah 'an al-jinnan,* al-Bahrein: al-Manamah Maktabat al-tawhid, 1999.

———. *al-Ghoul bayna al-hadith al-nabawi wa al-mawruth al-sha'bi*. Dammam: Dar ibn al-qayyim, 1989.

al-Suyuti, Jalal al-din 'Abd al-Rahman. *al-Haba'ik fi akhbar al mala'ik*. Cairo: Maktabtat al-qur'an, 1990.

———. *Laqt al-marjan fi ahkam al-jann*. Beirut: Dar al-kutub al-'ilmiyyah, 1986.

———. *al-Rahmah fi al-tibb wa al-hikmah*. Damascus: Maktabat al-hadarah, 1972.

al-Tabari, Muhammad ibn Jarir. *Tafsir al-qur'an*. Saudi Arabia: Dar al-turath al-'arabi, 1986.

———. *Tarikh al-rusul wa al-muluk*. Cairo: Dar al-ma'arif, n.d.

al-Tabatiba'i, Muhammad Husein. *al-Makhluqat al-khafiyyah fi al-qur'an*. Beirut: Dar safwan, 1995.

al-Tahanawi, Muhammad ibn 'Ali. *Mawsu'at istilahat al-'ulum al-islamiyyah*. Beirut: Dar khayyat, 1966.

al-Tahtawi, 'Ali Ahmad 'Abd al-'Al. *Fath al mannan bi ahkam al-jann*. Beirut: Dar al-kutub al-'ilmiyyah, 2005.

———. *Fath rab alfalaq: Sharh kitab bid' al-khalq*. Beirut: Dar al-kutub al-'ilmiyyah, 2004.

al-Tha'alabi, Ahmad ibn Muhammad. *Qisas al-anbiya'*. Cairo: Maktabat al-jumhuriyyah al-'arabiyyah, 1902.

Yaqut, ibn 'Abdullah al-Hamawi. *Mu'jam al-buldan*. Beirut: Dar ihya' al-turath al-'arabi, n.d.

al-Zabidi, Murtada. *Taj al-'arus min jawahir al-qamus*. 40 vols. Kuwait: Matba'at huku-mat al Kuwait, 1965–2001.

al-Zamakhshari, Abu al-Qasim Jarullah Mahmud ibn 'Umar. *al-Kashshaf 'an haqa'iq al-tanzil*. Cairo: al-Maktabah al-tijariyah al-kubra, 1953.

Zaydan, Jurgi. *al-A'mal al-kamilah*. Beirut: Dar al-jil, 1982.

IN ENGLISH AND FRENCH

Agrippa, Henry Cornelius. *The Philosophy of Natural Magic*. Secaucus, NJ: Univ. Books, 1974.

Amoli, Seyyed Haydar. *Inner Secrets of the Path*. Translated by Assadullah al-Dhakir Yate. Shaftesbury, Dorset: Elements Books, 1989.

Arberry, A. J. *The Koran Interpreted*. New York: Simon and Schuster, 1996.

Atkinson, James. *Laili and Majnun: A Poem from the Original Persian of Nizami*. London: A. J. Valpy Publishers, 1836.

Bachelard, Gaston. *Psychoanalysis of Fire*. Translated by C. M. Ross. Boston: Beacon Press, 1964.

Beal, Timothy K. *Religion and Its Monsters*. New York: Routledge, 2002.

Bernot, Denise, ed. *Génies, anges et démons*. Paris: Editions du Seuil, 1971.

Bevan, Edwyn Robert. *Sibyls and Seers: A Survey of Some Ancient Theories of Revelation and Inspiration*. London: George Allen and Unwin Limited, 1928.

Black, Jeremy A., and Anthony Green. *Gods, Demons, and Symbols of Ancient Mesopota-mia: An Illustrated Dictionary*. Austin: Univ. of Texas Press, 1992.

Bouché-Leclercq, A. *Histoire de la divination dans l'Antiquité*. 4 vols. Paris: Editions Ler-oux, 1882.

Briggs, Katharine M. *An Encyclopedia of Fairies: Hobgoblins, Brownies, Bogies, and Other Supernatural Creatures*. New York: Pantheon Books, 1976.

———. *The Fairies in English Tradition and Literature*. Chicago: Univ. of Chicago Press, 1967.

————. *The Personnel of Fairyland*. Oxford: Alden Press, 1953.

Budge, Wallis. *Amulets and Talismans*. New York: Carol Publishing Group, 1992.

————. *The Gods of the Egyptians: Studies in Egyptian Mythology*. New York: Dover Publications, 1969.

Buitenen, Van Johannes Adrianus Bernardus, ed. *Tales of Ancient India*. Chicago: Univ. of Chicago Press, 1959.

Burton, Richard, trans. *The Book of the Thousand Nights and a Night*. 20 vols. London: Burton Club, 1885.

Campbell, Joseph. *The Hero with a Thousand Faces*. 3d ed. New Jersey: Princeton Univ. Press, 1973.

————. *The Inner Reaches of Outer Space: Metaphor as Myth and as Religion*. Novato, CA.: New World Library, 2002.

Chaitanya, Krishna. *Sanskrit Poetics: A Critical and Comparative Study*. New York: Asia Publishing House, 1965.

Cheetham, Tom. *The World Turned Inside Out: Henry Corbin and Islamic Mysticism*. Woodstock, CT: Spring Journal Books, 2003.

Chevalier, Jean, and Alain Gheerbrant. *Dictionnaire des symbols*. Paris: Seghers, 1969.

Chittick, William. *Ibn al-Arabi Metaphysics of Imagination: The Sufi Path of Knowledge*. Albany: State Univ. of New York, 1989.

————. *Imaginal Worlds: Ibn al-Arabi and the Problem of Religious Diversity*. Albany: State Univ. of New York Press, 1994.

————. *The Self-Disclosure of God: Principles of ibn al-Arabi's Cosmology*. Albany: State Univ. of New York, 1998.

————. *The Sufi Path of Love: The Spiritual Teachings of Rumi*. Albany: State Univ. of New York, 1983.

Coomaraswamy, Ananda K. *Yaksas: Essays in the Water Cosmology*. New Delhi: Indira Ghandi National Center for the Arts; New York: Oxford Univ. Press, 1993.

Cooper, J. C. *An Illustrated Encyclopedia of Traditional Symbols*. New York: Thames and Hudson, 1978.

Corbin, Henry. *L'archange empourpé: Quinze traités et récits mystiques de Suhrawardi*. Paris: Fayard, 1976.

————. *Avicenna and the Visionary Recital*. Translated by Willard R. Tresk. Texas: Spring Publications, 1980.

————. *The Man of Light in Iranian Sufism*. Translated by Nancy Pearson. New York: Omega Publications, 1994.

————. *Spiritual Body and Celestial Earth: From Mazdean Iran to Shi'ite Iran*. Translated from the French by Nancy Pearson. New Jersey: Princeton Univ. Press, 1997.

———. *Swedenborg and Esoteric Islam.* Translated by Leonard Fox. West Chester, PA: Swedenborg Foundation, 1995.

———. *The Voyage and the Messenger: Iran and Philosophy.* Berkeley: North Atlantic Books, 1998.

Cousineau, Phil, ed. *The Way Things Are: Conversations with Huston Smith on the Spiritual Life.* Berkeley: Univ. of California Press, 2003.

Dalley, Stephanie. *Myths from Mesopotamia.* New York: Oxford Univ. Press, 1991.

Daniélou, Alain. *The Gods of India: Hindu Polytheism.* New York: Inner Traditions International, 1985.

Dodds, E. R. *The Greeks and the Irrational.* Berkeley: Univ. of California Press, 1951.

Drijvers, H. J. W. *The Religion of Palmyra.* Leiden: E. J. Brill, 1976.

Driver, G. R. *Witchcraft in the Old Testament.* Edmonds, WA: Sure Fire Press, 1994.

Durand, Françoise, and Christiane Zivie-Coche. *Gods and Men in Egypt, 3000 BCE to 395.* Ithaca, NY: Cornell Univ. Press, 2004.

Eliade, Mircea. *Images and Symbols: Studies in Religious Symbolism.* Translated by Philipe Mairet. New Jersey: Princeton Univ. Press, 1991.

———. *Myth and Reality.* Translated by Willard R. Trask. New York: Harper Torchbooks, 1975.

———. *The Myth of the Eternal Return: or, Cosmos and History.* Princeton: Princeton Univ. Press, 1991.

———. *Myths, Dreams, and Mysteries.* London: Harvill Press, 1960.

———. *The Sacred and the Profane.* Translated by Willard R. Trask. New York: Harcourt Brace and Company, 1959.

———. *Shamanism: Archaic Techniques of Ecstasy.* Translated by Willard R. Trask. New York: Pantheon Books, 1964.

Ellingham, Lewis, and Kevin Killian. *Poet Be Like God: Jack Spicer and the San Francisco Renaissance.* Hanover, NH: Univ. Press of New England, 1998.

Else, Gerald. *Plato and Aristotle on Poetry.* Chapel Hill: Univ. of North Carolina Press, 1986.

Entralgo, Pedro. *The Therapy of the Word in Classical Antiquity.* New Haven: Yale Univ. Press, 1970.

Fahd, Toufic. *La divination arabe: Etudes religieuses, sociologiques et folkloriques sur le milieu natif de l'Islam.* Leiden: E. J. Brill, 1966.

———, ed. *L'Arabie préislamique et son environnement historique et culturel. Actes du colloque de Strasbourg.* Strasbourg: Université des sciences humaines de Strasbourg, 1989.

Février, J. G. *La religion des Palmyriens.* Paris: Librairie Philosophique J. Vrin, 1931.

Flacelière, Robert. *Greek Oracles.* New York: W. W. Norton, 1965.

Fowden, Garth. *The Egyptian Hermes: A Historical Approach to the Late Pagan Mind.* Princeton, NJ: Princeton Univ. Press, 1993.

Frankfort, Henry. *Kinship and the Gods: A Study in Ancient Near Eastern Religion as the Integration of Society and Nature.* Chicago: Univ. of Chicago Press, 1948.

Frazer, James George. *The Golden Bough: A Study in Magic and Religion.* London: Oxford Univ. Press, 1994.

Friedlander, Paul. *An Introduction.* London: Routledge and Kegan, 1958.

Gager, John G., ed. *Curse Tablets and Binding Spells From the Ancient World.* Oxford: Oxford Univ. Press, 1992.

Glassé, Cyril, ed. *The Concise Encyclopedia of Islam.* New York: Harper and Row, 1989.

Goswami, Amit. *The Self-Aware Universe.* New York: Penguin, 1995.

Graves, Robert. *The White Goddess: A Historical Grammar of Poetic Myth.* New York: Farrar, Straus and Giroux, 1966.

Guénon, René. *Fundamental Symbols: The Universal Language of Sacred Science.* Translated by Alvin Moore Jr. Cambridge: Quinta Essentia, 1995.

————. *The Great Triad.* Translated by Peter Kingsley. Cambridge: Quinta Essentia, 1991.

Guillaume, Alfred. *Prophétie et divination chez les sémites.* Paris: Payot, 1950.

Haddawy, Husain, trans. *The Arabian Nights.* New York: W. W. Norton and Company, 1990.

Hamilton, Edith. *Mythology: Timeless Tales of Gods and Heroes.* New York: Penguin Books, 1982.

————, ed. *The Collected Dialogues of Plato.* New York: Pantheon Books, 1961.

Harf-Lancner, Laurence. *Les fées au Moyen Age: Morgane et Mélusine: La naissance des fées.* Geneva: Editions Slatkine, 1984.

Harpur, Patrick. *Daimonic Reality: A Field Guide to the Otherworld.* Ravensdale, WA: Pine Winds Press, 2003.

————. *The Philosophers' Secret Fire: A History of the Imagination.* London: Penguin Books, 2002.

Hastings, James, ed. *The Encyclopedia of Religion and Ethics.* 10 vols. New York: Scribner, 1928.

Haykal, Muhammad Husayn. *The Life of Muhammad.* Translated by Isma'il Raji al-Faruqi. Indianapolis, IN: American Trust Publications, 1976.

Hillman, James. *Revisioning Psychology.* New York: Harper Perennial, 1992.

Hirsch, Edward. *The Demon and the Angel: Searching for the Source of Artistic Inspiration.* New York: Harcourt, 2002.

Hirtenstein, Stephen, and Michael Tiernan, eds. *Muhyiddin ibn 'Arabi: A Commemorative Volume.* Rockport, MA: Element, 1993.

Hitti, Philip. *History of the Arabs.* London: Macmillan, 1943.

Homère. *L'Odyssée.* Translated by Mario Meunier. Paris: Editions Albin Michel, 1961.

Hooke, S. H. *Middle Eastern Mythology.* New York: Penguin Books, 1963.

————, ed. *Myth and Ritual: Essays on the Myth and Ritual of the Hebrews in Relation to the Culture Pattern of the Ancient East.* Oxford: Oxford Univ. Press, 1933.

Hughes, Merrit, ed. *John Milton: Complete Poetry and Major Prose.* New York: Odyssey Publishers, 1957.

Hulkrantz, Ake. *Soul and Native Americans.* Quebec: Spring Publications, 1997.

ibn al-Kalbi, Hisham. *The Book of Idols.* Translated by Nabih Faris. Princeton, NJ: Princeton Univ. Press, 1952.

ibn 'Arabi, Muhyi-al-din. *Fusus al-hikam.* Translated by Ra'uf Bulent. Oxforn, UK: Alden Press, 1986.

————. *Kernel of the Kernel.* Translated by Ismail Hakki Bursevi. Sherborne, UK: Beshara Publications, 1997.

————. *Shajrat al-kwan.* Translated by A Jeffrey. Lahore: Aziz Publishers, 1980.

ibn Kathir, Isma'il. *The Signs Before the Day of Judgment.* London: Dar al-Taqwa, 1992.

ibn Khaldun. *Introduction.* Translated by Franz Rosenthal. London: Routledge and Kegan Paul, 1958.

ibn Nabi, Malik. *The Qur'anic Phenomenon: An attempt at Understanding the Holy Qur'an.* Indianapolis: American Trust Publications, 1983.

ibn Qayyim al-Jawziyyah, Muhammad ibn Abi Bakr. *Medicine of the Prophet.* Translated by Penelope Johnstone. Cambridge: Islamic Texts Society, 1999.

ibn Sirin, Muhammad. *Dictionary of Dreams According to Islamic Inner Traditions.* Translated by Muhammad M. al-'Akili. Philadelphia: Pearl Publishing House, 1992.

ibn Taymiyah, Ahmad. *Struggle Against Popular Religion and Kitab iqtida' al-sirat al-mustaqim wa-mukhalafat ashab al-jahim.* Translated and annotated by 'Umar Muhammad Memon. Paris: Mouton-La Hague, 1976.

Ikhwan al-Safa'. *The Case of the Animals Versus Man Before the King of the Jinn: A Tenth-Century Ecological Fable of the Pure Brethren of Basra.* Translated by Lenn Evan Goodman. Boston: Twayne Publishers, 1978.

Jacobs, Joseph, ed. *Celtic Fairy Tales.* London: David Nutt Publisher, 1892.

James, William. *The Varieties of Religious Experience.* New York: Modern Library, 1991.

Jami, Nur al-din 'Abd al-Rahman. *Lawa'ih: A Treatise on Sufism.* Translated by E. H. Winfield and Muhammad Kazvini. London: Theosophical Publishing House, 1978.

Jastrow, Morris. *Aspects of Religious Belief and Practice in Babylonia and Assyria.* New York: B. Blom, 1971.

Jayyusi, Lena, ed. *The adventures of Sayf ben Dhi Yazn: An Arab Folk Epic.* Bloomington: Indiana Univ. Press, 1996.

Jeffers, Ann. *Magic and Divination in Ancient Palestine and Syria.* Leiden: E. J. Brill, 1996.

Joseph, Jacobs, ed. *Celtic Fairy Tales.* New York and London: G. P. Putnam's Sons, 1959.

Kasulis, Thomas P. *Shinto: The Way Home.* Honolulu: Univ. of Hawaii Press, 2004.

Khairallah, As'ad E. *Love, Madness, and Poetry: An Interpretation of the Magnun Legend.* Beirut: Orient-Insitut der Deutschen Morgenlndischen Gesellschaft, 1980.

Khan, Muhammad Muhsin. *Sahih al-Bukhari.* Translated by Muhammad ibn Isma'il al-Bukhari. Madinah: Islamic Univ., 1985.

King, L. W., trans. *Enuma Elish: The Seven Tablets of Creation.* 2 vols. Escondido, CA: Book Tree Publishers, 1999.

al-Kisa'i, Muhammad ibn 'Ali. *The Tales of the Prophets.* Translated with notes by W. M. Thackston Jr. Boston: Twayne Publishers, 1978.

Kishk, 'Abdul-Hamid. *The World of Angels.* London: Dar al-taqwa, 1999.

Kramer, Samuel Noah, and Diane Wolkstein. *Inanna, Queen of Heaven and Earth: Her Stories and Hymns From Sumer.* New York: Harper and Row, 1983.

Lamoreaux, John C. *The Early Tradition of Dream Interpretation.* Albany: State Univ. of New York Press, 2002.

Langton, Edward. *Essentials of Demonology.* London: Epworth Press, 1981.

Leeuw, G. Van der. *Religion in Essence and Manifestation.* New York: Harper and Row, 1963.

Ling, T. O. *Buddhism and the Mythology of Evil: A Study in Theravada Buddhism.* Oxford: Oneworld Publications, 1997.

Lings, Martin. *Symbol and Archetype: A Study in the Meaning of Existence.* Cambridge: Quinta Essentia, 1991.

Liu, James J. Y. *The Art of Chinese Poetry.* London: Routledge and Kegan Paul, 1962.

Livingston, Ray. *The Traditional Theory of Literature.* Minneapolis: Univ. of Minnesota Press, 1962.

Lorca, Federico Garcia. *In Search of Duende.* New York: New Directions, 1998.

Lorimer, David, ed. *The Spirit of Science: From Experiment to Experience.* New York: Continuum Publishing, 1999.

Luck, Georg. *Arcana Mundi: Magic and the Occult in the Greek and Roman Empire.* Baltimore: Johns Hopkins Univ. Press, 1985.

Macdonald, Duncan Black. *Aspects of Islam.* New York: Books for Library Press, 1971.

———. *The Religious Attitude and Life in Islam.* Beirut: Khayats, 1965.

Marquet, Yves. *La philosophie des alchemists et l'alchimie des philosophes: Jabir ibn Hayyan et les frères de la Pureté.* Paris: Editions Maisonneuve et Larose, 1988.

al-Mas'udi, 'Ali. *L'abrégé des merveilles.* Translated into French by Carra de Vaux. Paris: Editions Sindbad, 1984.

Mokri, Muhammad, ed. *Anges, démons et êtres intermédiares.* Paris: Labergerie, 1969.

Mullen, Theodore E., Jr. *The Divine Council in Canaanite and Early Hebrew Literature.* Harvard: Harvard Semitic Monographs 24, Scholars Press, 1980.

Mundkur, B. *The Cult of the Serpent: An Interdisciplinary Survey of Its Manifestations and Origins.* Albany: State Univ. of New York Press, 1983.

Murray, Penelope. *Genius: The History of an Idea.* New York: B. Blackwell, 1989.

Nadir, Albir Nasr. *Le système philosophique des Mu'tazilah.* Beirut: Editions les Belles Lettres, 1956.

Narvaez, Peter, ed. *The Good People: New Fairylore Essays.* Lexington: Univ. Press of Kentucky, 1991.

Nasr, Seyyed Hossein. *An Introduction to Islamic Cosmological Doctrines.* Albany: State Univ. of New York, 1993.

———. *Knowledge and the Sacred.* Albany: State Univ. of New York, 1989.

———. *Science and Civilization in Islam.* Cambridge, MA: Harvard Univ. Press, 1968.

al-Nawawi, Muhyiddin abu Zakariyya Yahya ibn Sharaf. *Riyad al-salihin.* London: Curzon Press, 1975.

Nitzche, Jane Chaucer. *The Genius Figure in Antiquity and the Middle Ages.* New York: Columbia Univ. Press, 1975.

Padel, Ruth. *Whom Gods Destroy: Elements of Greek and Tragic Madness.* Princeton, NJ: Princeton Univ. Press, 1995.

Parke, H. W. *Sibyls and Sibylline Prophecy in Classical Antiquity.* New York: Routledge, 1988.

Perrault, Charles. *Contes.* Paris: Collection de l'imprimerie nationale, 1987.

Pinch, Geraldine. *Magic in Ancient Egypt.* Austin: Univ. of Texas Press, 1994.

Plato. *Great Dialogues of Plato.* Translated by W. H. D. House. New York: New American Library, 1984.

Plutarch. *Essays.* Translated by Robin Waterfield and introduced by Ian Kidd. London: Penguin Books, 1992.

———. *Troublesome Things: A History of Fairies and Fairy Stories.* London: Penguin Books, 2001.

Rahman, Fazlur. *Health and Medicine in the Islamic Tradition: Change and Identity.* New York: Crossroad, 1987.

———. *Prophecy in Islam: Philosophy and Orthodoxy.* Chicago: Univ. of Chicago Press, 1979.

al-Razi, Abu Bakr Muhammad Zakariyya. *The Spiritual Physick of Rhazes.* London: J. Murray, 1950.

Razi, Najm al-Din. *The Path of God's Bondsmen from Origin to Return.* Translated by Hamid Algar. North Haledon, NJ: Islamic Publications International, 1980.

Romilly, Jacqueline de. *Magic and Rhetoric in Ancient Greece.* Cambridge, MA: Harvard Univ. Press, 1975.

Russell, Jeffrey Burton. *The Devil: Perceptions of Evil from Antiquity to Primitive Christianity.* Ithaca, NY: Cornell Univ. Press, 1977.

Saqr, Ahmad. *al-Jinn.* Lombard, IL: Foundation for Islamic Knowledge, 1994.

Savage-Smith, Emilie, ed. *Magic and Divination in Early Islam.* Burlington, VT: Ashgate/Variorum, 2004.

Schimmel, Annemarie. *Islam and the Wonders of Creation: The Animal Kingdom.* London: al-Furqan Islamic Heritage Foundation, 2003.

Schneweis, Emil. *Angels and Demons According to Lactantius.* Washington, DC: Catholic Univ. of America Press, 1944.

Schuon, Fritthjof. *The Feathered Sun: Plains Indians in Art and Philosophy.* Bloomington, IN: World Wisdom Books, 1990.

———. *The Transcendental Unity of Religions.* New York: Harper and Row, 1975.

Sendry, Joseph, ed. *John Keats: A Thematic Reader.* Glenview, IL: Scott, Foresman, 1971.

Shah, Idries. *Oriental Magic.* New York: Philosophical Library, 1957.

———. *World Tales: The Extraordinary Coincidence of Stories Told in All Times, in All Places.* New York: Harcourt Brace Jovanovich, 1979.

Sheldrake, Rupert. *The Sense of Being Stared At.* New York: Crown Publishers, 2003.

Smith, Huston. *Forgotten Truth: The Primordial Tradition.* New York: Harper and Row, 1976.

———. *The Way Things Are: Conversations with Huston Smith on the Spiritual Life.* Berkeley: Univ. of California Press, 2003.

———. *Why Religion Matters.* New York: Harper and Collins, 2001.

Smith, W. R. *Lectures on The Religion of the Semites: The Fundamental Institutions.* 3d ed. New York: Macmillan, 1927.

Starcky, Jean. *Palmyre.* Paris: Editions Adrien Maisonneuve, 1952.

Starcky, Jean, and Salah al-din al-Munajjid. *Palmyra, the Bride of the Desert.* Damascus: General Directorate of Antiquities, 1948.

al-Suhrawardi, Shihab al-din. *The Philosophical Allegories and Mystical Treatises.* Translated by Wheeler M. Thackston Jr. Costa Mesa, CA: Mazda Publishers, 1999.

———. *Treatises of Shihabuddin Yahya Suhrawardi.* Translated by Wheeler. M. Thackston Jr. London: Octagon Press, 1982.

Sutherland, Gail Hinich. *The Disguises of the Demon: The Development of the Yaksa in Hinduism and Buddhism.* Albany: State Univ. of New York, 1991.

Teixidor, Javier. *The Pagan God: Popular Religion in the Greco-Roman Near-East* Princeton, NJ: Princeton Univ. Press, 1977.

———. *The Panthéon of Palmyra.* Leiden: E. J. Brill, 1979.

Thompson, R. Campbell. *Semitic Magic: Its Origins and Development.* London: Luzac, 1908.

Thompson, Stith. *The Folktale.* New York: Dryden Press, 1946.

Todorov, Tzvetan. *Introduction à la littérature fantastique.* Paris: editions du Seuil, 1970.

Vadet, Jean-Claude. *L'esprit courtois en orient dans les cinq premiers siècles de l'hégire.* Paris: G. P. Maisonneuve et Larose, 1968.

Waite, Arthur Edward, ed. *Hermetic and Alchemical Writings of Paracelsus the Great.* Edmonds, WA: Alchemical Press, 1992.

Wallis, Richard T., and Jay Bregman, ed. *Neoplatonism and Gnosticism.* Albany: State Univ. of New York Press, 1992.

Watt, Montgomery. *Muhammad at Mecca.* Oxford: Clarendon Press, 1960.

———. *Muhammad at Medina.* Oxford: Clarendon Press, 1956.

Wentz, W. Y. Evans. *The Fairy-Faith in Celtic Countries.* Franklin Lakes, NJ: New Page Books, 2004.

Wolf, Fred Alan. *The Dreaming Universe: A Mind-Expanding Journey into the Realm Where Psyche and Physics Meet.* New York: Simon and Schuster, 1994.

Yeats, W. B. *Irish Fairy and Folk Tales.* New York: Boni and Liveright, 1979.

———. *Writings on Irish Folklore, Legend, and Myth.* London: Penguin Books, 1993.

Zajonc, Arthur, ed. *The New Physics and Cosmology: Dialogues with the Dalai Lama.* Oxford: Oxford Univ. Press, 2004.

Zwemer, Samuel M. *The Influence of Animism on Islam.* New York: Macmillan, 1920.

———. *Studies in Popular Islam: A Collection of Papers Dealing with the Superstitions and Beliefs of the Common People.* New York: Macmillan, 1939.

MISCELLANEOUS

Encyclopedia of Islam. Leiden: E. J. Brill, 1991.

The Holy Bible. Contemporary English Version. New York: American Bible Society, 1995.

ARTICLES AND CHAPTERS IN BOOKS

Albright, W. F. "Islam and the Religions of the Ancient Orient." *Journal of the American Oriental Society,* no. 60 (1940): 283–301.

Bulent Rauf. "Universality and ibn 'Arabi." *Journal of Muhyi ibn 'Arabi Society* 4 (1985): 1–3.

Fahd, Toufic. "Kihanah." *Encyclopedia of Islam* 4, (1991): 421.

al-Hakim, Sou'ad. "Knowledge of God in ibn 'Arabi." In *Muhyiddin ibn 'Arabi: A Commemorative Volume,* edited by Stephen Hirtenstein and Michael Tiernan 264–90. Rockport, MA: Element, 1993.

Jad'an, Fahmi. "Les anges dans la théologie musulmane" [Angels in Islamic theology]. *Studia Islamica* 41, (1975): 23–61.

Marquet, Yves. "Sabéens et Ikhwan al-Safa'." *Studia Islamica* 24 (1966): 35–80.

Raine, Kathleen. "The Underlying Unity: Nature and the Imagination." In *The Spirit of Science: From Experiment to Experience,* edited by David Lorimer, 216–20. New York: Continuum, 1999.

Steven Dick J., "Plurality of Worlds." In *Cosmology: Historical, Literary, Philosophical, Religious, and Scientific Perspectives,* edited by Norriss S. Hetherington, 515–32. New York: Garland Publishers, 1993.

Index

animals: in human-jinn interactions, 101–2; humans and jinn as, 172n. 47; in literature, 172n. 47; as mounts for jinn, 92, 170n. 13, 171n. 22; sacred, 90; sixth sense of, 89

Anima Mundi, 134

animic realm. *See* celestial realm

animism, xi, xvi

anthropology, evolutional, 169n. 62

Antichrist, 21–22, 155n. 31

Anton, John P., 163n. 22

Anubis, 90

Anwar al-tanzil wa asrar al-ta'wil (al-Baydawi), xxi

Apollo, 122, 123

Apollonius, 51

Apology (Socrates), xiv–xv

Arabian Nights, The: "Ajib and Gharib," 141; "Ali the Cairene and the Haunted House," 29–30; "The Fisherman and the Jinni," 23, 153n. 1; "Hasan of Basorah," 154n. 11; initiation stories of, 111–18; on invisibility, 23–24; on jinn's learning from humans, 29–30; "The King's Son and the Ogress," 140–41; love stories of, 108–18; *marid* in, 142; "The Merchant and the Jinni," 24, 109–10; "Nur al-din Ali and His Brother Shams al-din Muhammad," 31; popular Islam and, xx; "Porter and the Three Ladies," 23–24, 81, 111, 168n. 36, 173n. 25; "Prince Sayf al-Muluk and Princess Badi'at al-Jamal," 116–18; "Qamar al-Zaman," 16, 31; "Sayf al-Muluk and Badi'at al-Jamal," 16; on societies of jinn, 16, 154n. 11; "The Tale of Hasan al-Basri," 113–14, 173n. 31; "The Tale of Janshah," 111–13, 173n. 29; on wedding night abductions, 110–11

Arabic language, xvi, 29, 157n. 61, 159n. 27

Arabic letters, 82–83

Arab sagas: popular, 174n. 33

Aramaic, Western, 159n. 25

ara-mi-tama, xiii

Arberry, Arthur John, xix

Arjuna, 115

Art of Chinese Poetry, The (Liu), 133

Asag, 72

'asatir, 179

ascension, 161n. 65

al-'A'sha, 131–32

Asha'ira school, 22, 179

al-Ash'ari, Abu al-Hasan, 22

Asma' allah al-husna, 179

al-Asnam (The Idols), 179

'Asr (tribe), 179

Assyria, xiv, 71–72

Assyro-Babylonian culture, 54

astronomical charts, 54

atomic weapons, xvii

al-'Attar, Farid al-din, 53

Avicenna, xvii, 87–88

al-'Awd, Jiran, 70, 74

'azif, 74

al-Azraqi, Muhammad ibn 'Abdallah, 65

al-'azzaf, 167n. 15

'Azzah, Kuthayyir, 121, 126–27, 133

ba, xiv

Babylonia: animal forms in, 90–91, 170n. 5; divination in, 54–55; gene in, 38; magic in, 71–72; serpents in, 96; spiritual entities of, xiv; witches, 76–77

Bacon, Francis, xviii

Balqis, 104, 107, 172n. 4, 179

bani/banu: definition of, 179

Banu 'Amru ibn 'Amir (tribe), 63, 129, 179

Banu Ashja' (tribe), 179

Banu Dhi'b (tribe), 180

Banu Ghazwan (tribe), 180

Banu Sahm (tribe), 99, 180

Banu Shaysaban (tribe), 180